Spaces of Fiction / Fictions of Space

Also by Russell West-Pavlov

BODIES AND THEIR SPACES: System, Crisis and Transformation in Early Modern Drama

CONRAD AND GIDE: Translation, Transference and Intertextuality

FIGURES DE LA MALADIE CHEZ ANDRÉ GIDE

SPACE IN THEORY: Kristeva, Foucault, Deleuze

SPATIAL REPRESENTATIONS ON THE JACOBEAN STAGE: From Shakespeare to Webster

TRANSCULTURAL GRAFFITI: Diasporic Writing and the Teaching of Literary Studies

Spaces of Fiction / Fictions of Space

Postcolonial Place and Literary DeiXis

Russell West-Pavlov
Professor of Postcolonial Literatures
Free University of Berlin

First published 2010 by
PALGRAVE MACMILLAN

Palgrave Macmillan in the UK is an imprint of Macmillan Publishers Limited, registered in England, company number 785998, of Houndmills, Basingstoke, Hampshire RG21 6XS.

Palgrave Macmillan in the US is a division of St Martin's Press LLC, 175 Fifth Avenue, New York, NY 10010.

Palgrave Macmillan is the global academic imprint of the above companies and has companies and representatives throughout the world.

Palgrave® and Macmillan® are registered trademarks in the United States, the United Kingdom, Europe and other countries.

ISBN: 978-0-230-23776-6 hardback

This book is printed on paper suitable for recycling and made from fully managed and sustained forest sources. Logging, pulping and manufacturing processes are expected to conform to the environmental regulations of the country of origin.

A catalogue record for this book is available from the British Library.

A catalog record for this book is available from the Library of Congress.

10 9 8 7 6 5 4 3 2 1
19 18 17 16 15 14 13 12 11 10

Printed and bound in Great Britain by
CPI Antony Rowe, Chippenham and Eastbourne

For my wife Tatjana and our children
Joshua, Iva and Niklas

Contents

Conclusion: "Here Fix the Tablet" 206
Field – Grenville

Acknowledgements

This book has been coming together in fits and starts for a number of years. It took on its more or less final form, however, during a sabbatical spent with my family at the University of Melbourne, Australia, from October 2006 to March 2007. The sabbatical would not have been possible without the support of a number of organizations and individuals who aided and abetted me in that project.

I wish to thank the Arts Faculty of the Free University of Berlin for granting a sabbatical with the time and space to pay uninterrupted attention to such a project. The generous support of the German Research Council (Deutsche Forschungsgemeinschaft) made the six-month stay in Melbourne financially viable.

I am grateful to the Australian Centre and the Department of English at the University of Melbourne, and their respective directors, Professor John Murphy and Professor John Frow, for hosting me during that time. A more domestic roof over our heads in the beautiful grounds of Queen's College, University of Melbourne was made available by the Master of the College, Professor David Runia. It was there that many early-morning writing sessions took place. Our son Joshua especially appreciated the huge garden at Queen's and produced some of his first deictics within its bounds.

Professor Peter Otto and Professor Chris Wallace-Crabbe availed us of their warm hospitality during our stay. Professor Ken Gelder was and continues to be a source of support and encouragement.

Jens Elze and Dr Jennifer Wawrzinek were of assistance in fine-tuning a penultimate version of the book. An anonymous external referee made invaluable suggestions for improving that version. I am indebted to Jens Elze, Justus Makokha, Anja Schwarz and Jennifer Wawrzinek for broadening my horizons through productive suggestions and stimulating discussions.

RUSSELL WEST-PAVLOV
Berlin 2009

Note on Translations

Translations: English translations are taken from the most easily available editions; where such translations do not yet exist, the translations given are my own.

Introduction: DeiXis

There is a famous tale by Jorge Luis Borges, in which a character named Pierre Menard intends to re-write Cervantes' *Don Quixote* so as to produce "a few pages which would coincide – word for word and line for line – with those of Miguel de Cervantes" ["unas páginas que coincidieran – palabra por palabra y línea por línea – con las de Miguel de Cervantes"]. The project of re-writing the *Quixote*, in perfectly identical form, is of course perfectly unfinishable, and the narrator of the tale can only posit hypothetically the completion of this undertaking: "Shall I confess that I often imagine he did finish it and that I read the *Quixote* – all of it – as if Menard had conceived it?" ["Confesaré que suelo imaginar que la terminó y que leo el Quijote – todo el Quijote – como si lo hubiera pensado Menard?"].[1] In another less well-known story, Borges evokes a similar notion, that of a map which is perfectly accurate: "the College of Cartographers set up a Map of the Empire which had the size of the Empire itself and coincided with it point by point" ["los Colegios de Cartógrafos levantaron un Mapa del Imperio, que tenía el tamaño del Imperio y coincidía puntualmente con él"]. Such a map is not without disadvantages, however, despite its perfect accuracy, and for precisely this reason finally becomes obsolete: "Less Addicted to the Study of Cartography, Succeeding Generations understood that this Widespread Map was Useless and not without Impiety they abandoned it to the Inclemencies of the Sun and of the Winters. In the deserts of the West some mangled Ruins of the Map lasted on ..." ["Menos Adictas al Estudio de la Cartografía, las Generaciones Siguientes entendieron que ese dilatado Mapa era Inútil y no sin Impiedad lo entregaron a las Inclemencias del Sol y de los Inviernos. En los desiertos del Oeste perduran despedazadas Ruinas del Mapa ..."].[2]

What Menard attempts for a literary work, the cartographers of Borges' imagined empire attempt for a spatial text: namely, the flush fit of a text to its referents. Both undertakings are doomed. But Borges posits them as extreme examples – hubristic, excessive, utopian, in Marin's formulation[3] – which tell us, by dint of their very impossibility, about the manner in which both words and spatial signifiers function. By imagining a modern text which is perfectly identical with its historical avatar, and a map which is perfectly identical with the landscape it represents, Borges seeks to highlight the ineluctable difference and non-identical specificity which underpins representation, whether verbal or spatial.

Borges selects two absolute projects for the express purpose of registering their no less absolute failure. Italo Calvino offers a rather more differentiated view of the same problem. In an anthology of accounts of imaginary cities, Calvino's Marco Polo says to his patron, Kublai Khan: "No one, wise Kublai, knows better than you that the city must never be confused with the words that describe it. And yet between the one and the other there is a connection" ["Nessuno sa meglio di te, saggio Kublai, che non si deve mai confondere la città col discorso che la descrive. Eppure tra l'una e l'altro c'è un rapporto"].[4] In contrast to Borges' one-to-one correspondence of text or map to the respective signified, Calvino portrays a much looser rapport between spatial narrative and the spatial contours it represents. Correspondingly, that rapport is less vulnerable to failure. Because it makes more modest claims, it has less to lose.

Deixis, chiasmus, deiXis

This book is about the manner in which texts can describe space, and the ways in which those descriptions necessarily must be fictive: "the city must never be confused with the words that describe it", says Calvino's Polo. It is also, conversely, about the manner in which those texts, though they construct spaces as much as they describe them, also draw upon the material contours of those spaces and must, in turn, be informed by them: "between the one and the other there is a connection". It is a book, on the one hand, about the fictions of space, and on the other, the spaces of fiction.

The book takes as its over-arching eponymous metaphor the notion of deixis, the linguistic means by which a speaker anchors utterances in the concrete place of enunciation ('here', 'there', 'this table'). Deixis suits my purposes because it is an operation, drawn from language itself, which offers a general model, beyond its own limited and specific sites of implementation, of how language and space might interact.

Deixis can be understood, in a book as much about literature as about language, as modelling the tenuous grasp language has upon physical space. The parables chosen above from Borges and Calvino make concrete the way in which deictic markers are both *word* and *map* – and what such markers are capable of achieving or not.

However, the book also works with a second term drawn from the study of language, this time from the domain of rhetoric rather than of linguistics: chiasmus. Chiasmus is the figure of 'crossing' which structures, for example, the pair "spaces of fiction" and "fictions of space". Chiasmus is central to the task this book attempts because it models a relationship of reciprocity which, in contrast to traditional theories of deixis, can be found to hold between language and space. Language does not merely gain purchase upon space via the instrument of deixis. Conversely, space can be said to ground, indeed, more actively, to inform or infiltrate language. It is perhaps because Borges' texts and maps in the parables cited above seek to cover absolutely their referents, forgetting their derivative, even indebted relationship to their spatial partner, that they fail so spectacularly. Calvino's less grandiose form of spatial narrative stresses connection, rapport, and would thus appear more democratic, less concerned to obliterate that which is denoted by the signifier.

This book introduces a capital X into the word 'deixis'. In this way the very form of chiasmus is made to infiltrate the concept of deixis so as to produce the neologism 'deiXis'. 'DeiXis' is a tentative gesture seeking to represent, in typographical form, a mode of two-way, reciprocal interaction between language and space in literary texts. 'DeiXis' takes account of the manner in which literary texts model the spatial configuration of the world ("the fictions of space") as well as the manner in which those spatial configurations, although not available outside representation, also inflect texts and inform them according to their own patterns ("the spaces of fiction").

Such a relationship of reciprocity is highly significant. Structuralism and poststructuralism curtailed the sovereignty of the speaking subject by reminding it of its emergence out of the systematicity of language. Similarly, the pre-existing character of material space constitutes the environment out of which human activity, social, linguistic and cultural arises, as Grange has intimated:

> Without place, there would be neither language, nor action nor being as they have come to consciousness through time. Suppose there were no place. There would be no 'where' within which history could take

place. 'Where' is never a there, a region over against us, isolated and objective. 'Where' is always part of us and we are part of it.[5]

Likewise, Malpas has stressed that:

> Place is ... that within and with respect to which subjectivity is itself established – place is not founded *on* subjectivity, but is rather that on which subjectivity is founded. Thus one does not first have a subject that apprehends certain features of the world in terms of the idea of place; instead, the structure of subjectivity is given in and through the structure of place.[6]

The reciprocal model I am proposing in this book would stress the debt implicitly acknowledged by language to those spatial realities it engages with, even as it in turn moulds them through its discursive operations. In the face of what Irigaray has called "the forgetting of air" ["l'oubli de l'air"] – with a clear pun on the homonym "aire" ["area, place, space"] – this book seeks to restore a sense of debt, always already inscribed in language, to the places which enable it: "I am trying to retraverse all the places where I've been locked up or cast out so that he could constitute his here/there. I am trying to rediscover the possibility of a relationship with air/place. Isn't this necessary for me, well before I even start to speak?" ["J'essaie ... de retraverse tous les lieux où j'ai été exilée-enfermée pour qu'il constitue son là. ... J'essaie de retrouver la possibilité d'un rapport à l'air. N'en ai-je pas besoin, bien avant de commencer à parler?"].[7]

The spatial model proposed in this book would be one, in the words of Charles Tomlinson, "where space represented possibility and where self would have to embrace that possibility somewhat self-forgetfully, putting aside the more possessive and violent claims of personality."[8] This notion of self-abnegation has much in common with contemporary revisions of the rationalist and empiricist paradigm that has informed scientific experimentation since the Enlightenment. Rather than assuming the inanimate or at least 'soulless' character of the natural world, new ethical approaches to science stress the experimenter's debt to the objects of experimentation:

> the laboratory is also *a place saturated with obligations* ... we cannot avoid the conclusion that today's physicist *would not exist without the electron* (just as the molecular biologist would not exist without DNA) because most of the equipment inhabiting his laboratory presupposes its existence!

[le laboratoire est également *un lieu saturé d'obligations*. ... on devra conclure que le physicien d'aujourd'hui *n'est rien sans l'électron* (on le biologiste moléculaire sans l'ADN) car la plupart des dispositifs qui peuplent son laboratoire supposent son existence!][9]

The experimental scientist owes a debt to the supposedly inanimate entities upon whose existence his very work is predicated. This debt is not merely empirical, but takes on a genuinely ethical nature. The object of scientific experimentation imposes obligations upon the experimenting subject. In turn, this debt implies that the object is not merely passive, but has an agency which must be recognized, such that it emerges as another subject on a par with the experimenter. These reflections from recent studies of science function as an analogy for the way in which space can be conceived as a medium to which the human subject owes a debt.

Such indebtedness is part and parcel of the very process of nature-writing. The semantics of debt is explicitly engaged by the contemporary German poet Eva Strittmatter in a poem about the landscape outside of Berlin: "This earth won't let itself be traded with – it's not by chance that I'm descended from her" ["Diese Erde lässt nicht mit sich handeln. | Ich komm nicht umsonst aus ihr"].[10] The expression encoding a relationship of descendency, intimacy, genealogy, literally means "it's not for free". The natural environment eschews commodification, but by the same token imposes its own relationships of debt and obligation: the latter bonds combat the former reification. The title of the poem, "Mark", as in the Mark Brandenburg, also relates to the boundary "marking" territorial possession, to the currency which renders possession liquid, tradeable, to the marks left by writing, but of course also to the "remarking" in which pre-commodification relationships are re-enacted so as to remind us of where we come from.

Space, according to this conception, would not merely be a pre-existing scenario for events, it would gain an element of agency rarely ascribed to the natural world except when it escapes from human control. This forgetting of agency is posited upon a clear distinction between active humans and passive nature. The very essence of modernity, Bruno Latour has claimed, is predicated upon this "total separation of humans and non-humans" ["séparation totale des humains et des non-humains"].[11]

Yet such a radical division is far from self-evident. Indigenous thought, for instance, is diametrically opposed to such scissions. In his study of North-Western Arnhem Land culture, Ronald Berndt stressed that the interlinking clan-language pairs underlying that culture applied to the "whole of the human, non-human and natural environment".[12] Likewise, Eddie Kneebone says that "Aboriginal spirituality is the belief that all objects are living and share the same soul or spirituality that Aboriginals share."[13] A common soul assumes a common, if differentiated agency. "Aborigines envisage other species taking part in cultural activities ... The distinction between subject and object break down as people identify rocks, trees or birds as representations of their own beings."[14] This ascription of agency is evinced in the words of the Australian indigenous storyteller Bill Neidjie:

> That star e working there ... see?
> E working. I can see.
> Some of them small, you can't hardly see.
> Always at night, if you lie down ...
> look careful, e working ... see?[15]

In our rationalist world-view, stars do not "work". That is, the inanimate world does not possess agency. Bill Neidjie pre-empts this objection by remarking upon the "smallness" of stars. In other words, the apparent non-evidence of agency is merely a flaw of human perception. In Neidjie's conception of a natural world invested with counter-agency, the relationship is reciprocal:

> I love it tree because e love me too.
> E watching me same as you
> tree e working with your body, my body,
> e working with us.
> While you sleep e working.
> Daylight, when you walk around, e work too.
>   (*Story About Feeling* 4)

Here not only the human speaker but also the tree both possess agency, each in their own way. This installs a reciprocal relationship between human and nature, one that Neidjie expresses in chiastic form: "I love it tree because e love me too." The tree as a nexus of reciprocal human-natural relationships becomes a site of what I term in this book 'deiXis', where the capital X denotes the chiastic form appropriate to the crossing-over of mutual, interwoven conditions of possibility. DeiXis acknowledges the work done by humans in moulding space, but foregrounds the prior enabling work undertaken by space itself: "the social does not exist prior to place nor is it given expression except in or through place – and through spatialised, temporalised ordering … It is within the structure of place that the very possibility of the social arises."[16] Accordingly, DeiXis would be a mode of spatial representation which would "Let the ground rise up to resist us, let it prove porous, spongy, rough, irregular – let it assert its native title, its right to maintain its traditional surfaces."[17]

Given space?

But if space is there 'before' human actors, enabling their subsequent moulding of its contours, does this make it a tangible entity, a substance? Would not the notion of a spatial dimension endowed with an agency matching that of human actors merely restore an empirical notion of space, according to which "history changed society while geography provided the ground upon which history worked"?[18] Certainly, recent constructivist theories of landscape, for instance, that stress their operation as forms of cultural practice, are sceptical about seeing space "as an agent of power that is (or frequently represents itself as) independent of human intentions".[19] Setting up a reciprocity in which space is a no less active partner in the deictic process, it would appear, runs the risk of assuming that "space" is a naturalized given – thereby conferring upon deiXis as the essence of spatial language a reflective, mimetic, and ultimately ideological power.

Such a move would ignore the consensus, arrived at over several decades of spatial theorization, that space is the "product of interrelations … constituted through interactions, from the immensity of the global to the intimately tiny … always under construction."[20] Thus Edward Said could open his classic *Orientalism* by suggesting that "We must take seriously Vico's great observation that men make their own history, that what they can know is what they have made, and extend it to geography." This is because, he continued, "as … geographical and cultural entities – to say nothing of historical entities – such locales, regions, geographical sectors as 'Orient' and 'Occident' are manmade."[21] According to such theories, the notion of 'space' would thus encompass a bundle of reciprocal and multivectorial "spatial practices", among which hegemonic, power-serving "representations of space" would constantly intermesh with contestatory, user-owned "spaces of representation".[22]

DeiXis cannot afford to dispense with these theories. This complex and dynamic model of 'space' as a product and environment of spatial actors' practices, semiotic as well as material, underlies the explorations of the present book – but is supplemented by a corresponding model of the agency of space itself as a counterpoised network of dynamic, constantly changing, multivectorial relationships.

One recent theoretical example may point to a way of resolving this problem. The linguistically derived pragmatics of space elaborated by Michel de Certeau conceives of spatial practices as speech acts at the level of *parole* which make real an abstract spatial system at the level of *langue*. De Certeau is concerned to rehabilitate everyday spatial practices. He wishes, like Lefebvre, to re-endow the practices of ordinary women, men and children with their proper dignity and value.[23] Spatial practices are the ways humans make something of their environment: "The act of walking ... is a spatial acting-out of the place" ["L'acte de marcher ... est une *réalisation* spatiale du lieu"].[24] Social space is created by human practice out of the pre-existing raw materials of the place where that practice occurs, just as language works with the linguistic system manifest in prior speech acts.

By the same token, however, de Certeau comes very close to dispossessing space itself, making it merely the fabric created by human actions, forgetting that non-human actors (the elements such as water, air, gases, minerals, plants, and animals) have their own complex and dynamic practices which co-create the spaces equally configured by human actors. It comes as no surprise, then, to discover that the deictic concept which matches this Saussurean notion of spatial practice merely replicates the standard account of speaker-oriented deixis (see Chapter 1). The proximal/distal poles of deictic marking (*here* vs. *there*) are centred upon the human actor, just as the concretization of spatial language in the individual spatial *parole* re-awards the walker-speaker with agency: "In the framework of enunciation, the walker constitutes, in relation to his position, both a near and a far, a *here* and a *there*" ["Dans le cadre de l'énonciation, le marcheur constitue, par rapport à sa position, un proche et un lointain, un *ici* et un *là*"].[25] The walker constitutes space around her- or himself as formative actor.

Yet there is a site of ambivalence in de Certeau's theory which opens up alternative possibilities. He refers to the Saussurean notion of *langue*, the latent and purely abstract system underlying linguistic practice. *Langue* as system can only ever be posited as a hypothesis, because it is only accessible via the concrete speech acts (*parole*) which it is supposed to motivate. In de Certeau's spatial analogy, however, there is no abstract spatial system to be activated in the walker's "*parole*". There is merely the concrete place, itself the result of prior human practices of space (clearing, tilling, planting, excavation, building, demolition, renovation, etc.), which is then *re*-appropriated by the pedestrian. What emerges in the interstices of de Certeau's anthropocentric "arts de faire" is the shadow of a place which precedes and thus enables human spatial action. The walker's "near and ... far, ... *here* and ... *there*" ["*proche et ... lointain, ... ici et ... là*"] are deictic markers. They transpire to be, in the last analysis, instances of deiXis – that is, indices of the walker-enunciator's debt to a space which enables her or his practice. A visual index of this relationship of debt might be found in a tandem series of deserts photos by the Australian photographer Lyn Silverman. A horizontal series of outback horizon-and-sky photos is exactly matched by a second series, directly beneath it, of shots of the ground at the photographer's feet – sometimes even with the tips of her boots protruding into the bottom frame of the photo. The panoramic gaze above is always underpinned, literally in spatial terms of above/below, by intimate glimpses of the ground upon which the photographer stands: sand, gravel, sun-baked mud, with the occasional wiry desert flower. The series below makes up "a set of tracks ... a double lines, an exploration of reversibility, the trace of a movement on a strange, still space."[26] The ground under the photographer's feet enables the panoramas presented above.

The space that re-attains agency in the reciprocal mode we have been calling deiXis is not a given. Nor, conversely, is it merely the result of human practice. Rather, it is the embodiment of ongoing practices constituted by relationships between human and non-human actors. These non-human actors include the elements themselves, as acknowledged in Irigarary's work on air, water and earth, or in Simon Rodia's implementation of the raw materials, wood, stone, concrete, plastic, glass, or steel in the built environment.[27] Similarly, Australian indigenous thought concretely admits the agency of non-human actors by "anthropomorphizing" nature, as as indicated above in the extracts from Bill Neidjie's storytelling. Indeed, if one accepts the primacy that Australian indigenous dreaming narratives give to the ancestors and to the environment (essentially, they are one and the same), it might be more accurate to say that nature anthropomorphizes humans, creating humans in its own image. In the aphoristic title of a book by Deborah Bird Rose, "dingo makes us human".[28]

Such spatially informed modes of writing would participate in spatial politics, both as witness, but also as agent. This mode of literary spatial aesthetics would be part and parcel of historical process, recognizing that all history is the history of spatial experience, conflict and transformation. It would also be cognisant of the fact that neither experience, conflict nor transformation can occur without the medium of spatial semiotics, acknowledging thereby "the agency of space in the very thought that honours it".[29] Literary space would be a privileged form of representation which would specifically bear the burden of creating and transmitting meaning in the realm of spatial social existence. Yet that spatial social existence would also have contours of its own which make it not merely the passive site, albeit one constantly under construction, of the social world, but one endowed with forms of agency in its own right. Such agency becomes visible in the relationships of debt that, for instance, ecological discourses or indeigenous religious concepts insist upon. Indeed, the apparent collision between constructivist theories of space and empirical assumptions about space to be found in the notion of deiXis explored in this book are resolved in indigenous narrative. It is for this reason that the book turns, in its final chapters, to contemporary indigenous narrative as the exemplification par excellence of literary deiXis.

Tracks

The book is divided into two parts, following its title. Part I, 'the spaces of fiction', examines in detail the spatial contours of literature, beginning with theatre and moving on to prose fiction, so as to elaborate first the concept of deiXis which underpins this book, and then to develop a theory of narrative space which opens up the closure of chiasmus. Part II, 'the fictions of space', seeks to work out the consequences of such notions of literary spatiality in the domain of the postcolonial interface between Europe and its erstwhile colonies.

Part I, 'the spaces of fiction', is thus concerned to examine the microcosmic functioning of the mode of literary deiXis at a very detailed textual level.

Chapters 1 and 2 offer a reading of Samuel Beckett's *En attendant Godot* (1953)/*Waiting for Godot* (1956), so as to outline the notion of deiXis presented in this study. The first two chapters sketch a general theory of deiXis with reference to an artistic genre, theatre, in which deiXis works in immensely concrete ways. Theatre anchors the fictions of 'drama' within the very real here-and-now of a performance context without which it would remain mere script.

Beckett's play is particularly useful for this reading because it sits on the border between literary modernism and postmodernism, and thus embodies the two-stage perspective upon deixis which is introduced in these chapters. Chapter 1 embarks upon a critique of received notions of deictic language demonstrating that the customary conception of speaker-centered or 'egocentric' deixis, and revisions of it such as self-reflexive deixis, are patently inadequate; for they ignore the concrete spatial context in which deixis always occurs. This chapter draws upon the negative, modernist facet of Beckett's drama – the 'tragic' face of his *Tragicomedy in Two Acts*. In contrast, Chapter 2 proposes a notion of deixis which, in the manner we have sketched above, sees a fundamental reciprocity at work in spatial language. Spatial reference and spatial referents exist in a mutually constitutive and enabling relationship. The second facet of Beckett's *Tragicomedy*, namely, the more playful, postmodern side of the play, comes to the fore in this chapter, encapsulating the ineluctable imbrication of spatial language and its context. Chapter 2 concludes by evoking a concrete case of theatre-reception, Michel Foucault's debt to Beckett, so as to index the ways dramatic deiXis genuinely engages with a traceable social context.

Chapters 3 and 4 continue this concern with the social reception of literature in a specific locus by examining the manner in which narrative texts themselves dramatize the site of their reception. Chapter 3 utilizes Kristeva's notion of the "spatialization" of literature (resulting from her concept of intertextuality), in conjunction with Shklovsky's notion of narrative levels, to produce a spatial theory of narrative production. Each space of narration generates a contiguous space of narration in which the terms of the narrative are produced anew and differently. Chapter 3 begins with a comparison of the narrative situation of Conrad's *Heart of Darkness* (1899/1900), comparing it with its contemporary, Gide's *L'Immoraliste* (1902) [Engl. trans.: *The Immoralist*, 1960]. Chapter 4 continues this interrogation, via a reprise of theories of 'story' and 'discourse', with reference to two postmodern texts, Wolf's *Störfall* (1987) [Engl. trans.: *Accident*, 1989] and Dabydeen's *The Intended* (1991). These narratives include a *mise-en-abyme* of their own conditions of production, thereby gesturing towards their own conditions of *re*-production – physical, spatial conditions, embodied in the sites of re-narration, whose contours they in turn configure. In the debt which cannot be disguised by narrative agency, the mutuality that is deiXis comes to light.

In Part II, 'the fictions of space', the focus widens to include the global spaces of the colonial and postcolonial world. One might justifiably ask how the predominantly modernist focus of the first two chapters leads into the concerns of postcolonial writing. There are in fact many palpable links between these literary domains.

There is a growing body of criticism which acknowledges that Beckett was not merely an Irish author in exile or a reified exemplar of a universalized modernism. More significantly, he was a writer intent on opposing "authentic origins, history and language" as "crucial elements of national identity formation", in particular the sort of hypernationalism which emerged in post-independence Ireland.[30] In this respect, his quasi-postcoloniality had much in common with that of "semicolonial Joyce".[31] Beckett can therefore plausibly be seen as an artist "who by virtue of the concatenation of his geographical, temporal, linguistic and cultural locations is especially likely to have particular insight into one of the most important phenomena of his times: the end of imperialism as 'legitimate' political discourse."[32]

Likewise, Conrad is exemplary for the manner in which modernism and postcolonialism, often seen as having quite disparate agendas, are intimately linked.[33] The same might be said of Gide, who wrote some of his most important work as a response to prolonged stays in colonial North and West Africa. Wolf's and Dabydeen's work can be situated in the contemporary postcolonial and postimperial moment, thereby achieving the transition to the broad focus of the second part of the book. Thus Beckett, Conrad, Gide, Wolf and Dabydeen can be seen to be centrally concerned with issues of imperialism, whether colonial, postcolonial or neocolonial. The analysis of their texts concentrates upon the *spaces of narration* performed in these novels, embedded within *narrated spaces* of the colonial and postcolonial world as a global domain prefiguring our own supranational, global moment. These five authors offer a platform of detailed textual analyses that opens onto a wider panorama of over twenty-five poets, novelist and dramatists, many of whom wrote or write from outside of Europe, and exemplifying a plethora of contrasting perspectives on postcolonial space.

The second part of the book deals with deixis according to three modes of deictic representation (ego-centric deixis, self-reflexive deixis and spatio-centric deiXis) which are roughly aligned with the colonial period, the immediate post-independence period, and a later period in which the earlier optimism and jubiltation of national liberation had waned. Despite the hint of strict epochalization they may convey, these periods are understood very loosely and serve to indicate a general 'mood' or 'orientation' of deictic representation in the colonial and postcolonial world. They do not suggest that only one particular mode of deictic representation was at work at any given period, nor that these modes were always dominant in the same parts of the world at the same time. Nor should they be equated with Foucault's tripartite history of space (uncannily similar to Conrad's tripartiate history of Geography Fabulous, Geography Militant, and Geography Triumphant) or Soja's ternary First-, Second- and Thirdspace (itself playing upon Lefevbre's triad of spatial practices, representations of space and spatial representations).[34]

In the six chapters that make up Part II, I deal first with two modes of deixis in which space is the subaltern object of writing. First, I speak of colonial deixis, which corresponds to the standard account of speaker-centred or ego-centric deixis. I present post-independence deixis, which approximates in its functioning to self-reflexive deixis. I then move on to a third mode of deixis in which space emerges as the subject of writing. This is the mode of post-post-independence deictic marking – the 'deiXis' already sketched in the earlier chapters of this book. Here, space is envisaged as an active producer in its own right – as an agent which is also manifested in the putative 'givens' of specific places, givens which are all too easily mistaken however for the mere objects and arenas of human agency.

The second part commences in Chapters 5 and 6 with an examination of what W. J. T. Mitchell has called "imperial space", a mode of spatial representation that assumes a deictic activity firmly centered in European-speaker-centred deixis.[35] Chapter 5 briefly revisits the "spatial turn" in the humanities since the 1960s to suggest that the debates around the nature of social space themselves have reflected the changes in the deictic marking of space from the colonial, via the postcolonial, to the neo-colonial globalizing moments. Ondaatje's *The English Patient* (1991) and Desai's *The Inheritance of Loss* (2006) serve as textual exemplifications showing how the spatial amnesia operative since the Enlightenment has persisted into the present day, occluding the workings of imperialism and its avatars. Only recently has it been dispelled, allowing a novel perception of the specific fabric of space in the postcolonial world to emerge in which space figures with its own agency alongside that of humans.

Chapter 6 addresses more specifically the workings of imperial space, reading Conrad's *Heart of Darkness* (once again) alongside Naipaul's *A Bend in the River* (1979) to explore the colonial ideologies of the non-European world as a place without history – a place where space ostensibly eradicates time. This notion of timelessness underwrites the static but panoramic gaze evinced, for instance, in Robert Dunbar's poem *The Cruise: A Prospect of the West Indian Achipelago* (1835). A glance at Keats's 'On First Looking into Chapman's Homer' (1816) and Kipling's *Kim* (1901) shows how such panoramas were inevitably textual manifestations of imperial control (military and then economic) of colonial territory. The chapter closes by enumerating alternative perspectives that contested such fantasies of panoramic mastery, such as Césaire's *Cahier d'un retour au pays natal* (1956) [Engl. trans.: *Return to My Native Land* (1971)], Jean Rhys' *Wide Sargasso Sea* (1962), Roy's *The God of Small Things* (1997), or Rushdie's *Midnight's Children* (1981).

This contestation is pioneered, in the post-independence period, on the same deictic ground as that of colonial deixis. Chapters 7 and 8 suggest how this acceptance of the underlying premises of imperial deixis may have hampered the post-independence project of a self-reflexive mode of national deixis. In Chapter 7, this aporia is seen to be already intimated in a very early post-World War II poem by J. E. Clare McFarlane, 'On National Vanity' (ca. 1948). Seizure of the imperial-speaker-centred-deixis and its transfer away from the European metropolis towards the newly independent nation was problematic because it neglected to transform the speaker-centred structure of deixis itself. The persistence of such a structural continuity is explored in readings of Achebe's *Things Fall Apart* (1958) and Ngũgĩ wa Thiong'o's *A Grain of Wheat* (1967/1986), though the latter novel voices a suspicion that the self-reflexive national mode of deixis may not guarantee genuine political transformation.

Chapter 8 sharpens the critique of post-independence nationalism and its self-reflexive mode of deixis, exploring examples of such self-reflexivity across Davison's *The White Woman* (1994) with reference to Carter's work on colonial naming. The unbroken continuities between pre- and post-independence spatial regimes are instantiated via a reading of Kourouma's *Les Soleils des independences* [*The Suns of the Independences*] (1970). A closing examination of Wicomb's *David's Story* (2000) and Vassanji's *The In-Between World of Vikram Lall* (2003) shows how these tragic continuities have contributed to contemporary skepsis about national independence paradigms. Such narratives point the way to an alternative form of spatial marking that I have baptized as deiXis.

Finally, in Chapters 9 and 10 the book focuses upon narratives which re-discover or perpetuate an apparently lost but none the less enduring tradition that cedes speaker-centred deixis to nature itself, thereby enacting a reciprocal linguistic process of spatial performativity which I term deiXis – a version of nature glimpsed in poems by Fatoba or in Muecke's *No Road* (1997). Chapter 9 approaches these narratives negatively, reading texts such as Naipaul's *The Enigma of Arrival* [*Solibo the Magnificent*] (1987), Warner's *Indigo* (1992), or Chamoiseau's *Solibo Magnifique* (1988), which can only apprehend this mode of deictic intimacy and reciprocity in an elegiac tenor, registering the loss of such cultural legacies.

Chapter 10 reverses this perspective, employing Malouf's *An Imaginary Life* (1978), *Child's Play* (1982) and *Remembering Babylon* (1993), E. M. Forster's *A Passage to India* (1924), Ondaatje's *English Patient* (revisited) and Wright's *Carpentaria* (2006), to begin sketching a poetics reposing upon deiXis as a reciprocal form of spatial representation. The chapter concludes by listening to Australian indigenous storytellers, Kim Scott and Hazel Brown in *Kayang & Me* (2005) and Bill Neidjie in *Story About Feeling* (1989). The oral narratives passed on by these storytellers embody a contemporary deiXis which evinces the respectful acknowledgement of the spaces of the natural environment as the indispensable other upon whom human existence is dependent.

Part I
The Spaces of Fiction

1
Deixis and I

In *Finnegan's Wake* (1939), Joyce's encyclopaedic compendium of punning neologisms, he forges the pair "fullstoppers" and "semicolonials".[1] Grafted onto the punctuation marks 'full stop' and 'semicolon' are two geopolitical social categories from the age of high imperialism: the firmly-rooted citizen of the metropolitan colonizing centre and the quasi-colonial subject (the English-speaking Irish, South-African or Australian rather than the native Indian or African).[2] In contrast to the immobile identity of the metropolitan citizen, securely buttressed by the phrasal closure of the full stop, the "semicolonial" identity is defined by phrasal apposition. The semicolon separates but connects. As a punctuation mark it is already an uneasy mix of full stop and comma, of phrasal closure and intraphrasal segmentation (a "hybred", adds Joyce – *Finnegan's Wake* 152), destabilizing the singularity and incisiveness of the terminal dot. The "semicolonial" condition is one in which a distinctive identity is both enabled by its contiguous neighbours ('natives', 'Englishmen') – but also contaminated and cast into question by them. It is hardly surprising that the "semicolonial" subject, liminal from the outset, tends to be a traveller and exile. Though the "semiocolonial" subject often belongs to a so-called 'settler' colony, the juxtaposition of colonial periphery and European cultural affiliation makes for a generic 'unsettledness'. Whence the trajectory of a "semicolonial" writer such as Joyce via Dublin, Paris, Trieste, Zürich.

This opening chapter focuses on Joyce's equally semicolonial protégé: Samuel Beckett. The constitutive state of apposition generated in Beckett's peregrinations is only slightly less picaresque (Dublin, London, Paris, Roussillon). And, rather than the macaronic polyglot inventiveness of his mentor, an all-pervasive bilingualism is manifest in his apposition of English and French texts. This relation of apposition in

Beckett's *oeuvre* undermines any exclusive allegiance to an originary maternal language or an originary autochton territory. Languages and the spaces they are customarily identified with constantly unsettle each other. This chapter inaugurates an extended reading of *En attendant Godot* (1952) and *Waiting for Godot* (1956) – texts patently in apposition – in order to question the standard accounts of deixis.[3] For this reason, this chapter will consistently place Beckett's 'original' French versions before his 'derivative' English translations of his own texts. The theatre of this Anglo-Irish author does not 'originate' in his mother-tongue, but rather, in his adopted second(ary) French. Beckett's full-scale attack on 'here'-ness underlies the critique of language and nation implicitly mobilized by his work. The chapter embarks upon a critique of received notions of deictic language, demonstrating that the customary conception of 'egocentric' deixis, and revisions of it such as self-reflexive deixis, are patently inadequate; for they ignore the concrete spatial context in which deixis always occurs. This chapter focuses on the negative, modernist aspect of Beckett's drama – the 'tragic' face of his *Tragicomedy in Two Acts* – before turning, in the following chapter, to the more playful, comic, postmodern aspect of that drama.

Time and space in modernism

The confrontation of Beckett's characters with the aporias of time within modernism's general sense of apocalyptic disintegration ("Things fall apart", wrote Yeats in 'The Second Coming') is signalled from the outset by the title of Beckett's *En attendant ... /Waiting ...*[4] Beckett's interest in temporality – from his early work on Proust through to pieces such as *Endgame* or *Krapp's Last Tape* – is patently obvious. Yet the aporias of time and space are inextricably intertwined. Beckett's two tramp-like no-hopers, Vladimir and Estragon, struggle to ascertain whether it is Saturday – and which Saturday then? – or Sunday – or Monday – or perhaps Friday: Vladimir "[*regarde*] *avec affolement autor de lui, comme si la date était inscrite dans le paysage*" (*En attendant Godot* 18) – Vladimir "[*looks*] *wildly about him, as though the date was inscribed in the landscape*" (*Waiting for Godot* 15). Little help is coming from Beckett's bare stage. Vladimir and Estragon manifestly have considerable difficulties locating themselves in time – but even more so in space. They are waiting for Godot. That much is sure. But are they waiting in the right place? "*Tu es sûr que c'est ici?*" (*En attendant Godot* 16) – "You're sure it was here?", asks Estragon (*Waiting for Godot* 14). They have been told to wait in front of a tree. There are no others in sight, but this one looks more like a bush than a tree. Is it the right one? "Qu'est-ce que tu veux insinuer? Qu'on s'est trompé d'endroit?" (*En attendant Godot* 17) – "What are you insinuating? That we've come to the wrong place?" demands Vladimir (*Waiting for Godot* 14). In the context of Beckett's play, this uncertainty of spatial reference is centrally important. It makes it impossible to say whether the meeting with Godot will ever 'take place', as the 'place' remains radically undecidable. Thus the aporetic temporal axis of the play's action, with *waiting* as its paradigmatic mode of temporal being, is fundamentally dependent upon an equally aporetic spatial axis of reference.

The aporias of space (Yeats' "The centre cannot hold", for instance) have generally drawn less attention than those of time. When this has not been the case, it is often merely because, according to the customary logics of Modernism, space resurges as that default mode which comes to the fore when temporal schemes fail – as in Vladimir's bleak "Le temps s'est arrêté" (*En attendant Godot* 50) – "Time has stopped" (*Waiting for Godot* 36). In modernism, Joseph Frank has claimed, history becomes ahistorical – time becomes a continuum in which distinctions between past and present are wiped out. Past and present are then apprehended spatially.[5] If, as Foucault once quipped, time is generativity, fertility, productivity, in brutal contrast, space – in particular under the aegis of modernism – is decay, infertility, stasis.[6] Modernism, "finding the mirror of nature broken",[7] turned away from what had once symbolized organic continuity and tradition, or registered the fragments which remained:

> What are the roots that clutch, what branches grow
> Out of this stony rubbish? Son of man,
> You cannot say, or guess, for you know only
> A heap of broken images, where the sun beats,
> And the dead trees give no shelter, the cricket no relief,
> And the dry stone no sound of water.[8]

The landscapes of *The Waste Land*, as the title tells us from the outset, are landscapes of catastrophe and function as a metaphor for modern civilization devoid of all organic cultural resilience. In their purely symbolic value T. S. Eliot's panoramas of futility, aridity and destruction are landscapes "stripped down to [their] bare essentials" (in the words of Helen Gardner).[9]

In Beckett's play these spatial aspects are indexed less ostentatiously for the academic critic primarily interested in the verbal fabric of the drama and focused upon the script (despite, for instance, Estragon's angry "fous-moi la paix avec tes paysages" [*En attendant Godot* 86], "you and your landscapes" [*Waiting for Godot* 61]). They should be patently obvious, however, to the theatre critic observing the performance, where the bare stage and the leafless, skeletal tree resonate with the modernist failure of organic life, but more determinedly, advertise the paucity of spatial reference points. Estragon, after wondering whether this was the tree where they were supposed to await Godot, makes up his mind :

ESTRAGON: Pour moi, nous étions ici.
VLADIMIR: (*regard circulaire*). L'endroit te semble familier?
ESTRAGON: Je ne dis pas ça.
VLADIMIR: Alors?
ESTRAGON: Ça n'empêche pas.

(*En attendant Godot* 18)

ESTRAGON: In my opinion we were here.
VLADIMIR: (*Looking round*). You recognize the place?
ESTRAGON: I didn't say that.
VLADIMIR: Well?
ESTRAGON: That makes no difference.

(*Waiting for Godot* 15)

Or does it? Difference is at the heart of the problem. It has seeped into identity, thus ruining its coherence as a basis for meaning: "Je est un autre", as Rimbaud famously quipped in a letter of 1871. Difference also corrodes spatial identity. The identity of 'here', like that of 'now', has become radically uncertain. Language no longer fixes temporal or spatial meaning but appears to have come adrift. It merely "makes differences": "Tu en vois d'autres?", "Do you see any others?", as Vladimir asks (*En attendant Godot* 17/*Waiting for Godot* 14).

The "differences" of this universe are not merely punctual, as one might believe from Vladimir's later comparison with the Vaucluse (in English the Mâcon region): "tu ne vas pas me dire que ça (*geste*) ressemble au Vaucluse. Il y a quand même une grosse différence" (*En attendant Godot* 86) – "you can't tell me that this (*gesture*) bears any resemblance to ... (*he hesitates*) ... to the Mâcon country, for example. You can't deny there's a big difference" (*Waiting for Godot* 61). The difference is so immense as to admit of no convergence whatsoever. That is the import of Vladimir's indexical "ça"/"this" and his gesture, which simultaneously points at the place of its reference and disqualifies it as deserving of reference. (Even more drastically denuded of reference is Estragon's "geste vers l'univers" – *En attendant Godot* 19/"gesture towards the universe" – *Waiting for Godot* 16). The whole action of *Waiting for Godot* dramatizes the failure of convergence: Godot never materializes in the 'here' and 'now'; his and the other characters' paths never cross.

The collapse of spatial and temporal referentiality performed on Beckett's stage is part of the generalized failure of language which is registered by European writers from the turn of the twentieth century onwards and is neatly encapsulated in T. S. Eliot's 'Burnt Norton':

> Words strain,
> Crack and sometimes break, under the burden,
> Under the tension,
> Slip, slide, perish,
> Decay with imprecision, will not stay in place,
> Will not stay still.
> (*Four Quartets*, in *The Complete Poems and
> Plays of T. S. Eliot*, 175)

Language, once the vehicle of tradition and the transmitter of certainties, has been invaded by the uncertainties of spatial erosion. In Conrad's idiom, the traditional sense that "the earth ... is ... a standing place ... a place to live in", cedes to the Modernist shock of recognition: Marlow gasps that Kurtz "had kicked the very earth to pieces. ... I before him did not know whether I stood on the ground or floated in the air."[10] Spatial language, as a synecdoche for language in general, is cast free of its erstwhile moorings. Lefebvre, perhaps echoing Virginia Woolf in her essay 'Modern Fiction', even goes so far as to put an exact date of this dislocation of spatial parameters:

> The fact is that around 1910 a certain space was shattered. It was the space of common sense, of knowledge (*savoir*), of social practice, of political power, a space thitherto enshrined in everyday discourse, just as in abstract thought, as the environment and channel for communications; the space, too, of classical perspective and geometry, developed from the Renaissance onwards on the basis of the Greek tradition (Euclid, logic) and bodied forth in Western art and philosophy, as in the form of the city and town.

> [Vers 1910, l'espace commun au bon sens, au savoir, à la pratique sociale, au pouvoir politique, contenu du discours quotidien comme

de la pensée abstraite, milieu et canal des messages, celui de la perspective classique et de la géométrie, élaborée depuis la Renaissance,
à partir de l'héritage grec (Euclide et la logique), à travers l'art et
la philosophie de l'Occident, incorporé dans la ville, cet espace se
branle.][11]

If space as evinced in "the content of everyday discourse and ... the
milieu and channel of communication" has been thrown out of synch,
then it is hardly surprising that language has also been one of the primary sites of the interrogation which has ensued. In the century since
1910 *anno domini*, spatial language has been subjected to rigorous critical scrutiny. The place where much of that critical reappraisal has been
carried out has been fiction, envisaged as a laboratory of language.

This book explores various facets of the twinned critiques of spatial
language and linguistic space across modern fiction, poetry, and drama
in English and French. It suggests that the uncertainty evinced in and
vehiculed by spatial language may be salutary, pointing up (literally, as
will become clear in what follows) in the direction of an ethical relationship with our existential environment. Spatial language, so goes
the argument of this book, offers us, by virtue of its very fabric, a model
for ways of being in the world that commit us ineluctably to a socially
and politically informed solidarity with our fellow beings.

Deixis

But is the spatial unease tangible in Beckett's drama only a symptom of
a particular period of existential and epistemological turbulence? The
typically (post?)modernist passages from Beckett's *Waiting for Godot*
cited above may also reveal something quite distinct from the destabilizing influence of modernist linguistic scepticism. What Beckett's
text additionally evinces is an instability that is endemic to spatial and
temporal referentiality as such.

In an everyday linguistic context, spatial language tends to dispense
with substance, relying upon the proximity of the objects referred to.
Vladimir enquires where Estragon has spent the night. In a ditch, the
latter replies. And where, Vladimir asks? "(*sans geste*). Par là" (*En attendant
Godot* 10) – "(*without gesture*). Over there" (*Waiting for Godot* 9). In the spatial language of real-time-space situations (what theatrical performance
simulates, using the material of real-time-and-space itself) the content
omitted from the linguistic utterance is supplemented by the environment, aided sometimes by a gesture of pointing – or not, as the case

may be (*"sans geste* ... Par là"/*"without gesture* ... Over there"). The loss of spatial content at the level of the utterance may be compensated by the concretude of content at the level of context. The mechanics of pragmatics generally work with gesture, gaze, a nod of the head or an extended finger. Gesture is particularly important on the stage because it pins the dramatic text into the real context of the theatrical performance: "Gesture, in this sense, *materializes* the dramatic subject and his world by asserting their identity with an actual body and an actual space."[12] However, the gap between language and place can never be completely bridged. Beckett makes it a yawning chasm by cancelling the compensatory pointing (*"sans geste"* – *"without gesture"*) and refusing to fill it.

Gesture fulfils the vital role of rendering specific indicators which are notoriously vague: which night? which ditch? where is "over there"? These indicators function only differentially: "this Saturday, and not next Saturday" is a statement in which the two terms are mutually dependent upon each other for their meaning. That difference may be spanned by the fluid semiosis of indexical gesture or metacommentary. The chasm may continue to gape, leading to the mundane mis-communications of the sort that we all know so well: muddled-up meeting places, mutual misunderstandings. Modernism raises such failures of the spatial speech act to paradigmatic status. It loosens the tight bonds of reference until metaphor slackens into metonymy or its handmaiden indexicality. Beckett's minimalist stage, consciously flouting the realist conventions of the well-made-play, sheers off the physical docking-points for spatio-temporal reference. In so doing, his stagecraft lays bare the essentially aporetic nature of spatio-temporal denotation. Modernism does little more than parade the multivalency, and thus the emptiness, which inherently dogs linguistic reference.

What Beckett effectively mobilizes is an exploration of the hollowness of spatial signification – a hollowness generally elided by the pragmatic flexibility of everyday communication, but, because it is the linchpin upon which that flexibility hinges, easily becomes acute in a moment of cultural crisis. Beckett's theatre could be understood, to state the matter in more formal terms, as a historically specific localization of the perennial risks of deixis.[13] The term 'deixis' refers to words which anchor a discourse in a context, which, in Lyons' serviceable definition, "relate utterances to the spatio-temporal co-ordinates of the act of utterance".[14] Demonstratives such as 'this' or 'that', markers of space such as 'here' or 'there', pronouns such as 'she' or 'he' or 'I', markers of time such as 'yesterday', 'now', 'immediately' all serve to root a discourse within a context of enunciation.

These markers are in themselves empty of content. Their emptiness is the guarantor of their flexibility. Their hollowness does, however, make them perfect candidates for semantic confusion. By extension, as Levinson notes programmatically, "The importance of deictic information for the interpretation of utterances is perhaps best illustrated by what happens when such information is lacking."[15]

Deictics gain substance, then, only by being planted in the here and now of speech. As so-called 'shifters', mobile, polyvalent 'pointers' (from the Greek, δειξια, to point or refer [*OED*]) without substance of their own, they can serve in a multitude of situations. Accordingly, they structure the context in which they are implemented. The discourse they ground frames and configures a realm of material space, making it meaningful. But by the same token, it is only by virtue of that space that deictics take on a specific content. Without that concrete contextualization they remain empty, abstract, pure formalism. In turn, they owe their meaning to the ground in which they anchor their act of enunciation.

In deixis discourse and context are interdependent. Their relationship is one of reciprocal definition, each giving the other what it lacks. Reciprocity is at the heart of deictic operation. Deixis can be said to propose a basal model of ethics arising out of the spatialized speech or discourse situation. It offers a pattern of constant, performative give-and-take grounding the very possibility of speech-in-context.

This book opens with the issue of deixis in order to create a model of the way in which language and context interact in relationships of mutual interdependence. Spatiality is not a secondary aspect of language, a subsidiary domain which is laid bare only when language in its linear, teleological, communicative function falters. Rather, spatiality is the place where language is revealed for what it is, namely, the site of human existence as reciprocality from beginning to end. Thus spatiality becomes the literal locus of an ethical mode of linguistic being in the world. Literary works which foreground spatial thematics, I argue, cannot but draw attention to their own fabric, their inherently spatial language and, by the same token, point to the networks of reciprocal and ethical relationships in which they, their authors and their readers willy-nilly find themselves.

The following chapter (Chapter 2) returns to deixis to explore more thoroughly the nature of reciprocity in spatial language. The present chapter prepares that task by proceeding via counter-examples: first, the predominant models of deixis which privilege egocentricity; and secondly, the briefly envisaged alternative of deictic self-referentiality. At each juncture, I will turn to Beckett's *En attendant Godot/Waiting for*

Godot, in part because the drama rehearses a variety of possible stances with regard to spatiality but also, in the final analysis, because drama (as an art form) itself incorporates the sort of spatial reciprocity I am seeking to elucidate here. I will be citing, as is already clear, both Beckett's French 'original' and his subsequent English (self)-translation because this textual duality constitutes a first index, by virtue of its multiplicity, of the reciprocity of theatrical performance text and the contextual *here* in which it is staged.

Egocentric deixis

Shortly after Pozzo's arrival on the stage with Lucky, Vladimir and Estragon dare to ask why the unfortunate "carrier" is not permitted to put down his baggage. Pozzo deigns to explain, but prefaces his explanation with a lengthy preamble:

> POZZO: (... *se revaporise la gorge, remet le vaporisateur dans sa poche*). Je suis prêt. Tout le monde m'écoute? (*Il les regard tous les trois, Lucky en dernier, tire sur la corde*). Alors quoi? (*Lucky lève la tête*). Je n'aime pas parler dans le vide. Bon. Voyons. (*Il réfléchit*).
> ESTRAGON: Je m'en vais.
>
> (*Waiting for Godot* 41)

> POZZO: (... *sprays his throat again, puts back the vaporizer in his pocket.*) I am ready. Is everybody listening? Is everybody ready? (*He looks at them all in turn, jerks the rope.*) Hog! (*Lucky raises his head.*) I don't like talking in a vacuum. Good. Let me see. (*He reflects*).
> ESTRAGON: I'm going.
>
> (*Waiting for Godot* 30)

It is Estragon's disgusted announcement of his departure which alerts us to the hidden spatial dimensions of Pozzo's discourse. Estragon's intended exit, like so many others in the play, comes to nothing. It is vitiated by Pozzo's vaguely threatening spatio-temporal marker: "Réfléchissez, avant de commettre une imprudence. Mettons que vous partiez maintenant, pendant qu'il fait encore jour, car malgré tout il fait encore jour" (*En attendant Godot* 38) – "Think twice before you do anything rash. Suppose you go now, while it is still day, for there is no denying it is still day" (*Waiting for Godot* 29). Pozzo's threat means nothing. It does, however, lay bare the latent coercion in the situation of discourse: "Je suis prêt. Tout le monde m'écoute?" – "I am ready. Is everybody listening?" That Pozzo's long-awaited speech is so long in coming merely underlines its capacity to polarize the figures on stage into a hierarchy of speaker and listener positions.

To this extent, it fulfils the central criteria for deixis as it has been understood in most twentieth-century accounts. Two instances of this commonplace will suffice for the moment. Kryk, for example, claims: "The crucial role of deixis ... [is to allow] the speaker to anchor his utterances in an extra-linguistic world."[16] Jones notes acidly: "It is rather ironic that deixis is often cited as proof of the interdependence between language structure and communicative function and yet communication is quite often pictured as an act of pure self-expression by a lone individual."[17] A second instance of the same commonplace is provided by Brown and Yule. Regarding the spatial deictic 'here', they claim that "the interpretation of the spatial range of the expression ... on any particular occasion of use will have to be sought in the context of what *the speaker* is talking about."[18] "Again, no mention of hearer," observes Jones sardonically.[19]

In Beckett's drama, Pozzo is the embodiment of such notions of speech-in-situation as being defined exclusively by the-speech-of-the speaker. Vladimir and Estragon are in thrall to the pending explanation of Lucky's servitude, itself tantalizingly delayed by Pozzo's suggestion that he too should be party to the meeting with Godot (*En attendant Godot* 39/*Waiting for Godot* 29). They may not be tethered at the end of a rope like Lucky but they are positioned no differently by Pozzo's discourse. Whence Vladimir's equally discursive attempt to break out of the discursively-constructed deictic place of listener: "Je m'en vais" – "I'm going". Resisting the overpowering egocentricity of Pozzo's discourse, he tries in vain to convert an already peripheral but static discursive position into a patently centrifugal vector of escape.

If we are to attempt seriously to elaborate a model of reciprocity as the determining function of deixis, we must inevitably cast into question the dominant tenor of most extant studies of deictic language. Most commentary on deixis, of which I will cite only a few salient examples, assumes its inherent egocentricity. Beginning with Karl Bühler's pioneering work, theorists of deixis have repeatedly stressed the agency of the human speaker wielding the linguistic tools of deixis. Bühler, in 1934, programmatically foregrounded the egocentric aspect of deixis. The "deictic field" ["Zeigfeld"] is anchored in what he called the

"Origo": "From the *origo* of the visible here, all other positions are indi-cated verbally" ["Von der Origo des anschaulichen Hier aus werden sprachlich alle anderen Positionen gezeigt"].[20] This theory of deixis is egoistical, not reciprocal. As Jones observes, "It is important to note that despite Bühler's acknowledgement of the social nature of the communi-cative event ... the first casualty of his psychologically based theory of the deictic field is the addressee or receiver who is simply missing from the coordinate system ... This a-social, one-sided focus is typical of the standard account."[21]

Bühler's perspective set the tone for much later work on deixis, beginning with Bertrand Russell, who called deictic markers "egocen-tric particulars".[22] Burlakova finds that egocentricity is "a fundamental characteristic of deixis in contemporary linguistics".[23] Green likewise accepts that "there is a centre of orientation in deixis which is invari-ably egocentric".[24] Only Levinson more cautiously claims that "it is generally (but not invariably) true that deixis is organized in an ego-centric way".[25]

Contemporary linguistics has thus built, explicitly or otherwise, upon the assumption of the perceptual egocentrism inherent in deixis.[26] Lyons claims that "The canonical situation-of-utterance is egocentric in the sense that the speaker, by virtue of being the speaker, casts himself in the role of ego and relates everything to his viewpoint. He is at the zero-point of the spatiotemporal co-ordinates of what we will refer to as the deictic context."[27] Little has changed since Bühler, except that Lyons, perhaps unwittingly, makes more explicit the manner in which the subject's experience of itself is at heart autopoetic. The subject gains a sense of selfhood in the very action of "casting itself" as an ego. What Lyons usefully highlights here is the manner in which the self believes in its own agency, one that is based upon a self-reflexive gaze. That gaze embodies the "leurre de l'identification spatiale" ["lure of spatial iden-tification"] that Lacan sees at the heart of the mirror stage.[28] According to the dominant model, in deixis this spatial identification takes place following the logic of 'Here I am – therefore I am.'

Jones notes the connections between the individualism of Bühler's theories, and the central role of individualism in founding the empiri-cism which marks his approach:

> Bühler's work on deixis is essentially nothing more than a translation
> of this philosophical individualism into a theory of language, via an
> empiricist psychology of human action and perception. The reason,
> I would argue, for the universal acceptance of Bühler's conceptual

framework lies in its conformity with the prevailing individualism and subjectivism (in empiricist and rationalist versions) of the
Western philosophical *Weltanschauung*.[29]

Since Locke, empiricism has entailed a rigorous separation of things-
in-the world which are perceived as ideas-in-the mind by a perceiving
individual. Locke defines as "determinate" or "clear ideas" *"that simple
appearance, which the Mind has in its view, or perceives in it self, when
that Idea is said to be in it"*. He subsequently defines as "determined"
or "complex ideas" those ensembles constructed of *"a determinate
number of certain simple or less complex Ideas, joyn'd in such a proportion and situation, as the Mind has before its view, and sees in it self, when
that Idea is present in it, or should be present in it, when a Man gives a
name to it."*[30] The individual's understanding of the world, marked by
clarity and analytical construction on the basis of atomized conceptual units, depends for its certainty upon the scission of inner and
outer worlds. This scission in turn is projected upon the "clear ideas"
and their distinction from each other and then finally upon a clear
sense of selfhood. Deixis, according to what Levinson categorizes as
the "proximal" and "distal" markers 'here' and 'there' respectively,[31]
is assimilated to a dichotomized world with a subjective interiority at
its centre. This eradication of all potentially blurred boundaries can in
turn be expressed in a gruff empiricism which sees external objects in
their ipseity reduced to the sum total of sensations, which are then said
to be perceived 'within' the self.

This system is patently tautological. It depends upon a constant cir-
culation between outer and inner worlds that is persistently elided so
as to establish the illusion of pragmatic clarity. In this circularity one
can catch a glimpse of the newly emergent human being identified by
Foucault as "the locus of an empirico-transcendental doublet ... that
paradoxical figure in which the empirical contents of knowledge necessarily release, of themselves, the conditions that have made them
possible" ["lieu d'un redoublement empirico-transcendental, ... cette
étrange figure où les contenus empiriques de la connaissance délivrent,
mais à partir de soi, les conditions qui les ont rendus possibles"].[32] The
human subject emerges as the subject and object of its own knowledge.
In other words, this human being knows itself on the same terms as
it knows the other objects constituting the ensemble of its empirical
knowledge. Pope's "Know then thyself"[33] comes to describe an individual which assumes its own pre-existence as the basis of its perception, ignoring the manner in which that 'perception' has created the

ostensibly perceiving self. Similarly, the egocentric theory of deixis posits a self wielding deictic instruments whose action, and the environment acted upon, found the self that supposedly masters them.

Deixis, in the egocentric account, is predicated upon the centrality of a clearly-marked individual consciousness, neatly cordoned-off from its surroundings and anchoring itself in that context by means of deictic buoys cast into the environs. What can be detected in this account, however, are two alternative approaches to deixis which we will consider below. On the one hand, in the tautological character of the empiricist notion of thought and language, there slumbers the shadow of a self-reflexive notion of deixis which will emerge under the aegis of modernism. We will turn to this notion in the next section. On the other hand, in the elided but ongoing exchanges between the environment and the individual's senses, there is to be found the germ of a contextual and reciprocal model of deixis which this book seeks to elaborate as a model for literary deiXis in general. This model is the subject of Chapter 2.

Self-reflexive deixis

Vladimir enquires, in an exchange already quoted above, where Estragon has spent the night, to which the latter replies: a ditch. In an everyday linguistic context, spatial language tends to dispense with substance, relying upon the proximity of the objects referred to: "VLADIMIR: (*épaté*). Un fossé! Où ça? ESTRAGON: (*sans geste*). Par là" (*En attendant Godot* 10) – "VLADIMIR: (*admiringly*). In a ditch! Where? ESTRAGON: (*without gesture*). Over there" (*Waiting for Godot* 9). In the absence of a gesture anchoring the "par là"/"over there" in a specific region of the stage-space, Estragon's deictic marker can only make sense by its differential relationship to his own 'here'. Stripped of its connection to the place, it refers only to its own constitutive instance – and place – of enunciation. In turn, the space it points to to is projected by its own deictic activity. The situated speech act, ostensibly grounding the speaking self, is merely suspended between the terms 'here' and 'there'. Beckettian deixis is riddled with tautology upon tautology.

If the egocentric core of deixis is merely a mirage, an infolding of the world, a gesture of "casting" which retroactively produces a self around that casting, is deixis itself not, in turn, a tautology? Perhaps, as some recent theoreticians of deixis have suggested, spatial indexicality does nothing but point to itself. In place of the person-centred model of deixis, this approach posits an anonymous discourse-centred perspective, totally erasing the subjective human element.

Roland Barthes, in a treatise on classical rhetoric, identifies *topography* (the description of places) as one of the many *topoi* or commonplaces available to the rhetoritician. Why topoi? According to Aristotle memory places (or spatial mnemonics) helped the speaker to find the particular rhetorical resource to be implemented in a particular context.[34] Topography is thus a janus-faced entity. On the one hand, it is a description of real places turned towards the physical world, while on the other it is merely one scion of the large family of rhetorical topology. A deictic marker such as 'here' is ambiguous, pointing as it does to a location both in space and in discourse. Topography simultaneously charts real geographies *and* one mental region of the larger territory constituting the topology of rhetorical topoi. The 'here' of physical topography would seem far more real than the 'here' of rhetorical topology. This hierarchy is predicated, however, on a progressive distance (or abstraction) from the concrete referent of the deictic 'here'.

Yet this assumes that one stakes out a conceptual position which gives priority to real landscapes. If one approached the distinction between topography and topology from another direction, however, things would look rather different. Suppose one regarded the topography/topology divide from the perspective of the latter, giving weight to the discursive face of topography. Topography would then appear merely as a subset of a superior linguistic mega-set. Topography itself would be susceptible of further subdivision into sub-sub-sets. Let us take the conveniently binary topography of "Country and City"; its first term could in turn be opened up to produce the subsidiary "Garden and Wilderness", and so on. The putative physical referent of topography would then begin to evaporate as layer after layer of sub-topographies imposed themselves between language and its physical referent. Spatial signifiers would not lead us to spatial signifieds, but merely to an endless chain of further spatial signifiers. Even if at some point we were none the less to emerge from this linguistic thicket into nature 'itself', we would discover that nature 'itself' is ineluctably inscribed with cultural meanings. Nature abounds with metaphors: the fields of England are a patchwork; the country is covered in a blanket of snow. Even the negation of metaphor contained in the term "the incomprehensible bush" is, paradoxically, a way of making it comprehensible, a way of reducing the excess of signification in nature.[35] Nature, from this point of view, is always already culture – or linguistic culture at least.

The manner in which nature is always already riddled with language can be instantiated in Beckett's *Waiting for Godot*, where there is a brief attempt on the part of Estragon to flee the bleakness of the place where he and Vladimir find themselves. Estragon evokes memories of the Holy Land, or, to be more precise, of maps of the Holy Land:

> Je me rappelle les cartes de la Terre sainte. En couleur. Très jolies. La mer Morte était bleu pâle. J'avais soif rien qu'en la regardant. Je me disais, c'est là que nous irons passer notre lune de miel. Nous nagerons. Nous serons heureux. (*En attendant Godot* 14)

> I remember the maps of the Holy Land. Coloured they were. Very pretty. The Dead Sea was pale blue. The very look of it made me thirsty. That's where we'll go, I used to say, that's where we'll go for our honeymoon. We'll swim. We'll be happy. (*Waiting for Godot* 12)

The Promised Land is true to its name by virtue of the fact that it cannot be present, it must be in the future: "c'est là que nous *irons* passer notre lune de miel. Nous *nagerons*. Nous *serons* heureux" – "that's where *we'll* go for our honeymoon. *We'll* swim. *We'll* be happy." The discourse of a promised land is constructed around a deferral of the spatial referent. That referent occurs merely at the end of a string of textual associations, the Bible and its coloured maps. The desires evoked by the idea of the Holy Land are so patently utopian that the spatial signifiers remain with no other signified than that of their own discourse. This is hardly a surprise. As the capital letters alert us already, the Holy Land is not a place. It the spatial signifier *par excellence*, the Place of all Places in the Book of Books. It is the paradigmatic site of spatial reference within the paradigmatic text. Because all spatial signification in the Bible is laid under the originary curse of expulsion from Eden, all spatial semiosis is consequently condemned to remain incomplete.

In Jakobson's formulation of this aporia, the topographical code has no referent. Indeed, it can have no referent, except for the topographical message itself. This is the turn of phrase that Jakobson employs to characterize "shifters", that is, indexicals (pointers) or deictic markers. He notes that "shifters are distinguished from all other constituents of the linguistic code solely by their compulsory reference to the given message."[36]

Jakobson captures a prevalent post-Lapsarian attitude to deixis which has constituted one of the possible reactions towards the egocentric account of deixis. That attitude deems that deictics cannot express the will of a speaker because the speaker is nothing more than the fleeting instantiation of a linguistic convention. Benveniste, writing in the 1950s, was already exploring the aporetic character of deixis and, as part of a chain of argumentation to which we will return later, self-referentially folding deixis back into its constitutive code. Benveniste claims that the singularity of the *I* [*je*] is the contextual singularity of a 'shifter', an empty signifier whose very paucity of content permits it to do service in a multitude of situations. It permits a subject to "cast" itself (to echo Lyons' phrasing), to mould itself, but also, to throw itself into new situations. Benveniste writes: "It is by identifying himself as a unique person pronouncing *I* that each speaker sets himself up in turn as the 'subject'" ["C'est s'identifiant comme personne unique pronon-çant *je* que chacun des locuteurs se pose tour à tour comme 'sujet'"].[37] He continues by noting that *I* [*je*] is "a unique but mobile sign ... which can be assumed by each speaker on the condition that he refers each time only to the instance of his own discourse" ["un signe unique, mais mobile ... qui peut être assumé par chaque locuteur, à condition qu'il ne renvoie chaque fois qu'à l'instance de son propre discours"].[38] 'I' simply constitutes a position within the linguistic system or *langue*, given con-cretude by the discourse as *parole*. The identity of both *je* and of *tu* are collapsed into the speech situation itself: "Their relationship with *I* will be shown by defining them: *here* and *now* delimit the spatial and tem-poral instance coextensive and contemporary with the present instance of discourse containing *I*" ["On mettra en évidence [la] relation [d'*ici* et *maintenant*] avec *je* en les définissant: *ici* et *maintenant* délimitent l'instance spatiale et temporelle coextensive et contemporaine de la présente instance du discours contenant *je*"].[39] Benveniste folds the putative individuality of the 'I' back into the singularity of a speech act. That singularity is marked by the deictics *here* and *now*.

Levinson notes a similar formulation on the part of other linguists such as Reichenbach, who "argued ... that all indexicals involve an element of **token-reflexivity**, i.e., refer to themselves, so that, for exam-ple, *I* means 'the person who is uttering this token of the word *I*'."[40] By extension, the 'here' of this 'I' is nothing more than the 'here' con-structed in the moment of enunciation. 'Here' is nothing more or less than the 'here' fleetingly crystallized by the enunciation itself.

Deixis, modernity, postmodernity

These moves to make deixis a purely self-referential process, in which the deictic marker is anchored neither in the egocentricity of a speak-ing self nor in the putative reference of an extra-linguistic context, but merely in its own ephemeral discursive performativity, can be related to a specific moment in mid-twentieth-century thought. Deictic self-reflexivity is symptomatic, in its resonances with the modernist mood of solipsism, of a specifically late-modernist reaction to its predecessor. Conrad's pessimistic statement, "It is impossible to convey the life-sensation of any given epoch of one's existence. ... We live, as we dream – alone" (*Heart of Darkness* 172) resurges in postmodernism's celebration of an all-encompassing discursive hall of mirrors.

Without even a lonely subject (the legacy of modernism and its melancholy) to support it, postmodernism is left with something akin to Marlow's biscuit-tin steamer: "She rang under my feet like an empty Huntley & Palmer biscuit-tin ... she was nothing so solid in make, and rather less pretty in shape" (*Heart of Darkness* 175). Navigating the steam-boat among the snags and shoals of the great river is a treacherous business. The steam-boat's own noise does nothing to establish a spatial location, other than marking itself as the floating source of the ruckus of modernity: "I could only hear the heavy splashing thump of the stern wheel..." (*Heart of Darkness* 199–200).

Yet there is a significant episode in which the steam-boat resonates with the din caused by its captain and mechanic who are capering on the metal deck in the deep of the night. Marlow and his mechanic are anticipating the arrival of the rivets they need to repair the gashed hull of the steamer: "I slapped him on the back and shouted, 'We shall have rivets!' He scrambled to his feet exclaiming, 'No! Rivets!' as though he couldn't believe his ears" (*Heart of Darkness* 176). If the steamboat becomes a metonymy of the self-propelling but empty subject, rivets, by contrast, may figure the manner in which that subject emerges out of intersubjectivity and out of an underlying spatiality.

Rivets are insignificant in themselves. They have no function except as connectors. They hold together the metal sheets of the steamer's hull just as, for an instant, they hold together its crew-members. Rivets are the catalyst for the minimal community which crystallizes briefly in the African night. But they also point to the way in which the hollow echoes of modernity's paddle-steamer are not merely indicative of solipsism, but also of the way any community, in order to coagulate, also needs a place. Rivets are very much like linguistic 'shifters' – the deictic markers which can be used interchangeably to point to an infinite variety of concrete 'heres' and 'theres'. Deitic rivets anchor a speaker and a listener into a shared 'here', but they also connect those discursive agents to the very place of their communication: the ringing metal deck upon which Marlow and his mechanic caper and dance, the river which carries them along on their journey, and the jungle which, for all its inscrutability, nevertheless frames their nightmarish odyssey.

Should one interpret the rivets Marlow demands but apparently never receives merely as an element of the paddle-steamer, itself figuring an isolated subject in the midst of an indecipherable chaos? In that case, they function as a metaphor of self-reflexive deixis, autotelic, indeed autistic, simply wrapping speaker-centred deixis back in upon itself.

Might one, alternatively, interpret the rivets, shipped from Europe, easily transportable ("Three carriers could have brought all that was wanted to set that steamboat afloat" – *Heart of Darkness* 174), as minute entities within a larger context of travel, trade and imperial conquest? Then they would perform a connective function in which innumerable overlapping spaces and their respective complexities enabled the discourses which referenced them. At this juncture, deiXis as a mode of reciprocal joining of language and space emerges in the interstices of the Conradian text.

The sound of Marlow and his mechanic resonates with the jungle: "A frightful clatter came out of that hulk, and the virgin forest on the other bank of the creek sent it back in a thundering roll upon the sleeping station" (*Heart of Darkness* 176). Conrad's text takes a first step, albeit in the semi-autistic mode of echo and "echonomics",[41] towards a recognition of dialogue with place – a dialogue that may redeem the self-referential deixis of modernism and point a way to what we are calling deiXis.

2
From Deictics to DeiXis

What options remain after the solipsism of autoreflexivity? Are there alternatives to these extreme polarizations of person-centred and depersonalized deixis? In one of Vladimir and Estragon's futile dialogues they discuss the Vaucluse (in Beckett's English version the Mâcon country) where, in better days, they worked as grape-pickers. In Beckett's French original, Vladimir remembers the name of the farmer and the place; in the subsequent English translation, these details have slipped his mind. Estragon fares no better, not even having noticed such trivial details:

> VLADIMIR: Pourtant nous avions été ensemble dans le Vaucluse, j'en mettrais ma main au feu. Nous avons fait les vendanges, tiens, chez un nommé Bonnelly, à Roussillon.
> ESTRAGON: (*plus calme*) C'est possible. Je n'ai rien remarqué.
> VLADIMIR: Mais là-bas tout est rouge!
>
> (*Waiting for Godot* 86)

> VLADIMIR: But we were there together, I could swear to it! Picking grapes for a man called ... (*he snaps his fingers*) ... can't think of the name of the man, at a place called ... (*snaps his fingers*) ... Can't think of the name of the place, do you not remember?
> ESTRAGON: (*a little calmer*) It's possible. I didn't notice.
> VLADIMIR: But down there everything is red!
>
> (*Waiting for Godot* 62)

The exchange appears to embody all the ambient loss of spatial reference that one comes to associate with Beckett's modernism. Yet despite the ferocious evacuation of spatial meaning (even more marked in English than in the French), there is an equally sustained marking of spatial axes of 'non-reference' – that is, a mode of spatial reference that, though hardly susceptible of categorization under the regime of positive denotation, none the less continues to be active in other ways, in particular, the indexical or metonymic mode of deixis. First there is the axis of 'egocentricity' ("j'en mettrais ma main au feu" – "I could swear to it!"). Then there is the axis of descriptive spatial reference ("Mais là-bas tout est rouge!" – "But down there everything is red!"). Additionally, intercalated between these two, there is the axis of intersubjective communication ("tiens..." – "do you not remember?"). None of these axes of deictic reference, whether performative (swearing), denotative (description), or interrogative-intersubjective (remembering) can fix place (though the vague French "chez un nommé Bonnelly, à Roussillon" is still stronger than its English equivalent). None the less, they continue to index it even in the moment of its absence – an absence which is representational as much as mnemonic.

This triptych of the aporia of deictics, however, points the way to an alternative vision of deictic marking. Each of these axes of spatial 'non-reference' can be related to a specific perspective upon deixis. The performative "I could swear to it!" could be taken as indicative of the egocentric and self-reflexive functions of deixis discussed in the previous chapter. They tacitly found what is generally accepted as the denotative function, though this is largely disqualified under the aporetic representational regime of modernism. There remains an axis of 'interrogative deixis' which is more apposite to our purposes, one which can be identified here in very schematic terms as the intersubjective function. In what follows I will be using this latter deictic function (linguistic pointing as the establishment of a shared social space) as the basis for a more extensive notion of spatial reciprocity in deictic activity.

This chapter pursues that more radical conception to elaborate a notion of deixis which sees a fundamental give and take at work in spatial language. Spatial reference and spatial referent exist in a mutually constitutive and enabling relationship. In this chapter it is the second facet of Beckett's *Tragicomedy*, namely, the more playful, postmodern side of the play, that encapsulates the ineluctable imbrication of spatial language and its context. This reciprocity will be instantiated in a brief anecdote from the reception of Beckett's theatre. In that reception there can be detected an index of the ways dramatic deiXis genuinely engages with a traceable social context.

Deixis as contextual reference

Recent developments in theories of deixis have seen a shift away from both egocentricity and self-reflexivity towards what Jones calls "socio-centric" approaches.[1] Hanks for instance stresses that "Verbal deixis is a central aspect of the *social* matrix of orientation and perception through which speakers produce context."[2] Even where lip service is still paid to the dominant egocentric approach, another emphasis is becoming evident. Grewendorf, Hamm and Sternefeld, for example, stress the "context-ual dependence" ["Kontextabhängigkeit"] of deictic markers, defining them as "expressions whose denotation is dependent upon the speaker or the place of expression or the time of expression" ["Ausdrücke … deren Denotat vom Sprecher bzw. dem Äußerungsort bzw. dem Äußerungszeit abhängt"].[3] It is significant that this approach stresses the dependence of the deictic speech act not merely upon the speaker's central function, but also upon the time and the place. These latter two factors are sequentially subordinated to the speaker, but the repeated conjunctive "or" ["bzw."] tends to flatten out the customary hierarchy of subject and site.

The sustained interrogation of the assumed egocentricity of deixis can be traced back as far as the mid-1950s to Benveniste's deconstruction of the putative substance of individual subjectivity. Benveniste begins by exposing the substance of selfhood, the felt consistency of the 'I', the *je*, as merely arising out of a discursive context whose personal contours are multiple, a conglomeration of selfhoods. Any discursive context must by definition be occupied by at least two actors, a sender and a recipient of the speech act:

> But as soon as [a speaker] declares himself a speaker and takes on his language, he implants the other opposite himself, whatever degree of presence he may attribute to this other. Every utterance, whether explicit or implicit, is an allocution, and assumes the presence of an allocutor.

> [Mais immédiatement, dès qu'il se déclare locuteur et assume sa langue, il implante l'*autre* en face de lui, quel que soit le degré de présence qu'il attribue à cet autre. Toute énonciation est, explicite ou implicite, une allocution, elle postule un allocutoire.][4]

The texture of the felt subjectivity associated with the utterance 'I', clearly constituted out of an intersubjective context, is a function of the situation. It is not an essential characteristic of the selfhood doing the uttering. This produces a situation which can only be a shared context of intersubjectivity. This sharing does not logically admit of a hierarchy. As Jones notes: "In a relational opposition of this kind (*I–you*) there is no logically central term. It is as inaccurate and misleading ... to call the speaker the central person in communication as it would be to call either the husband or wife the 'central partner' in marriage."[5]

Jones dismantles the assumed hierarchy of a deictic 'I' over a deictic 'you'. Once this process of dismantling has been begun, it is difficult to stop it. Anna Fuchs continues this demolition of hierarchies by turning her attention to the customary privileging of a physical speech-situation over other potential contexts. She objects to the habitual assumption that deixis refers primarily to concretely localizable situations. She extends Jones' assault on 'egocentricity' in deixis to take in what one might term 'corporeo-centricity'. 'Here', she points out, often refers not merely to the speaker's bodily position ("Deitic theory has unduly isolated the 'situation of speech' aspect, and in a superficial manner at that"[6]), but rather can refer to many various 'heres', including discursive (Vladimir's "Where was I" – *Waiting for Godot* 12) or even imaginative or abstract frameworks. Whence the polysemic interrogation uttered by Vladimir: "Que faisons-nous ici, voilà ce qu'il faut se demander" (*En attendant Godot* 112) – "What are we doing here, *that* is the question" (*Waiting for Godot* 80). This anguished question is clearly one which refers at one level to the bleak locality where he and Estragon wait for Godot, but no less so to their equally grim existential condition. By extracting deixis from its customary context of the immediate physical environment Fuchs opens it up to more figurative, but equally 'real', contexts such as "the shared knowledge contexts (or 'frames', 'scenes', 'background', etc.) activated in communication".[7] These contexts vitiate any attempt to ground them in a particular speaker's egocentric vision, indeed, to individualize them at all. They become instead a common discursive ground for communication: "the shared-knowledge 'world segment' the utterance addresses".[8]

Fuchs effectively widens the frame of reference of deixis to include a much larger range of 'heres' beyond the immediate temporal or physical environment of the respective utilizers of deictic markers. The result is to project the mutually constitutive intersubjectivity of the 'horizontal' *I–you* axis (Benveniste) onto a 'vertical' axis of speech act and enabling frame. In other words, the deictic process and the contexts (or frameworks) it refers to exist in a situation of mutual interdependence in the same way as the 'I' and the 'you' of interpersonal deixis. What we are talking about *here* (my own formulation is deliberately performative of Fuchs' innovation) could thus go as far as referring to some sort of Foucauldian *episteme* – that underlying system of epistemological conditions that enable some forms of knowledge and prohibit others at any given point in time. 'Here' can refer to the very discursive 'conditions of possibility', the foundations explored by Foucault's 'archaeologies', that enable its own enunciation.[9]

Fuchs widens the definition of deixis to include other socio-centric contexts of communication ranging from shared intersubjective frames of reference to the epistemic conditions of possibility of a broad-based discursive formation in the Foucauldian sense. In so doing, she allows something to become visible which destabilizes deixis as the work of human communities of communication. Fuchs' wider definition of deixis begins to articulate a sense of the way in which deixis may not merely be reciprocal at the intersubjective level, but more radically, at the speaker-context level as well.

Fuchs' theory of deixis thus casts into question the primacy of human deixis over the context it refers to. This primacy is helpfully articulated by Lyons in his observations about the relationships between speakers and context in the standard account of deixis: "By deixis is meant the location and identification of persons, objects, events, processes and activities being talked about, or referred to, in relation to the spatiotemporal context *created and sustained by the act of utterance and the participation in it*, typically, of a single speaker and at least one addressee."[10] The context is sustained by utterance and the demonstrative forms of the utterance remain empty until they find a context.

Jones may contest the speaker-centricity of this notion of deixis, but he shares with Lyons an underlying assumption about the anthropocentricity of deixis. That anthropocentricity is expressed by the concept of intentionality. Deixis, for Jones, is intersubjective, but none the less embedded within *intentional* social interaction: "My argument, then, is that there is no such thing as a 'perceptual *here*' or 'perceptual deixis'; there are no deictic expressions which do not assume for their interpretation a social context of intentional action."[11] Jones, while dismantling egocentricity in deixis and replacing it with sociocentricity, leaves a *spatial* egocentricity intact. Speakers (in the plural) craft deictic language among themselves, rather than around a central speaker, but they still wield it over and above the context they refer to. Intention continues to be understood as the force that patterns the broader context. Doubtless Jones wishes to preserve collective social agency here in a broadly historical-materialist perspective. However, in the context of spatial theory, such anthropocentric intentionality is highly problematic.

The most cogent formulation of intention as the central agency in the configuration of social and material space is produced by Maurice Merleau-Ponty in his influential work on the phenomenology of perception. The essence of space in its pure and originary form, according to Merleau-Ponty, is that it is structured according to the subject's intentions. Space is understood not as something which precedes the subject, an already given landscape into which she or he strolls, but rather as a fluid environment which forms itself under her or his gaze. Merleau-Ponty's theory revolutionizes notions of Euclidean space in that it questions the pre-existence of space-as-container, claiming on the contrary that space is malleable, a fluid medium susceptible to crafting by human agency. Merleau-Ponty thus forges a

> new conception of intentionality ... Space is not the setting (real or logical) in which things are arranged, but the means whereby the position of things becomes possible. ... I catch space at its source, and now think the relationships which underlie this word, realizing then that they live only through the medium of a subject who traces out and sustains them.
>
> [nouvelle conception de l'intentionnalité ... L'espace n'est pas le milieu (réel ou logique) dans lequel se disposent les choses, mais le moyen par lequel la position des choses deviennent possible. ... je ressaisis l'espace à sa source, je pense actuellement les relations qui sont sous ce mot et je m'aperçois alors qu'elles ne vivent que par un sujet qui les décrive et qui les porte.][12]

Merleau-Ponty's theory of spatiality is one which no longer follows the realist postulates of a Euclidean topography. It has already shifted in the direction of a nascent constructivism, but one which is configured according to the dictates of a subject held responsible for making its place in the world and only susceptible of eluding that role at the cost of bad faith. Merleau-Ponty abolishes space as a given but does not abolish the subject as its centre of gravity. The spatial referent no longer commands reference, forcing spatial language into a subordinate, descriptive role. But intention none the less continues to function as the guiding vector of that language, assuring a residual egocentricity under the guise of intersubjectivity or 'sociocentricity'.

Such intentional vectors of deictic activity, are however patently deconstructed in *Waiting for Godot*. It can hardly be a coincidence that Beckett's play, staged initially in Paris in 1953, came only a few years after Merleau-Ponty's celebrations of intention. In Beckett's 'riposte' inertia, rather than intention, appears to be the defining characteristic of stage characterization. Intention is inadequate to allow the subject to configure space. As if to dispel any residual doubts about Beckett's abolition of intention the closing lines of the play reiterate the recurring leitmotif of paralysis:

VLADIMIR: Alors, on y va?
ESTRAGON: Allons-y.
　　　　　(*Ils ne bougent pas*)
　　　　　　(*En attendant Godot* 134)

VLADIMIR: Well? Shall we go?
ESTRAGON: Yes, let's go.
　　　　　(*They do not move*)
　　　　　　(*Waiting for Godot* 94)

Deictic intention has patently become untenable under modernism. The alternatives are bleak: the purely self-reflexive deictics of a solipsistic and ultimately placeless world or the absolute vitiation of the vectors of intention. One other option may emerge, namely, in a more moderate refutation of deictic intention, a form of reciprocity.

The social context provides the conditions under which intention can be exercised, the channels in which it can find expression, indeed the forms which it will take. It is worth recalling Marx's comments on intention in a historical framework: "Men make their own history, but they do not make it under circumstances chosen by themselves, but under circumstances directly found, given and transmitted from the past" ["Die Menschen machen ihre eigene Geschichte, aber sie machen sie nicht aus freien Stücken, nicht unter selbst ausgewählten, sondern unter unmittelbar vorgefundenen, gegebenen und überlieferten Umständen"].[13] What holds good for Marx on the diachronic plane of history holds equally well for a reciprocal theory of deixis on the synchronic plane of spatial contextuality. Space is not a given – we contribute to its making. But if we are involved in the making of space it is not solely on terms dictated by ourselves.

The putative speaker-identity (the origin or "origo" of Bühler's deictic theory, the "ego" of Lyons' semantics) is merely a reciprocal construct in which deixis depends upon context, and context upon deixis. The attempt to ground deixis in an originary speaking identity tumbles back into a groundless, reciprocally constitutive relationship between language and its context in which each is equally dependent upon the other to come to being. Neither language nor the context is previously there grounding the other. On the contrary, they ground each other in a mutual dialogue of place and communication. Chiastically formulated, language grounds place and place grounds language.

Deixis as reciprocity

There are few props on Beckett's stage. Two of the most prominent are the removable, and frequently removed, elements of Estragon and Vladimir's costumes: their boots and hats. As hollow receptacles, mobile signifiers of the self which have their own existence but no pragmatic utility when not connected to a bearer, they are literal embodiments of the 'shifter' – empty, susceptible of assuming a practical significance in a multitude of situations, belonging to no-one in any intrinsic manner but able to be donned by the next best comer. Estragon removes his boots at nightfall, only to discover, at the beginning of Act II, that they have been taken away and replaced by another pair which, it transpires, fit better than the original set (*En attendant Godot* 94–8; *Waiting for Godot* 67–70). It is the exchangeability of boots and also their connective role (they mediate between the subject and the ground he stands upon) which make them a powerful concrete metaphor of the deictic function. In this tragicomedy of postmodern spatial aporia, they take on an unexpected significance. In one of Beckett's inimitable mime scenes, Estragon wrenches off his shoe, peers inside, rummages about inside with his hand, upturns it, shakes it about, checks whether there is not something that has fallen out, sees nothing but none the less peers inside again. Estragon affirms that there is nothing inside:

VLADIMIR: Fais voir.
ESTRAGON: Il n'y a rien à voir.
VLADIMIR: Essaie de la remettre.
ESTRAGON: (*ayant examine son pied*). Je vais le laisser respirer un peu.
VLADIMIR: Voilà l'homme entier, s'en prenant à sa chaussure alors que c'est son pied le coupable. (*Il enlève encore une fois son chapeau, regarde dedans, y passé la main, le secoue, tape dessus, soufflé dedans, le remet.*) Ça devient inquiétant.
(*En attendant Godot* 12–13)

VLADIMIR: Show me.
ESTRAGON: There's nothing to show.

VLADIMIR: Try and put it on again.

ESTRAGON: (*examining his foot*). I'll air it for a bit.

VLADIMIR: There's man all over for you, blaming on his boots the faults of his feet. (*He takes off his hat again, peers inside it, feels about inside it, knocks on the crown, blows into it, puts it on again*.) This is getting alarming.

(*Waiting for Godot* 11)

This elaborate mime demonstrates, beyond the trace of a doubt, that the boots are empty inside: "Il n'y a rien à voir", "There's nothing to show". None the less, they are full of meaning. By the same token, the mime displays the social value of deixis: to create a force field arising out of the mutually constitutive relationship between spatial language and its material context or conceptual framework.

"Fais voir" – "Show me", commands Vladimir, thus engaging in a per-locutionary act whose very content, etymologically speaking, is deic-tic (Greek δεικτικ = able to show [*OED*]). The action of showing, even if there is no content, nothing to be shown, lays bare the real role of deixis. Indeed, the fact that there *is nothing to be shown* demonstrates even more clearly the functioning of deixis. Showing, show (with a knowing gesture towards the theatricality of the performance which the audience is in that moment watching) is an empty gesture which none the less creates a community.

Beckett's drama performs the absence of meaning, spatialized on stage, but it also performs meaning as social process. In its acting out of the former the play is quintessentially modernist; in its dramatization of the latter it is no less *post*modernist. On the one hand, deixis is an empty vessel, one entirely apposite as a means of expression for the spa-tial wasting of modernity. On the other, the very hollowness of deixis also offers the ideal receptacle for showing a performative sociability, one in which a common spatial framework is made available as the condition of possibility of a social commonality. Deixis, like sociability, has no inherent content, it does not admit of any form of meaning that is fixed in advance. Rather it must be negotiated in every successive situ-ation. As Husserl says, the word "here" "switches from case to case, and again from person to person" – and "does this on each occasion using a new meaning" ["hier" ... "wechselt von Fall zu Fall und wechselt wieder von Person zu Person" ... "thut dies immer mittels neuer Bedeutung"].[14] Deixis thus triangulates between place, subject and speech act, each of which must be posited anew in concert with the others with every suc-cessive evocation of socio-linguistic place.

In Beckett's play deixis is symbolized concretely by the removable, exchangeable boots. Beckett's theatrical boots are on the borderline between the absurd, which declares the bankruptcy of (spatial) meaning, and the postmodern, which examines the processes by which (spatial) meaning is produced as a site for sociability. Of course the boots are empty – how could it be otherwise when Estragon has just removed them? More importantly, without that emptiness they would not function as boots, just as the hat into which Vladimir peers would not function as a hat without its constitutive hollowness.

Similarly, "blaming on his boots the faults of his feet" is a turn of phrase that asks us to redirect our attention from expressive substance of language (here, of spatial language, in particular deixis) to its virtual capacities. The hollowness of spatial language (its virtuality) is not to be blamed for the uncertainty of the communality that it may facilitate. On the contrary, that hollowness is the very condition of possibility of any common social fabric which is to emerge out of the reciprocity between spatial language and spatial referent. The vacuity of spatial language (its virtual character) is the guarantor of the virtual potential of any community which projects a future for itself and, in so doing, weaves the ongoing fabric it harbours.

This is all the more so in the case of theatrical deixis, the stage language which refers both to a real and a fictional here and now. Together, these two aspects of theatrical deixis (the space of the theatre and the fictive world which is conjured up within that space) present a framework which can be entered into by an audience. Theatrical deixis can facilitate the creation of an imagined fictional universe within a concrete, experiential site of performance, indexed by Estragon's reference to the theatre building, "Au fond du couloire, à gauche" (*En attendant Godot* 48) – "End of the corridor, on the left" (*Waiting for Godot* 35).[15] However, theatrical deixis cannot guarantee that creation, nor vouch for the understandings, readings, interpretations, criticism, etc., which may be produced as a result of the meeting of language, stage space, and audience. Vladimir's oxymoronic "Nous sommes cernés ... (*geste vers l'auditoire*) Là il n'y a personne" (*En attendant Godot* 104)/"We're surrounded ... (*Gesture towards front*) Not a soul in sight" (*Waiting for Godot* 74) gathers up the theatre's constitutive dependence upon the audience, but also the impossibility of predicting the identity of that audience or the potential infinity of its responses. Theatrical deixis in both its textual (dramatic) and performance (theatrical) manifestations invites a potentially infinite series of contextualizations ranging from the actor who learns her or his lines, and then plays a character upon the stage, via the audience who partakes of the performance, through to the theatre critic who passes judgement or the student or scholar who forges a new interpretation. These contextualizations are infinite because they are never in themselves complete. The productivity of theatrical space, like that of deixis, depends upon its emptiness (whence the title of Peter Brook's ground-breaking manifesto[16]) rather than being undermined by it. Theatrical deixis functions in a multitude of quite specific contexts with which it enters anew on each occasion into a reciprocal and productive relationship, facilitating a community of spectatorship or readership or understanding by turns.

In the case of Beckett, the realization (in the sense of 'making real') of multiple contexts which crystallize around the play and its spatial referents is already inscribed from the outset by its bilingual existence. Beckett wrote *Godot* first in French, and then produced an English translation shortly afterwards.[17] Beckett's own project of self-translation anticipated from the moment of its inception at least two communities of reception which would enable performance: the French and the English. Each instance of performance, however, would also reconfigure that already multiple dramatic text or script. Translation can be seen as a fundamentally deictic activity to the extent that its function, by definition, is to open up new contexts for the texts. Translation has its entire *raison d'être* in its assumption that there is a (different) context of reception that the text can only vaguely anticipate but towards which it reaches, and upon which it depends for its actualization. Translation thus makes explicit the latent deictic dynamic of any literary act. Like deixis itself, translation is thus essentially futuristic, inherently anticipating but by the same token unable to provide guarantees for the spaces where it will be received.

Beckett's characters may appear to be locked into a universe where nothing happens. But in the Beckettian world which is shared by the audience, however, much has happened since 1953 when the play was first staged. There have been hundreds of performances, each one different to the others which have preceded it, with no prospect of the creative potential of the drama ever being stemmed. One famous spectator at an early Paris performance of Beckett's *En attendant Godot*, Michel Foucault, typifies the play's capacity to generate reiterated avatars of itself in ever new contexts. In an interview given in 1983 Foucault recalled the impact which Beckett's play had upon him as a student:

> I belong to that generation who as students had before their eyes, and were limited by, a horizon consisting of Marxism, phenomenology,

and existentialism. Interesting and stimulating as these might be, naturally they produced in the students completely immersed in them a feeling of being stifled, and the urge to look elsewhere. I was like all other students of philosophy at that time, and for me the break was first Beckett's *Waiting for Godot*, a breathtaking performance.

[J'appartiens à cette génération de gens qui, lorsqu'ils étaient étudiants, étaient enfermés dans un horizon qui était marqué par le marxisme, la phénoménologie, l'existentialisme, etc. Toutes choses extrêmement intéressantes, stimulantes, mais qui entraînaient au bout d'un certain temps un sentiment d'étouffement et le désir d'aller voir ailleurs. J'étais comme tous les étudiants de philo à cette époque-là, et pour moi, la rupture est venue avec Beckett : *En attendant Godot*, un spectacle à vous couper le souffle.][18]

The caesura evoked by Foucault inaugurated his subsequent writing. Beckett triggered a rupture, or at least stood for the triggering of a rupture that took Foucault away from the teleology of Marxism, from the pristine basal experiences sought for by phenomenology, and from the sovereign self celebrated by existentialism. That fundamental fracture catapulted him towards the poststructuralism for which he would become famous: the analysis of the discontinuities of history, of the discursive conditions making possible putatively originary experiences, and of the specific history of knowledge which created the self-knowing self as the centrepiece of Enlightenment rationality.[19] Foucault acknowledged Beckett's crucial role on only a few occasions, at intervals of several decades: first with the brief quote in his famed "What is an author?" ["Qu'est-ce qu'un auteur?"] lecture in 1969; then in his inaugural lecture at the Collège de France in 1970; and finally in the 1983 interview quoted above.

Foucault's lecture on authorship held up Beckett's plea in favour of anonymity as a salutary reminder of the arbitrary, aleatory character of authorship. Foucault underlined the emergence of authorship as a contingent historical category:

Beckett nicely formulates the theme with which I would like to begin: "'What does it matter who is speaking,' someone said, 'what does it matter who is speaking.'" In this indifference appears one of the fundamental ethical principles of contemporary writing.

[Le thème dont je voudrais parler, j'en emprunte la formulation à Beckett : "Qu'importe qui parle, quelqu'un a dit qu'importe qui parle." Dans cette indifférence, je crois qu'il faut reconnaître un des principes éthiques fondamentaux de l'écriture contemporaine.][20]

That lecture suggested that authorship might be no more than a historically produced discursive slot, empty in itself but serving an important organizing function. The author, according to Foucault's reading, is a function which organizes and disciplines a chaotic textual field, a role which could be assigned to historical figures who had indeed produced texts, but was certainly not an essence of selfhood. The inaugural lecture reversed the customary enshrinement of the author by seeking to underline the historical character of discourse in its institutional frameworks. The institution, Foucault suggested, masked the disciplining, organizing power of the author function by setting up rituals of inauguration that would consecrate the subject as the officially sanctioned producer of discourse – rituals such as the inaugural professorial lecture, precisely that ritual which Foucault, by inaugurating his own discourse with such words, was in the process of lampooning. In this way, the institution inflated the author function so as to cushion the individual's entry into what was, in actual fact, a field of struggle.

A discursive participant such as himself, Foucault suggested, was assigned the space of an author, ritualized by a ceremony of origins, precisely in order to elide the more effective power struggles at work in the same space. This space was explicitly identified by an interviewer in 1973 as "the space of the lecture theatre at the Collège de France" ["l'espace de la salle du Collège de France"].[21] The answer to the question Beckett asked and Foucault reiterated ("What does it matter who speaks?", "Qu'importe qui parle ?") is thus double. On the one hand, it does not really matter *who* the author is, as long as the function itself is operative. On the other hand, it *does* matter very much whether someone can be identified as the ostensibly coherent centre of a conflict-ridden field of discourses.

Foucault opened his inaugural lecture at the Collège de France by calling it a "very provisional theatre" ["ce très provisoire théâtre"].[22] The term "theatre" clearly resonates with the Beckettian theatre which, by his own account, had triggered his personal assault on the common-sense conventions of philosophical thought. Foucault's theatricalization of the lecture theatre opened with an unmistakeable allusion to Beckett's *L'Innommable/The Unnameable*:

> Behind me, I should like to have heard (having been at it long enough already, repeating in advance what I am about to tell you) the voice

of Molloy, beginning to speak thus: "I must go on; I can't go on; I must go on; I must say them until they find me, until they say me – heavy burden, heavy sin; I must go on ..."

[J'aurais aimé qu'il y ait derrière moi (ayant pris depuis bien longtemps la parole, doublant à l'avance tout ce que je vais dire) une voix qui parlerait ainsi: "il faut continuer, je ne peux pas continuer, il faut continuer, je vais donc continuer, il faut dire des mots, tant qu'il y en a, il faut les dire, jusqu'à ce qu'ils me trouvent, jusqu' à ce qu'ils me disent, étrange peine, étrange faute, il faut continuer ...".][23]

By citing the voice of Beckett's protagonist talking about talk itself, Foucault achieves two things. On the one hand, he points out the manner in which discourse is always there before the subject, offering it a place to speak from, founding the author rather than originating from it. On the other, he is performatively rehearsing the manner in which discourse also creates a community of speakers who are borne along not merely as subjects by the discourse itself but as a collectivity emerging out of the sociability of discourse. Foucault is speaking back to Beckett, as it were.

Foucault's tribute to Beckett is thus twofold. In part, he honours the sceptical modernist side of Beckett's play, which insists upon the reduction of individuals to hapless language-ridden marionettes. But equally, he honours the residual germ of hope in Beckett's work, more manifest in the theatre than in the prose, which reposes upon the social nature of theatre *per se*. The theatre, quite simply, is a space where people come together.

In his own particular way, Foucault is acknowledging the way in which Beckett's theatre has enabled his own performance. Beckett was the voice, echoing through the lecture hall of France's most prestigious university institution, the Collège de France, which created the space in which Foucault spoke and his audience listened.

A decade apart from each other, both of these brief tributes to Beckett literally placed the speaker within a network of discourse, public space, and discursive and non-discursive politics. There is therefore nothing nihilist about the deictic work done by Beckett's *Waiting for Godot* with its stripped stage and its un-moored spatial reference. On the contrary, in the absence of clear deictic anchoring, it creates a space in which what Bakhtin/Vološinov called "addressivity" is raised to a higher power.[24]

The intensely social character of deixis as manifested in Beckett's drama, and borne out by its Foucauldian avatars, may serve to dispel some theoretical puzzlement over literary manifestations of deictics. Two scholars have recently noted: "In contrast to everyday situations, written texts are only anchored in the here-and-now of a determined speech situation by virtue of mediation" ["Anders als beispielsweise ein Alltagsgespräch sind geschriebene Texte nur vermittelt im *hic und nunc* einer bestimmten Sprechsituation verankert"]. That is to say, the deixis to be found in a literary text is not immediately present but is carried itself by a printed medium which must be activated in a given context by a reader. Taking up Bühler's time-honoured terminology, they enquire: "What is the 'origo' of a novel ...?" ["Was ist die 'origo' eines Romans ...?"].[25] It becomes clear that there is no single "origo" in such a text. Rather, deictic marking ocurrs out of the reciprocal interaction of more than one instances.

Indeed, what Beckett apears to be suggesting, and what is bodied forth by Foucault's tribute to him, is that space itself is the guarantor of sociability, the forum in which social relationships can come to be: "Place is ... that within and with respect to which subjectivity is itself established – place is not founded *on* subjectivity, but is rather that on which subjectivity is founded."[26] Spatial language is the fabric out of which social relationships are woven, because spatial language itself never ceases to remind one of one's debts to the place in which one stands.

DeiXis

In one of Beckett's most brilliant non-verbal scenes, Estragon and Vladimir engage in a hilarious exchange of hats. Vladimir scoops up Lucky's hat, putting it on his head and at the same time passing his own hat to Estragon. Estragon in turn places Vladimir's hat on his head, giving his own hat back to Vladimir. Vladimir sets Estragon's hat on his head, returning with the other hand Lucky's hat to Estragon. Estragon put on Lucky's hat, handing Vladimir's hat back to its owner – and so on and so forth (*En attendant Godot* 101/*Waiting for Godot* 71–2). The scene rests upon one of the few moments of spatial convergence in the play: "Je ne me suis donc pas trompé d'endroit" – "I knew it was the right place", comments Vladimir upon finding Lucky's bowler. He assumes that this marker reveals the identity of the spaces occupied on successive days (*En attendant Godot* 101/*Waiting for Godot* 71).

The abandoned bowler hat also functions as a trace of the other duo of the play, Pozzo and Lucky. Lucky's hat signals that despite their absence, they are soon to arrive again from off-stage. The hat is a mobile marker of something which is outside the closed world occupied by

Estragon and Vladimir, an 'exterior' that is also occupied by the *deus ex machina* Godot. Within the spatial semiotics of theatre, the off-stage is a hybrid space that is part fictional 'real world' and part contiguous with the 'real' real world.[27] It is hybrid in a manner not dissimilar to that of the audience space. The space of the audience is clearly demarcated from the stage and its fictions, but none the less a realm where the members of the audience agree, temporalily, to suspend disbelief and enter the fictional world of the drama. The hat is, therefore, a trace of this outside world in the Derridean sense: the presence of something which is absent, the absence of a putative presence beyond fiction. For that reason, its entry via the duality of Estragon and Vladimir's hats is a signal that something beyond the immediate fiction has intervened to open up the claustrophobia of the Beckettian universe.

The manner in which Lucky's hat prises apart a closed duality to make a more open triad can be understood as an analogy for the way in which deixis can also be understood as referring neither to a world dominated by the speaker (egocentric deixis) nor to an instance of pure discursive self-reflexivity (self-reflexive deixis). Rather, Lucky's hat, by virtue of its mobility, connects the dualistic closure of Estragon and Vladimir's waiting to an external referent by a modality which is neither that of presence or absence (the implications of egocentric and self-reflexive deixis respectively), but rather of indexicality. Indexicality is a looser mode of connection based upon association, causality or contiguity, and is thus situated somewhere between the extremes of presence or absence.

A purely structuralist vision of language would dispute the necessity of a referential ground, claiming that reference is a function of differential relationships within the system of *langue* itself. The shifter is empty, and gains its content only from the immediate message in which it is implemented – not from the context. Thus Jakobson sees the deictic shifter as the spatial code's reference to the spatial message which instantiates it.[28] However, if we are to understand deixis as a reciprocal relationship between indexical signs and their material or non-material spatial referents, we must have recourse to some other model of the sign.

A Peircean, and thus triadic, model of linguistic operation (including not only the sign itself, the capacity in which it functions, whether iconic, indexical or symbolic, but also its *object* or that for which it stands) would re-introduce the ground upon which linguistic production willy-nilly depends.[29] Peirce's theory is flexible enough, with its comprehensive catalogue of sign-referent types, to offer alternatives to the on-off binary of absence or presence. Indexicality in particular is a mode of deictic anchoring which reconnects discourse to its context without having to accept the dominant, masterful mode of reference which goes hand in hand with the achievement of referential 'presence' guaranteed by egocentric deixis. Indexicality suggests that a degree of spatial 'presence' can be evoked in language without the commanding gaze or monological dominantion inherent in speaker-centred deixis.

Accordingly, deixis does not merely anchor discourse in a context, it plainly anchors context in a discourse. The deictic relationship between discourse and context, one could say, is one of mirror-image inversion. In searching for a formulation which expresses the mutual interdependence and reciprocal grounding of language and place, of deictic language and its material spatial referents, I have chosen a time-honoured rhetorical device to give it form: that of chiasmus.

Jakobson's work upon duplex structures, in particular shifters, focuses upon their tendency to fold the code back upon the message.[30] In other words, their code, or basic framework of meaning-making, becomes self-referential, rather than speaking about a more properly 'referential' context. Julia Kristeva, however, draws out another aspect of this duplicity. She appropriates this aspect of Jakobson's research to exemplify Bakhtin's notion of "ambivalence", that is dialogicity, in language. Such "ambivalent" enunciations direct attention to their inherent capacity to meaning different things in the mouth of different speakers. All duplex structures both use *and* point to the code or the message and thereby implement what Althusser named "internal distantiation" ["distanciation interne"].[31] To that extent they make language foreign to itself from within but, paradoxically, also point to the foreignness which surrounds it: "The term 'ambivalence' implies the insertion of history (of society) in the text, and of the text in history" ["Le terme d' 'ambivalence' implique l'insertion de l'histoire (de la société) dans le texte, et du texte dans l'histoire"].[32] Kristeva's chiastic formulation, which envisages all literary texts as being invaded by their environment, and their environment as pervaded by textuality, is thus predicated upon the notion that shifters in Jakobson's sense, in contradistinction to the auto-reflexivity he ascribes to them, are reciprocally entwined in the space they index, as is that space in them. Kristeva's use of chiasmus to embody this relationship sanctions the implementation of chiasmus as the central figure underlying deixis as I conceive of it in this book.

The rhetorical figure of chiasmus (mirror-image inversion as the symmetrical crossing of two terms) can be imagined as a spatial figure which inflects what I henceforth will call 'deiXis'. Chiasmus, in Greek, means 'crossing', the 'chi' transcribing the Greek letter 'χ' (chi), which embodies the operation it designates. By 'deiXis' I mean an interlocking of discourse and context in which a reciprocal anchoring and framing of language and space occurs. This, literally, takes place in the form of a crossing.

Deixis, one linguistic mechanism, leads us back to chiasmus, another linguistic (rhetorical) mechanism. DeiXis, the composite term that we have coined here, does not mean that reality dissolves into rhetoric. There is no ground for epistemological panic. The recognition that our world is pervaded by language, and our language by the world, is a fairly down-to-earth recognition. But the fading of reality into the chiastic rhetorical structures of deiXis does mean that reality is only accessible, manageable, operable, with the help of rhetoric. And this rhetoric is, inevitably, spatially inflected.

DeiXis as emplotment

DeiXis, for all its patently spatial dimensions, also evinces a temporal aspect. In its perennial un-determinedness it inevitably maps the changing parameters of concrete space. DeiXis becomes the receptacle for a narrative of space in its historical transformations. In Beckett's drama, Pozzo very briefly swaps places in his imagination with his underling Lucky: "POZZO: Remarquez que j'aurais pu être à sa place et lui à la mienne. Si le hazard ne s'y était pas opposé. A chacun son dû" (*En attendant Godot* 43) – "POZZO: Remark that I might just as well have been in his shoes and he in mine. If chance had not willed otherwise. To each one his due" (*Waiting for Godot* 31). Pozzo's imagination of reciprocal place-swapping is chiastic in both its content and form ("j'aurais pu être à sa place et lui à la mienne" – "I might just as well have been in his shoes and he in mine"), and forms a minimal fiction, a virtual plot. Pozzo immediately recognizes the danger of such perfect symmetry and retreats to a narrative of chance and moralism.

Chiasmus, the 'X' at the heart of deiXis, can serve not merely as a static figure of speech but may equally well provide a figure of emplotment. If one bears in mind that chiasmus operates along the phrasal chain, then it becomes possible to imagine chiasmus working as a device of plot construction at the macro-level of the larger narrative. Richard Aczel summarizes the chiastic intrigue of an Elizabethan novel by Robert Greene: "Wit rejects wisdom, abandons friendship for love: abandoned by love, regains friendship and elects wisdom over wit." Such rhetorical figures are not inherent in the text, however, but must be activated by readerly (rhetorical) participartion: "Unlike a 'rhetoric of fiction', which reifies the text as a finished rhetorical product, a rhetoric of reading insists that texts only have a meaningful existence within the acts, strategies and traditions of reading in which they are perpetually produced."[33] Between the spatial figure of chiasmus as a figure of emplotment and its identification as such by a canny reader, there exists a relationship which is analogous to the openness of deiXis. It is only in the reciprocal cooperation of textual strategies and reading strategies that rhetorically-structured plot-motifs come to be. The text's exploits remain inert if not 'discovered' by a reader, while the reader's appetite for elaborate rhetorical forms remains unsatisfied until it has found a concrete instantiation of the rhetorical flourishes which inhabit her or his imagination. Thus even the temporal dimensions of chiasmus inevitably lead us back to the spatial insertion of deiXis – that is, to the contextualizations of readerly textual competence.

But how much readerly participation would really be demanded by a narrative built around the figure of chiasmus? Chiasmus as a figure of plotting appears not to leave much room for narrative unpredictability – nor for readerly intervention. Indeed, the very attraction of chiasmus comes from the neatness of its operation. It works in a manner which is perfectly symmetrical and balanced. Chiasmus is a trite figure of the aleatory as closed perfection. By the same token, it is a figure of restricted, controlled change, one which poses no risk, which involves no experiment. The two symmetrical halves of *En attendant Godot/Waiting for Godot* are inaugurated by a performative instance of chiasmus. At the beginning of Act I, Estragon is taking off his boots, those concrete embodiments of the mediating function of 'empty' deixis. At the beginning of Act II, in contrast, he is barefoot and soon to be pulling on another pair of boots. These inaugural gestures trigger the subsequent dramatic action, marking a minimal difference which is, to all intents and purposes, no difference at all. The on-off of a pair of boots, ceding to the off-on of another pair of boots, guarantees a minimal narrative which is nothing more than the *status quo* endowed with a sheen of dynamism.

However, if deiXis is really a task undertaken by shifters, then the relationship of crossing is one of crossing between changing elements. Under such conditions, change must be guaranteed on both sides. In its instantiation in deiXis, chiasmus must be rethought not as a figure of mere mirror-inversion but as a more radical form of change.

DeiXis, the marking of place within the expanse of language, is only ever a temporary event. It must be constantly renewed and constantly re-asserted because place itself, far from being the stable ground of enunciation, is constantly in process. Space is a phenomenon caught in a constant process of transformation, on the same plane as the society whose dimensions, volumes and relationships it materializes and forms.

DeiXis is thus always contaminated by the shifting linguistic landscapes to which it points. DeiXis functions like a foreign language within a language, opening up its interior space to the outside. DeiXis, with its crossed arms, makes language a border checkpoint where dialects meet, converge and diverge again like trajectories coming from outside, meeting at the centre and continuing their path back towards the distant horizon of the linguistic community and beyond to who knows where. DeiXis is a figure which brings togther two instabilities. It thus fuses the constant inventiveness and heterogeneity of the linguistic landscape and the uneven openness of coextensive spaces.

DeiXis, as a reciprocal interlocking of space and language, by which one grounds and frames the other so as to produce a spatial-linguistic event, is never a permanent state of affairs. DeiXis describes the mutual interaction of language-as-translation-approximation and space-as-potential-for-unending-exploration. An event of deiXis, because it stages the meeting and fusing of two mobile entities, becoming-language and becoming-space, also offers a basal model of narrative progression. As Foucault once commented, "An event is not a segment of time, it is, in fact, an intersection between two durations, two speeds, two evolutions, two lines of history" ["Un événement, ce n'est pas un segment de temps, c'est au fond l'intersection entre eux durées, deux vitesses, deux évolutions, deux lignes d'histoire"].[34] If Foucault suggests that any event has a spatial character, then this notion has been recently corroborated by Massey's formulation of something similar, but not quite identical. Massey argues that Laclau's "proposal for a 'radical historicity' could be even more radical were it to be spatialised: that is, were he to recognise from the outset that space is indeed, as he says, 'an event'".[35] Where Foucault had claimed that the event was spatial, Massey, via Laclau, proposes that space is 'evenemential' or event-like. The chiasmic mirroring that emerges here may hint at ways of translating Massey's central concern, namely, of escaping notions of the immobility of space so as to re-connect spatial theory with a radical politics of social transformation.[36] In turn, the mobilization instigated by this instance of chiastic thinking may suggest possibilities for opening up the chiasmus at the heart of deiXis.

It may be possible to read chiasmus not as a dual, but as a triadic figure, if we supplement the two sets of legs by the point of their crossing.

The point of crossing is, strictly speaking, not a space at all, but merely a point, a coordinate of no dimensions. In this respect, the crossing of chiasmus appears to be as intangible and elusive as the vanishing point in perspective painting. The vanishing point is the site where convergent lines merge at the horizon, the place where objects of perspectival representation become invisible. The vanishing point is the degree zero of perspectival representation, the point where all values = 0. It is a purely ideal point, the site at which the illusory character of perspectival representation is laid bare.

But wait. Like borders of any type, once adequately magnified, the crossing reveals itself as a space, a zone, a blurred domain where one territory shades over into another. Only in the *idea* of perspectival painting does the vanishing point actually occupy the null space of zero values. Only in the *idea* of chiasmus is the crossing of the two arms an invisible moment of convergence. In the phrasal flow of chiastic text that point of crossing is figured by a comma, a line-break or enjambement, or quite simply, a space.

In Pozzo's hypocritical imagination of a chiastic reversal of fates, this point of crossing is signalled by a copula ("et" – "and") and its surroundings spaces ("et" – "and"). This is exemplified in a passage already quoted above: "POZZO: Remarquez que j'aurais pu être à sa place et lui à la mienne. Si le hazard ne s'y était pas opposé. A chacun son dû" (*En attendant Godot* 43) – "POZZO: Remark that I might just as well have been in his shoes and he in mine. If chance had not willed otherwise. To each one his due" (*Waiting for Godot* 31; underlining added). The complex transitional space at the mid-point of chiasmus, by virtue of its tangible blankness, figures the invisible materiality of the point of chiastic crossing. The crossing is the point where balanced duality is revealed as a heterogeneous field of forces. For in Pozzo's phrasing, the chiastic structure of reversal, which he evokes purely as a rhetorical move (hiding behind the fatalistic alibi of "hazard"/"chance" and the moralizing excuse of "dû"/"due"), highlights an emplotment which lays bare a narrative of power and privilege. The "et"/"and" is not merely additive but reveals itself as a gear-change between regimes of inequality. The apparently chronological role of the copula, linking two segments in a narrative chain, is revealed as the spatial interface between regions of unequally distributed resources. History is always a history of place, we learn paradoxically, from "semi-colonial", crypto-post-nationalist Beckett. The fictions of space that are analysed in the rest of this book thus enact a series of localized regions with which reciprocal ethical relationships are set up in successive and contiguous spaces of fiction.

3
Narrative Space

"I have a voice ... and for good or evil mine is the speech that cannot be silenced", says Conrad's loquatious Marlow (*Heart of Darkness* 187). And with good reason. In the century since the novella's publication (1899/1900) Marlow's narrative has repeatedly informed other literary texts: *Heart of Darkness* furnished the vocabulary and imagery of Eliot's 'The Hollow Men' (1925); of Louis Ferdinand Céline's *Voyage au bout de la nuit* (1932) [*Journey to the End of the Night*]; Michel Leiris's *L'Afrique fantôme* (1934); V. S. Naipaul's *An Area of Darkness* (1964) and *A Bend in the River* (1979); not to mention more recent avatars such as Liam Davison's *The White Woman* (1991); Timothy Findley's *Headhunter* (1993); and Zakes Mda's *Heart of Redness* (2000).[1] Conrad's novella has become part of the cultural history of our time, marking, if only symbolically, not merely the beginning of modernist questioning of language and its capacity to tell the truth about the world, but also an early index of the still distant collapse of the colonial order. The language of *Heart of Darkness* has continued to resonate down the century at successive moments when writers have questioned their culture and nation.

In Walter Benjamin's terms, *Heart of Darkness* has generated its own "after-life" ["Überleben"], consisting of re-readings, re-writings and re-appropriations undergone by the text since its original appearance.[2] This and the following chapter trace a number of Conradian echoes across the twentieth century. I begin with André Gide's *L'Immoraliste* (1902) [Engl. trans., *The Immoralist*, 1960] and continue with David Dabydeen's *The Intended* (1991) and Christa Wolf's *Störfall* (1987) [Engl. trans. *Accident*, 1989] in the subsequent chapter.

In this double chapter I explore the notion of a spatial narration which builds upon the concept of intertextuality to expand the Russian Formalist notion of levels of narration. My articulation of Kristevan intertextuality and its "spatialization of literature" upon the Shklovskian notion of the act of narration/narrative of actions takes account of what Edward Said has called "the conditions ... by which a story's telling becomes necessary". Said focuses upon Conrad's "attention to the persuasively realistic setting of the tale's presentation", and this attention will provide the starting point for my analysis.[3] It is the space of narrative and the manner in which it engenders not only further narratives but also their respective contiguous spaces that I pursue across this century-long genealogy of Conradian avatars.

Narratives, however, generate their contiguous spaces of narration again and again only because they need those spaces to enable their own narration. The generative activity of narrative, an activity which spawns stories upon stories is not merely active. It is also profoundly dependent upon the spaces in which those stories can be told. The very act of space-creation betrays the debt that narrative owes to the spaces which sustain it. These chapters thus approach deiXis as the marking of relationships of reciprocal enablement between narrative and context.

Afterlife

The 'afterlife' of *Heart of Darkness* can be said to commence immediately after its appearance. The opening pages of Conrad's novella bear close comparison with those of a novel published almost co-terminously by the French writer André Gide:

> The sea-reach of the Thames stretched before us like the beginning of an interminable waterway. In the offing the sea and the sky were welded together without a joint ...
>
> Between us there was, as I have already said somewhere, the bond of the sea. Besides holding our hearts together through long periods of separation, it had the effect of making us tolerant of each other's yarns – and even convictions. ... Marlow sat cross-legged right aft, leaning against the mizzen-mast. ... We felt meditative, and fit for nothing but placid staring. The day was ending in a serenity of still and exquisite brilliance. The water shone pacifically; the sky, without a speck, was a benign immensity of unstained light ...
>
> And at last, in its curved and imperceptible fall, the sun sank low, and from glowing white changed to a dull red without rays and without heat, as if about to go out suddenly, stricken to death by the touch of that gloom brooding over a crowd of men. ...

"And this also," said Marlow suddenly, "has been one of the dark places of the earth." *(Heart of Darkness* 135–8)

Uncanny parallels with Conrad can be found in the opening passage of Gide's *L'Immoraliste* [*The Immoralist*] of 1902.[4] The same ingredients are present: the view out over an open expanse at dusk; a bond of friendship between a group of males which is strong enough to render conversation superfluous; and the abruptly inaugurated narrative of one in their midst:

[I am writing to you under a sky of flawless blue; during the twelve days that Denis, Daniel and myself have been here, there has not been a single cloud nor the slightest diminution of sunshine. ... You know what ties of friendship bound Michel, Denis and myself together – a friendship which was strong even in our school days, but which every year grew stronger. A kind of pact was concluded between us four ...

Until night came we barely exchanged a dozen words. ... we went up on to the terrace, where the view stretched away into infinity, and all three of us, like Job's comforters, sat down and waited, watching and admiring the day's abrupt decline over the incandescent plain.

Here is the story, just as Denis, Daniel and I heard it. Michel told it us on the terrace, as we were lying beside him in the dark and the starlight. At the end of his tale we saw day rising over the plain. Michel's house looks down on it ...

When it was night Michel said: ... (*The Immoralist* 4, 5, 6–7)]

[Je t'écris sous un azur parfait; depuis les douze jours que Denis, Daniel et moi sommes ici, pas un nuage, pas une diminution du soleil. ... Tu sais quelle amitié de college, forte déjà, mais chaque année grandie, liait Michel à Denis, à Daniel, à moi. Entre nous une sorte de pacte fut conclu ...

Jusqu'à la nuit nous n'échangeâmes pas dix paroles. ... Puis nous montâmes sur la terrasse d'où la vue à l'infini s'étendait, et tous trois, pareil aux trois amis de Job, nous attendîmes, admirant sur la plaine en feu le déclin brusque de la journée.

Je t'adresse donc ce récit, tel que Denis, Daniel et moi l'entendîmes: Michel le fit sur sa terrasse où près de lui nous étions étendus dans l'ombre et dans la clarté des étoiles. A la fin du récit nous avons vu le jour se lever sur la plaine. La maison de Michel la domine ...

Quand ce fut la nuit, Michel dit: ... (*L'Immoraliste* 369, 370, 371)]

The resemblances are striking. They can easily be enumerated in narratological terms. First, both share the presence of a frame narrator whose addressee is external to the text, thereby framing the incipient narrative: "'And this also,' said Marlow suddenly ..."; , "Quand ce fut la nuit, Michel dit ..."/"When it was night Michel said ...". Second, both texts dramatize the small group of listeners furnishing an immediate figure of the potential recipients of the text. Third, Conrad and Gide both present the embedded narration of an ambivalent and guilt-ridden protagonist; it takes the form of a long monologue in which the search for self-knowledge is hampered by self-deception and manipulation of the hearers.[5] Fourth, both novels describe panoramic site of narration with clear connections to the British and French colonial empires and their tales of conquest. Finally, the scrupulous attention to the details of light, weather and diurnal rhythms staking out the spatial and temporal conditions of narrativity – all of these elements are shared by the two texts. Both authors are manifestly concerned to present, via the dramatization of the scene of storytelling, what I call in this chapter spatialized narration.

A spatial rapport implicitly links the two texts. They were almost perfectly contemporaneous with each other and therefore cannot be linked by diachronic connections such as a traceable "influence". Instead, their relationship to one another appears as one of contiguity.

Gide would invest a huge amount of effort in furthering the translation of Conrad's works into French and making him known to a Francophone audience from the First World War onwards. Paradoxically, however, Gide read *Heart of Darkness* for the first time only in 1917, and its influence can be seen most clearly even later, for instance in his journal of the African journey of 1925–7, entitled *Voyage au Congo*. The travel narrative was dedicated to Conrad's memory and was replete with explicit references to *Heart of Darkness*: "I'm re-reading *Heart of Darkness* for the fourth time. It's only upon seeing the country it speaks of that I appreciate its utter brilliance" ["Je relis le *Coeur des Ténèbres* pour la quatrième fois. C'est seulement après avoir vu le pays don't il parle que j'en sens toute l'excellence"].[6]

In 1902, when *L'Immoraliste* was published, however, Gide had not even heard of Conrad. Another decade was to pass before he would read the Polish-English author. The close resemblance of the two narratives (not only in their opening scenes, but also in the African trajectories and Nietszschean destinies of their respective protagonists) thus constitutes an uncanny form of impossible intertextuality, one independent of any clearly identifiable influence. Gide was not averse, in other contexts, to identifying paradoxical instances of such impossible intertextuality. In January 1940 he noted in his diary, "Amusement upon discovering in Hugo's *Légende des siècles* a half-line from Mallarmé's 'Brise Marine'" ["Amusement de découvrir dans Hugo (*Légende*; livre VI, I, Le pont), un hémistische de Mallarmé (*Brise marine*)"].[7] Gide is clearly delighted to find that the great novelist and poet of the early nineteenth-century has been reading his modernist successor Mallarmé. Then common-sense comes to the fore, and Gide half-heartedly wonders whether Mallarmé was perhaps distantly recalling Victor Hugo's poetry. But his immediate impulse is to delightedly posit a paradoxical reverse intertextuality, a perverse achronology in which the earlier author alludes to the successor he could not have known. In such achronologies, linear lines of influence are discarded for modes of connection that often appear as spatial relationships.

This 'virtual' intertextuality provides an extreme instance of the brutal scission of influence and textual interconnection effected by Kristeva's novel concept of intertextuality: "any text is constructed as a mosaic of quotations; any text is absorbtion and transformation of another. The notion of *intertextuality* replaces that of subjectivity, and poetic language is read as at least double" ["tout texte se construit comme mosaïque de citations, tout texte est absorbtion et transformation d'un autre texte. A la place de la notion d'intersubjectivité s'installe celle d'*intertextualité*, et le langage poétique se lit, au moins, comme double"].[8] Kristeva's displacement of "intersubjectivity" ["intersubjectivité"] aims, in the first instance, at a depersonalization of Bakhtin's concept of 'dialogicity'. Kristeva's depersonalization reposes upon a shift of emphasis from dialogic 'word' to 'dialogic' (inter)textuality. However, her shift also constitutes a snide dismissal of the theories of literary influence which had hitherto configured accounts of literary diachronicity in terms of authorial agency and linear filiation.

In this respect, the inexplicable but undeniable resemblance between the opening passages of *Heart of Darkness* and *L'Immoraliste* exemplifies the absolute banishment of theories of conscious authorial influence, setting in its place a kinship which is clearly exclusively textual and denued of the slightest empirical trace of personal connection. (The two texts are temporally virtually synchronous, stripped of the diachronic connections central to the influence-theories Kristeva was seeking to question.[9])

Both texts are at pains to lay bare the intersubjective workings of narrative itself. However, it is striking that their dramatizations of the narrative process, albeit peopled by narrators and narratees, stresses the space and interstitial place of narrative. In this way, both Conrad and Gide offer models of narrative that eschew any easily linear notion of unmediated narrative transmission. In this chapter I wish to pursue this notion of spatialized narrative by utilizing Kristeva's theory of intertextuality to 'delinearize' Shklovsky's concepts of narratives levels (story vs. discourse). Successive appropriations of *Heart of Darkness* by Gide, Christa Wolf and David Dabydeen will provide the starting point and textual impetus for these theoretical explorations.

Spatial narration

The notion of spatial narration is one which becomes prominent in Kristeva's early semiotic work. In the essay on Bakhtin in which the notion of intertextuality is introduced for the first time, she explicitly conceives of narration as a spatial undertaking:

> Defining the specific status of the word as signifier for different modes of (literary) intellection within different genres or texts puts poetic analysis at the sensitive centre of contemporary 'human' sciences – at the intersection of *language* (the true practice of thought) with *space* (the volume within which signification, through a joining of differences, articulates itself).
>
> [L'établissement du statut spécifique du mot dans les différents genres (ou textes) comme signifiant des différents modes d'intellection (littéraire) place l'analyse poétique au point névralgique des sciences 'humaines' aujourd'hui: au croisement du *langage* (pratique réelle de la pensée) et de l'*espace* (volume dans lequel la signification s'articule par une jonction de différences).][10]

Literary activity occurs at the point where language as 'material thought' meets meaning as a conjunction of differences: that is, meaning as a heterogeneous space of dispersal rather than a homogenous point. Meaning, since de Saussure's "*c*at-*b*at-*m*at" contrasts (so-called 'pertinent oppositions'), does not reside *in* the sign, but is generated in the differential interval *between* signifiers. Difference, the nub of modern thought on linguistic meaning, spatializes the generation of meaning by locating them in an interval, a space-between.

What may this spatiality of poetic language be said to consist of? Kristeva elaborates further on the principle parameters of this spatialized differential poetics:

> Confronted with this spatial conception of language's poetic operation, we must first define the three dimensions of textual space ... These

three dimensions or coordinates of dialogue are writing subject, addressee, and exterior texts.

[Face à cette conception spatiale du fonctionnement poétique du langage, il est nécessaire d'abord de définir les trois dimensions de l'espace textuel ... Ces trois dimensions sont: le sujet de l'écriture, le destinataire et les textes extérieures (trois éléments en dialogue).][11]

The word, or spatialized term of differential meaning, is thus located within a three-dimensional realm, constituted by sender, addressee and past and present texts. These three dimensions are then re-defined, not entirely consistently, along the two-dimensional horizontal/vertical opposition (with the third dimension of depth perhaps remaining implicit):

The word's status is thus defined *horizontally* (the word in the text belongs to both writing subject and addressee) as well as *vertically* (the word in the text is oriented toward an anterior or synchronic literary corpus).

[Le status du mot se définit alors *a)* *horizontalement*: le mot dans le texte appartient à la fois au sujet de l'écriture et au destinataire, et *b)* *verticalement*: le mot dans le texte est orienté vers le corpus antérieur ou synchronique.][12]

The word or term of meaning as a nexus of language and space is thus doubly located within a sender/recipient relationship and within a field of prior pre-texts and contemporary con-texts. This apparent reduction of the three-dimensionality of textual space to a flatter two-dimensional surface should not worry us unduly, as Kristeva will subsequently dimiss the latter dualism. Modifying Bakhtin's emphasis upon addressivity, she will subsequently privilege the latter field of textuality as the site of *inter-textuality*.

In the case of the relationship between Conrad's *Heart of Darkness* and Gide's *L'Immoraliste*, it is indeed the latter field, that of textuality, and in particular that of a synchronic literary corpus, which seems to be the site of the relationship between the two novels. We cannot plausibly posit Conrad as the sender and Gide as the recipient in a relationship of influence. This is so because a genuine relationship of influence (the first component) would only develop subsequently with a verifiable record of Gide's reception of *Heart of Darkness* during the First World

War. Genuine influence postdated the uncanny echoes in *L'Immoraliste* by fifteen years.

Here any intertextuality is an intertextuality entirely without influence, indeed, without contact of any sort between the two authors at this point in time. The rapport between Conrad's *Heart of Darkness* and Gide's *L'Immoraliste* is a literal *inter-textuality* in which texts, and not writers, communicate with each other.

It is precisely this sort of depersonalization of the subject–addressee relationship which Kristeva is seeking, as her subsequent qualification makes patently clear:

> The addressee, however, is included within the book's discursive universe only as discourse itself. He thus fuses with this other discourse, this other book, in relation to which the writer has written his own text. Hence the horizontal axis (subject-addressee) and vertical axis (text-context) coincide, bringing to light an important fact: each word (text) is an intersection of words (texts) where at least one other word (text) can be read.
>
> [Mais dans l'univers discursif du livre, le destinataire est inclus uniquement en tant que discours lui-même. Il fusionne donc avec cet autre discours (cet autre livre) par rapport auquel l'écrivain écrit son propre texte; de sort que l'axe horizontal (sujet-destinataire) et l'axe vertical (texte-contexte) coïncident pour dévoiler un fait majeur: le mot (le texte) est un croisement des mots (des textes) où on lit au moins un autre mot (texte).][13]

Kristeva's comments are highly apposite in relationship to *Heart of Darkness* and *L'Immoraliste*: the addressee of both narratives is already integrated within the text itself as an instance of discourse. The addressee-as-discourse is concretized via the levels of embedded narration which structures both novellas: by the marking of sociability as storytelling in *Heart of Darkness* ("Between us there was ... the bond of the sea. ... it had the effect of making us tolerant of each other's yarns" – *Heart of Darkness* 135–6) and by the epistolary opening of *L'Immoraliste* ("*A MONSIEUR D. R. | Président du Conseil*" – *L'Immoraliste* 367 ["TO MR. D. R., PREMIER OF FRANCE" – *The Immoralist* 4]). All too often, narrators and narratees are only present as voices: "It had become so pitch dark that we listeners could hardly see one another. For a long time already [Marlow], sitting apart, had been no more to us than a voice" (*Heart of Darkness* 173); "Quand ce fut la nuit, Michel dit ..." (*L'Immoraliste* 371)

["When it was night Michel said: ..." (*The Immoralist* 7)]. The narrator is a discourse predicated upon a narratee also instantiated as discourse: "[Marlow's] remark did not seem at all surprising. ... It was accepted in silence. No one took the trouble to grunt even" (*Heart of Darkness* 139); "Mes chers amis ... si je vous appelai brusquement ... c'est pour vous voir, et pour que vous puissiez m'entendre. ... J'ai besoin de parler, vous dis-je" (*L'Immoraliste* 372) ["For, if I summoned you suddenly ... it was solely to see you and so that you could hear me out ... I need to speak, I tell you" (*The Immoralist* 8)].

Where Bakhtin is unable to clearly distinguish, according to Kristeva, the two axes of sender-recipient and text-context, it is for the simple reason, she claims, that they are of the same nature. Conrad's and Gide's mobilization of successive narrative levels admirably demonstrate the manner in which the dialogue between narrator and narratee and between text and context are discursive functions. The fundamentally identical nature of these two relationships leads Kristeva to collapse the difference between inner and outer forms of textual intercommunication in a formulation which has since become famous: "The notion of *intertextuality* replaces that of subjectivity" ["A la place de la notion d'intersubjectivité s'installe celle d'*intertextualité*"].[14]

However, another route of enquiry is left unexplored by Kristeva. In her eagerness to depersonalize the dialogicity of Bakhtin's poetics ("this dialogue counts the *person* out" ["ce dialogue met la *personne* hors circuit"][15]), she converts the Bakhtinian word into a shimmering text, and the speaker of the word into an anonymous textuality. This move has contributed to a salutary liberation from author-based criticism, and has opened up a rich field of intertextual interconnections which would otherwise have remained largely invisible to critics.

It does, however, elide the fact that at some residual but none the less significant level, narration assumes a narrator and a narratee. Narration, however much it may be understood as a textual dynamic, assumes some degree of agency, both at its source and at its destination. Without some active instance of transmission and reception, it is difficult to explain just those processes of transformation which intertextuality so clearly documents.

The erasure of the inner-textual configuration of voices and the extra-textual (and intertextual) arrangements of voices, as a spatial operation, is less a piece of theoretical sophistry than something that literary texts, as so often, undertook well before theory recognized the fact. Conversely, by virtue of their dramatization of fictional voices and their (sometimes) visible human bearers, texts may equally well point up the instances of agency of textual transformation. This does not mean that they assume real authors or readers, but rather, in their operations upon narrative (often embodied in characters) they may situate the interstitial transformations of textual material in a spatial field which is that of the narrating-receiving society.

Shklovsky's machines

In order to revamp Kristeva's notion of intertextuality so as to restore the missing element of 'subjectivity' and agency (that of textual transformation, not that of the 'sovereign subject') it may be helpful to invoke Bakhtin's contemporary, Viktor Shklovsky. Shklovsky's notion of narrative levels, the instances of *fabula* and *sujet*, of story-content and narrative discourse (*story* and *discourse*, the now widely-accepted equivalent terms established by Chatman, will be used hereafter in italics[16]), may allow us to locate the respective productive and receptive-productive instances of textual agency that go to make up the space of narrative action.

Shklovsky's iconoclastic theory of plot-formation de-naturalizes a process hitherto taken for granted by splitting storytelling into its constituent parts. In a succinct reformulation of a notion originally developed together with Eichenbaum, Shklovsky explains in his influential study *The Theory of Prose*, "The concept of plot (*syuzhet* [or *discourse*]) is too often confused with a description of the events of a novel, with what I'd tentatively call the *story* line (*fabula*)" ["Поняне сюжета слишком часто смешивют с описанием событий – с тем, что предлагаю условно назвать фабулой"].[17] Rather than simply 'telling a story', literature is conceived of as functioning by virtue of the combination of several formal elements. Shklovsky splits 'storytelling' into 'story-line' (*story*) and the process of its 'telling' (*discourse*). Then he goes a step further, envisaging the events recounted in a novel (the *story*) not as a content to be presented by the mediating form of the storytelling (the *discourse*), but rather, as material serving the process of storytelling: "На самом деле фабула есть лишъ материал для сюжетного оформления" (*О Теории Прозы* [*O Theorii Prosy*] 204) ["As a matter of fact, though, the story line is nothing more than material for plot formation" (*Theory of Prose* 170)]. The telling (*discourse*) is not at the service of the content (*story*); on the contrary, content (*story*) is subordinated to the telling (*discourse*). For Shklovsky, it is not the events of a narrative that take precedence, but their configuration in the narration.

In *Literatura i kinematograf* (1923) [*Literature and the cinematographer*], Shklovsky defines the *story* as "the material for narrative construction".

That raw material is significant only in so far as it is subsequently converted into the literary artefact. As Erlich explains: "The 'fable' [*story*] of *Anna Karenina*, for example, can be stated in one brief sentence: this paraphrase, however, would not even hint at the richness and complexity of the novel. Art in general, and art of fiction in particular, stands or falls with organization."[18] It is only by elaborating, reworking, distorting or refracting a basic sequence of events that a tale emerges.

Shklovsky focuses upon radical texts such as Sterne's *Tristram Shandy*, in which there is so much juggling in the *discourse* that the *story*, though almost entirely coherent and susceptible of reconstruction, becomes virtually unrecognizable.[19] The Sternian narrator's attempts to elucidate the genesis of his own writing project only generate a plethora of words obscuring that originary process, and, comically, hindering his own birth: "I declare that I have been at it these six weeks, making all speed I possibly could, – and am not born: – I have just been able, and that's all, to tell you *when* it happened, but not *how*; – so that you see that the thing is yet far from being accomplished."[20] The *story* is lost under the process of narrative *discourse*. Sterne enacts in his novel what Shklovsky is trying to carry out in the realm of narrative theory. In other words, he attempts to bar the *story*-line sequence as the cause and motivation of the *discourse*-construction. *Discourse*-construction becomes an end in itself.

Although the two terms (*story* and *discourse*) are inherently interdependent (and the two functions in reality inseparable within the concrete instance of the fiction), what appeals to Shklovsky is the illusion of the elimination of any prior story-line, the non-narrative core which is subsequently worked up into narration. This move in turn facilitates Shklovsky's demonstrative rejection of an exterior 'motivation' for literary activity – and of his denial of a social context and referent outside the text. For in his utter antagonism to an older school of literary criticism that sees the text as a mere vehicle for a moral or a message, Shklovsky is determined to ignore possible ideological or thematic contents of the work, making content a mere function of form. He embodies a radically materialist approach to art, regarding it as a set of formal devices that speaks, through its very mode of operation, of itself and not of anything extraneous to it. Paradoxically, this produces a notion of materialist criticism deprived of a concept of a social context of production.[21]

It is for this reason that one has good grounds for querying Shklovsky's interpretation of the narrative functions of *story* and *discourse*. Shklovsky caps the story-line, making of it a formal resource which sidelines content and theme, so as to intensify the conception of literature as materialist process. But by introducing the notion of story-line (*story*) as material that is produced or worked-up in the plot (*discourse*), Shklovsky effectively amputates a further instance of production by limiting it to the writerly activity and neglecting the activity of the consumer of literature, the reader. His theory of narrative can benefit by extension of the *story/discourse* distinction in a direction hitherto little explored, that of reader-reception. In this way, his theory of narrative construction becomes more than an explanation of linear reconfiguration of temporality, namely, a spatialized theory of narrative instances linked by their synchronous transformation of other narrative materials.

The absence of the reader in Shklovsky's theory can be exemplified in the notion of the literary text as machine. Peter Steiner has closely examined Shklovsky's affection for a machine analogy of language: the idea of the literary text as a machine whose mechanisms could be investigated and precisely documented allows him to bracket the 'what' of literature in favour of the 'how'. Thus form is freed from its previous subservience to content; the innovative concentration on form in turn facilitates the careful description of the mechanisms of the literary work.[22]

The machine analogy is one which, curiously enough, Conrad also used, though with a shiver of repugnance far removed Shklovsky's malicious delight:

There is a – let us say – a machine. It evolved itself (I am severely scientific) out of a chaos of scraps of iron and behold! – it knits. I am horrified at the horrible work and stand appalled. ... the most withering thought is that the infamous thing has made itself; made itself without thought, without conscience, without foresight, without eyes, without heart. ... It knits us in and it knits us out. It has knitted time space [*sic*], pain, death, corruption, despair and all the illusions – and nothing matters.[23]

Conrad's notion of a textual machine which "knits" is clearly related to the textile metaphorics of "yarning", present from the outset in *Heart of Darkness*: "the bond of the sea. ... [made] us tolerant of each other's yarns" – *Heart of Darkness* 135–6). The "yarn" is an inherently sociable and communal form of storytelling. Like Shklovsky's textual machine, Conrad's knitting machine appears to bracket off human agency, becoming autonomous in its terrible impersonality. Yet Conrad's machine also generates 'yarns' of various types. This yarning-machine cannot but integrate in some way a talking community and communicational sites: "It knits *us in* and it knits *us out.*" Conrad's and Gide's constant mobilization of narrators/narratees and the enactment of their role (whether "in" or "out" of the 'space' in which narrative occurs and upon which it depends) complicates Shklovsky's text-machine concept.

Literary texts, in their frequent dramatization of the scene of narration and their creation of narrator-protagonists, situate 'within' the functioning of the text itself a group of actors who are not merely 'described' by it, but from whom its narrative functioning as a whole is derived. Positing a group of agents 'inside' the text as its dynamic principle in turn opens up the possibility of similar actors 'outside' the text whose agency is equally potent and equally central to the functioning of the 'machine': "It knits us in and it knits us out." Significantly, Conrad's text eschews the hermeneutical mode which the frame narrator explains as placing "the whole meaning of which ... within the shell of a cracked nut ... inside like a kernel". Instead, the meaning of Marlow's yarns "was not inside like a kernel but outside, enveloping the tale which brought it out only as a glow brings out a haze, in the likeness of one of these misty halos that sometimes are made visible by the spectral illumination of moonshine" (*Heart of Darkness* 138). This comment points not only to the immediate context of reception of Marlow's narrative (that of the circle of friends sitting on the deck on the yawl anchored in the Thames) but also to the frame narrator whose comments, "enveloping the tale which brought it out", establish the virtual space of readerly reception. Conrad's analogy of the moonlight and the halo also points to later instances of reception and appropriation of Conrad's novella, some of which will be explored in the following chapter. Similarly, Gide distinguishes, in the 'paratextual' preface to *L'Immoraliste*, "l'intérêt réel d'une œuvre et celui que le public d'un jour y porte" (*L'Immoraliste* 368) ["the real interest of a work and the interest taken in it by an ephemeral public" (*The Immoralist* ix)], implying the agency of generations of future, more perceptive readers in the reception of the work. The knitting/yarning-machine is never set off from its environment. And that environment, the space of narration, facilitates the functioning of the text as much as it is created by the text.

An instructive comparison can be found in Terry Eagleton's use of the metaphor of theatrical production as an analogy for the text's production of prior ideological material. The theatrical metaphor avoids the pitfalls of the machine metaphor by necessarily including an instance of author–audience relations.[24] Where Shklovsky's mechanistic analogies aim to isolate the text from its social environment so as better to show up its workings (which it in turn 'lays bare' in a purely autotelic process) literary texts such as Conrad's and Gide's persist in portraying themselves as entities with a plurality of human faces and concomitant narrative places.

Clearly, if the text-machine is inherently social, then only a further community, that of future readers, could possibly make sense of it. Whence a modified notion of the narrative process, not just as a reworking of the *story* but rather, as an embedded, constantly layered process which involves and implicates a community of recipients. In the reading of avatars of *Heart of Darkness* presented in the following chapter, that process would appear to be potentially infinite, constantly generating new texts which grow out of Conrad's novella, itself understood as a non-originary instance of *story* persistently inviting conversion into *discourse*. Such insistent foregrounding of the processes of literary crafting (what Shklovsky called the 'device') does not merely guarantee renewal within the literary tradition, as Shklovsky claimed.[25] Rather, it underwrites literature as a collective productive process, as a communal undertaking. And that communal undertaking assumes a communal space in which narrative can take place.

In other words, the dual notion of *story* and *discourse* needs to be supplemented by what Chatman has called *story*-place and *discourse*-place.[26] It is significant that though Chatman can conceptualize *story*-place, categorizing it under narrative "existents", he has nothing further to say about *discourse*-place. The question of the mode of existence of such "existents", and of the spatial substrata they may depend upon, which brings us close to the deiXis which is the subject of this book, is ignored in Chatman's discussion. The reason for this strange inattention to *discourse*-place may be his commitment to a narrative theory whose primary epistemeological interest is directed to temporality. The following discussion will seek to rectify this weakness by demonstrating that *discourse*-place is of central importance in the generation of narrativity.

Shklovsky's spaces

The abstract distinction between *story* and *discourse*, though analytically useful, is inherently spurious for two reasons. First, because the two levels of narration can only occur together in a productive process, the narrated events are never available outside the process of narration. The point of suture between material and production is always situated at the point where one level of the *story-discourse* production process is converted by the act of reception into a successive level of *story*. Marlow's monologue is interrupted at strategic points by his listeners on the deck:

> "But I felt it all the same; I felt often [the inner truth of the jungle's] mysterious stillness watching me at my monkey tricks, just as it watches you fellows performing on your respective tight-ropes for – what is it? half-a-crown a tumble –"
>
> "Try to be civil, Marlow," growled a voice, and I knew there was at least one listener awake besides myself. (*Heart of Darkness* 183–4)

The recurring hinge upon which the process of textual (re)production turns is the act of reception. Marlow's story can only be constituted as *discourse* with the help of his listeners. The text repeatedly highlights this process.

Second, *discourse*-production process at one level of narration can become the *story*-material in a further level of reception, and so on *ad infinitum*. The listening "I" of "I knew there was at least one listener awake besides myself" is a storyteller for us as readers. The *discourse* level of the listener's reconstruction of Marlow's *story* becomes in turn the *story* which we reconstruct in the *discourse*-work of reading.

The logical result of this infinitely repeatable transformation of *discourse* into *story* (and *vice versa*) is that the opposition between the two terms threatens to dissolve altogether. In the last analysis, it is only possible to employ the terms *discourse* and *story* under erasure ('*sous rature*'). If *discourse* and *story* are inextricably linked by a constantly productive process, the one recurrently taking the place of the other as one level of narrative process succeeds another, then in principle the global process of narrative production is susceptible of infinite extension, and therefore always resists containment. If we can extend the *story-discourse* production process 'inwards' through the successive levels of embedded communicative systems, we can also extend it 'outwards', thus exploding the very limits designed to be put in place by this conceptual pair in its original formulation – namely, the exclusion of the social context from the analysis of formal textual devices. The transformative relationship *story-discourse* in turn becomes, under the gaze of the reader and her or his critical scrutiny, the *story*-element of a further *story-discourse* transformation.

Implicitly, Shklovsky develops a materialist theory of narrative production which dynamizes the literary artefact and replaces this with a notion of material process. Such a process, however, inherently contains within itself the power to resist closure. Whence the error of comments such those of Adorno in his *Aesthetic Theory* [*Ästhetische Theorie*]:

> That is why the relation of art to society is not to be sought primarily in the sphere of reception. This relation is anterior to reception, in production. Interest in the social decipherment of art must orient itself to production rather than being content with the study and classification of effects that for social reasons totally diverge from the artwork and their objective social content.

> [Darum ist das Verhältnis der Kunst zur Gesellschaft nicht vorwiegend in der Sphäre der Rezeption aufzusuchen. Es ist dieser vorgängig: in der Produktion. Das Interesse an der gesellschaftlichen Dechiffrierung der Kunst muß dieser sich zukehren, anstatt mit der Ermittlung und Klassifizierung von Wirkungen sich abspeisen zu lassen, die vielfach aus gesellschaftlichem Grunde von den Kunstwerken und ihrem objektiven gesellschaftlichen Gehalt gänzlich divergieren.][27]

Adorno's mistake is to assume that the process of production resides only in the space of the writer and not in the space of the reader. In contrast, the manifold strategies of multiple embedding employed by Conrad's and Gide's texts show the productive process occurring both in the events recounted by the text, in the recounting itself, and in the reader's reception of that narrative. This (at least) triple process of production, and the sheer impossibility of its containment, is acknowledged by Wolfgang Iser in laying down one of the founding principles of reader-response criticism in his claim to the effect

> that the indeterminate elements of literary prose – perhaps even of all literature – represent a vitall link between text and reader. They are the switch that activates the reader into using his own ideas in order to fulfil the intention of the text. This means that they are the basis for a textual structure in which the reader's part is already incorporated.

> [daß der Unbestimmtheitsbetrag in literarischer Prosa – vielleicht in Literatur überhaupt – das wichtigste Umschaltelement zwischen Text und Leser darstellt. Als Umschaltstelle funktioniert Unbestimmtheit insofern, als sie die Vorstellungen des Lesers zum Mitvollzug der im Text angelegten Intention aktiviert. Das aber heißt: Sie wird zur Basis einer Textstruktur, in der der Leser immer schon mitgedacht ist.][28]

It is worth noting that literary texts do not merely contain, however, punctual "points of uncertainty". They dramatize spaces of reader-reception, interstitial spaces of interpretive "free play", as part of their narrative in ways that far outstrip the meagre and occasional freedoms imagined by Iser.

If Kristeva's notion of intertextuality can be productively modified by comparison with Shklovsky, Shklovsky can in turn be helpfully inflected by comparison with Kristeva. Intertextuality can be understood as being dramatized spatially by *story/discourse* transformations undertaken by narrators and narratees within the text itself. Significantly, such notions are already anticipated, but not expanded, by Kristeva when she notes that "the subject of the word, stratified into loctutor and inter-locutor, embodies the only possible geography of resemblance" ["le sujet de la parole, stratifié en locuteur et inter-locuteur, incarne la seule géographie possible du vraisemblable"].[29] It is the double relationship between the narrator and narratee, in which they are both object for the other's subject-position, that is already prefigured within the narrator her- or himself as a split subject (as Kristeva suggests earlier, as simultaneous subject of the 'énoncé' or utterance, and of the enunciation or utter-ing[30]). Here Kristeva is drawing implicitly upon Benveniste's work on deixis. This suggests that discourse must always be anchored in a con-crete context, whence the importance of temporal and spatial deictics: "*I* can only be identified by the instance of discourse that contains it ... It has no value except in the instance in which it is produced" ["*je* ne peut être identifié que par l'instance de discours qui le contient ... Il ne vaut que dans l'instance où il est produit"].[31] However, discourse is also given concrete meaning by being inserted in an intersubjective context; it is the presence of an interlocutor that gives the shifter 'I', for instance, a framework in which it can assume an identity of its own. 'I' is an empty signifier given meaning only by the presence of a 'you' or a 'she'/'he'/'we': "the Word of a locutor listening to itself in its *inter-*locutor" ["la Parole du locuteur s'écoutant dans son *inter-*locuteur"].[32]

Accordingly, deixis, in its function of anchoring spoken discourse in a social context (making it 'discourse' as social practice), points to the intersubjectivity underlying subjectivity, to the social space marked out by the act of identifying subjectivities who speak. These subjectivities are made possible by language and its categories but also by the differ-ential relationships with other subjectivities. Social space founds narra-tion and is founded by it, and narrative subjectivity grows out of social space.[33] The 'I' of the 'enoncé' or utterance is dependent upon the 'I' of the 'énonciation' or uttering, which in turn is dependent upon an superiority of the historical paradigm in an interview with a geographers' collective banished that hegemony to a bygone age: "Space was treated as the dead, the fixed, the immobile. Time, on the contrary, was richness, fecundity, life, dialectic" ["L'espace, c'était ce qui était mort, figé, non dialectique, immobile. En revanche, le temps, c'était riche, fécond, vivant, dialectique"].[5] The reversal of hierarchies which established spatial studies entailed a denigration of temporal, teleological thought typified in the structuralist privilege of synchronic analysis over diachronic description. This reversal has proved very durable, with a recent discussion of postmodern space still declaring, "The withering away of the authority and certainty of our historical sense has another side ... namely, the reaffirmation of our spatial imagination."[6]

Yet Foucault himself stressed, in a famous paper on "different spaces" that "this does not really amount to a denial of time; it is a certain way of handling what is called time and what is called history. ... Space itself, in the Western experience, has a history" ["il ne s'agit pas par là de nier le temps; c'est une certaine manière de traiter ce qu'on appelle le temps et ce qu'on appelle l'histoire. ... l'espace lui-même, dans l'expérience occidentale, a une histoire"].[7] Such careful differentiation, indeed, can already be detected in Edward Soja's project, which does not rescue spatiality at the expense of temporality, but rather, attempts "to spatialize the historical narrative".[8] Doreen Massey has recently excavated the structuralist tendency to define the spatial aspect of social practice exclusively in negative opposition to the temporal. This negative definition of space, she argues, resulted in a bloodless and abstract conception of spatial practice which effectively neglected much of the dynamic, living texture of human spatial existence: "(Spatial) order obliterates (temporal) dislocation. Spatial immobility quietens temporal becoming. It is, though, the most dismal of pyrrhic victories. For in the very moment of its conquering triumph, 'space' is reduced to stasis. The very life, and certainly the politics, are taken out of it."[9] Massey's study, significantly, cites the first and more famous of Foucault's utterances quoted above, but nowhere registers the second, more judicious assessment.[10] Thus her corrective to the one-sided and excessively abstract spatial analysis of structuralism in part merely targets a straw man. It ignores the ongoing tradition of historico-spatial analysis which emerged alongside and often in open competition to structuralism – a tradition evinced, for example, in Kristeva's own description of her forging the notion of intertextuality as "a way of making history erupt at the very heart of structuralist analysis" ["une manière de faire intervenir l'histoire ... au coeur même de l'analyse structurale"].[11]

These polemics within the emergent spatial disciplines (including geography as it increasingly relinquished mere empiricism and fore-grounded its own epistemological project) are interesting for their own sake. But they may also be understood as echoes of broader and more significant shifts in the conceptualization of space. These debates about spatial theory can be conceived of as replicating various modes of spatial representation across a century which has seen a transition from colonial hegemony, via post-independence nationhood, to a more sceptical understanding of the simultaneously post- *and* neocolonial world order. The theoretical debates thus echo concomitant modula-tions from an elision of the global project of imperialism and colonial-ism as a patently spatial undertaking, via a hypertrophied privileging of essentialized space during the immediate post-independence era in the postcolonial world, towards a more differentiated understanding of postcolonial space in recent decades.

The first two moments of spatial conceptualization – the imperial and/or colonial, and the post-independence – can be seen as being characterized by two broadly dominant modes of deictic action. In the imperial/colonial mode the standard, egocentric – or Eurocentric – form of deixis could be said to have been dominant. In the subsequent post-independence phase, the self-reflexive mode of deixis can be seen to succeed the standard mode as hegemonic alternative. In the third phase, a mode of deixis comes to the fore which balances the agency of space with that of its human inhabitants.

These specific moments of spatial conceptualization have their own clearly political logic. It was in the interests of imperialism to deal with space either by suppressing it (whence the purely culturalist, indeed temporal narratives of the white man's burden or *la mission civilisatrice*) or by treating it purely empirically (the task of imperial geography in its mundane descriptive guise). Significantly, as Anne Godlewska and Neil Smith point out, "stories of the 'Age of Empire' generally either erase the geography of empire and the role of geographical knowledge in imp-erial expansion or else treat geographical questions as an inert back-drop to historical events."[12] Imperialism thus mobilized what Lefebvre has identified as the two most powerful illusions regarding space: on the one hand the illusion of its transparence, on the other the illu-sion of its substance ("la transparence de l'espace"; "la substantialité de l'espace").[13] Both strategies worked to elide the material spatial practices of conquest and settlement of territories, displacement and resettlement of populations, and the exploitation of natural resources. I contend that these elisions of material space can be traced in the histories and stories interlocutor. The self of the énoncé or utterance is in a sense produced by the other of enunciation. The value of Shklovsky's theory of narrative levels is that it renders possible an analysis of the manner in which the 'I' of enunciation is the result of a productive narrative process. This process, however, is spatial process insofar as it is one buttressed by deixis (linguistic 'pointing'). The asocial linearity of the *story/discourse* concept, originally a notion based upon temporal juggling, needs to be spatialized by careful attention to the dramatized presence of narratees within the text. Both Conrad and Gide do this.

Significantly, if one looks at the visual elements in Shklovsky's *Theory of Prose*, it transpires that he is indeed interested in spatial issues. His reproduction of the squiggly diagrams in *Tristram Shandy* portraying the digressions which make up its plot structure effectively draws attention back to the visual and spatial dimensions of narrative.[34] Shklovsky, then, may not have been totally indifferent to the impulse to spatialize the temporalities of *story* and *discourse* so clearly manifest in literary works. A production of narrative that is carried out in an intersubjective context would indeed not occur if there were no interlocutor there to listen. This interlocutor is the bearer of an inter-locution that creates an interstitial space of narrative. Such spatiality, though dramatized within the text, cannot be contained by the boundaries of the text. Rather, this spatiality demands to be pursued beyond the boundaries of the text, in an analysis of other literary works that engage upon the same production of the non-originary generator of narrative. We now turn in the following chapter to several other avatars of *Heart of Darkness* that exemplify such narrative generativity.

4
Anadiplosis

Douglas Hurd, the British Foreign Minister at the time of the Rwanda genocide, on one occasion excused British diplomatic inactivity during that crisis by dismissing the region as a "heart of darkness" better left to its own barbaric devices. Perhaps Hurd was also echoing the patently Conradian title of Naipaul's famous travel narrative, which, though documenting a tour of the Indian subcontinent, was penned by one who shared Hurd's disparaging attitude towards the non-European world and who was eager to claim Conrad as a colonial predecessor and master.[1]

Clearly, *Heart of Darkness* has produced a surplus of spatial meanings which continue to buttress the colonial meanings it in part contains and acknowledges. Conrad's text remains massively present within the field of neocolonial relations of cultural hegemony. Given the persistence of such text-borne stereotyping, the active resistance of other writers and readers, already dramatized within the text but never susceptible of containment, is highly significant.

The differing resonances of a text such as Conrad's for hegemonic colonial and neocolonial power and for its oppponents are already anticipated by the spaces which separate narrator and narratee, storyteller and listener, within the text. These interstitial spaces are zones of contention in which tolerance and intolerance alike (" 'Try to be civil, Marlow,' growled a voice" [*Heart of Darkness* 184]) govern the contrary purposes for which *story* is converted into *discourse*. This chapter continues the meditation upon narrative space inaugurated in the previous section. It does so by pursuing Conradian avatars in two contemporary texts: David Dabydeen's *The Intended* of 1991, and Christa Wolf's slightly earlier *Störfall* of 1987 [English translation, *Accident*, 1989].[2] In these texts one finds ever-expanding ripples of textual productivity.

Such productivity can never be subsumed to a single ideological telos but rather, translates the undisciplined paths of fictional proliferation itself. Yet, precisely because these texts are concerned with the global spaces of postcolonial migration and postmodern nuclear contamination, the manner in which space itself constitutes the precondition for narration never ceases to underwrite textual productivity.

Postcolonial intertextuality

In a postcolonial context the notion of intertextuality becomes an important instrument of theoretical analysis and, for writers aware of their task, of cultural intervention. In acknowledging the significance not just of debt or appreciation in the relation of one text to another but also of disturbance or conflict, in relation both to the source and to the target system,[3] intertextuality can take account of colonial and neocolonial struggles acted out at the level of the text. Genette's typology of the forms of "transtextuality" of which intertextuality is merely one of several variants (such as metatextuality or commentary, parody, pastiche, etc.), or models of macro-intertextuality such as Lotman's typologies of cultural exchange, offer the possibility of mapping intertextual relationships within broader cross-cultural configurations.[4] The *location* of intertextual relations takes on considerable importance in this context. David Dabydeen's novel *The Intended* explores the interrelated spaces of the writer, reader or student in relationship to the literary text and the broader social context in which reading takes place. As the comparison of Conrad and Gide in the previous chapter has already shown, these spaces are once again the interstitial spaces of a spatialized collective narrativity figured from the outset within the text itself.

Dabydeen's protagonist, a Guyanese adolescent completing his high-school education in 1970s South London, sees a literary education as the route of escape from his impoverished immigrant condition. Dabydeen is concerned with the motivations for and the contexts in which reading, and intertextual reading in particular, is enacted. Whence the care he takes to indicate the actual conditions and spaces of reading in *The Intended*. The protagonist and his friends meet out of school hours to cram for their exams:

> Shaz would come round each Sunday to gain guidance for his 'A' level literature exam. ... Joseph would tag along now and again and listen to us analysing Conrad's *Heart of Darkness*. The two of them sat on the bed and I, the professor, took the chair. I would select key

> passages from the text, read them aloud and dissect them in terms
> of theme and imagery, as I had been taught to do by our English
> teacher. (*Intended* 94)

Conrad's *Heart of Darkness* figures within *The Intended* as the principal
pedagogic text through which reading skills, and thus access to hegemonic English culture (inculcated by "our English teacher" and subsequently endorsed by examination results and university entrance)
is transmitted to a young generation of immigrants. The formation of
a neocolonial subjectivity based upon social betterment via cultural
assimilation is parodied by the proleptic assumption of the 'professorial' role. The identity construction of "I, the professor" is predicated
upon a quite clear narrative trajectory (obviously calqued on the public
persona of Naipaul):

> I wanted to be somebody and the only way to achieve this was to
> acquire a collection of good examination results and go to university.
> Everything was planned: I would try for top grades in my three 'A'
> levels, then I'd do a B.A. degree at Oxford or Cambridge and then a
> Ph.D. I would write books, and one day become a celebrity, or writer.
> (*Intended* 113)

Clearly the practice of reading is deeply implicated in the transmission
and 'reproduction' of cultural values and social relations in Bourdieu's
sense.[5] In *The Intended* the reproduction of social values is enacted both
through the educational narrative inherent in the novel and the intertextual indices of textual production strewn through the text.

There are many varieties of intertextuality at work in *The Intended*.
Dabydeen himself has commented on the deep personal intertextuality
which links him to Wilson Harris, Sam Selvon or Kamu Braithwaite.
Other critics have explored the intertextuality, doubtless partly satirical, that connects Dabydeen to Naipaul.[6] Here, however, it is worth
exploring the intertextual relationship to Conrad because it is the most
explicitly 'marked' form of intertextuality,[7] without a doubt intention-
ally so (the novel's Conradian title *The Intended* is an index of this) and
clearest exemplification of the processes I want to illustrate.

In *The Intended* intertextuality is activated in the moment of reading
and discussion so as to become a site of micro-cultural contestation.
The narrator takes on the pedagogic persona constantly performed in
school, one by which he proleptically rehearses his own successful integration into and thus reproduction of the dominant cultural, social

and economic system. His Rastafarian friend Joseph, however, persists in asking "daft questions" "which my training in theme-and-imagery spotting didn't equip me to answer fully" (*Intended* 99), making intertextuality the site of a 'conflict of interpretations' and thus of the disrupted transmission of hegemonic white cultural values.[8]

Two examples will demonstrate the way Dabydeen employs intertextuality so as to place it in a conflicted social field. The first example occurs during one of the informal after-school reading sessions during which Conrad's text becomes the theatre of a struggle of interpretative modes. The narrator's docile 'new critical' close-reading methods compete with Joseph's hallucinatory, quasi-mystical Rastafarian mode of eschatological glossing:

> "But what 'bout the way he talk 'bout black people?" Joseph persisted ... "What black people?" I asked uncertainly.
>
> He snatched *Heart of Darkness* from my hand and peered at the page, unable to decipher the words ... "Where the bit about them lying under trees dying?" he demanded, shoving the book at me.
>
> I flicked through, found the passage and read it aloud to him. "That's part of the theme of suffering and redemption which lies at the core of the novel's concern," I stated cogently and intelligently, putting the book down.
>
> "No, it ain't, it about colours. ... The white light of England and the Thames is the white sun over the Congo that can't mix with the green of the bush and the black skin of the people ..." (*Intended* 97–8).

Dabydeen is concerned to make sure that these intertextual passages are clearly marked. Indeed, he is simply making explicit, albeit massively so, one of the basic tenets of the theory of intertextuality: namely, that the intertext must be readable, figurable.[9] In the words of Worton and Riffaterre reformulating Peirce, intertextuality must pass via an interpretant.[10] It is for this reason that the passage contains a clear reference to the Conradian pretext.

Of greater significance is Joseph's tendency to treat colours as objects – a tendency akin to the treatment of words as 'things' that Freud finds employed by dream-language.[11] In this manner Dabydeen focuses attention on the text and the way its elements become opacities susceptible of manipulation. These strategies are indices of the activation of that 'pre-text'. Such modes of activation range from the haptic and physical exchange, to the implementation of an educationally-based discourse of interpretation, and its resistance: " 'No it ain't' ". The thematics of the passage, the ubiquitous question of 'colour' can be found in the 'pre-text', what Kristeva terms the "genotext" (the latent productive substrata of the intertextual relation then emerging in the manifest "phenotext"[12]):

> My purpose was to stroll into the shade for a moment; but no sooner within that it seemed to me I had stepped into the gloomy circle of some Inferno. ... Black shapes crouched, lay, sat between the trees leaning against the trunks, clinging to the earth, half coming out, half effaced within the dim light, in all the attitudes of pain, abandonment and despair. ... They were dying slowly – it was very clear. ... Then glancing down, I saw a face near my hand. The black bones reclined with one shoulder against the tree ... The man ... had tied a piece of white worsted round his neck ... Was it a badge? – an ornament – a charm – a propitiatory act? (*Heart of Darkness* 156–7)

In the Conradian "genotext" the thematics of colour, so central to all discourses of racism, is subject to a further strategy of activation. That activation of the hermeneutic mode confronted with a choice between badge/ornament/charm/propitiatory act is posed however in an uncertain, questioning manner. Thus even the "genotext" is, it would appear, always already a "phenotext" processing a prior signifying material, a material so resistant that it generates the modernist text in its archetypical mode of self-reflexive, meta-interpretive query.

The second example, in which the boys decide to document on film their differing opinions about Conrad's *Heart of Darkness*, also includes a clear reference to a prior passage in the novella. Once again, the mode of activation of the "genotext" at the level of the "phenotext" is foregrounded:

> we began ... analysing passages in Conrad's novel. Shaz, the camera focused on him, made strenuous efforts at eloquence. ... Unfortunately it was on one of those frequent occasions when Joseph had pressed the wrong combination of switches so that nothing was recorded on the tape. Shaz broke out in indecent expressions, accusing him of primitive incompetence. "You're just like one of those savages chewing bones on the river bank and scooting off whenever the white man blows the steamer-horn." As if to prove the point about Joseph's incomprehension of white man's technology, he picked up the book, found the passage about the African fireman and read it triumphantly aloud to the camera, telling Joseph to roll the film ... finally exploding in

an outburst about the stupidity of niggers and how unscientific they were. (*Intended* 106)

Analysis, interpretation, reading and performance are clearly all ways of making the text work in a given social situation. Shaz, one of the protagonist's British-Asian friends, claims with reference to technology that the Rastafarian "African" Joseph is not capable of performing such techniques of interpretation. The nostalgic "African" topoi of Rastafarianism are turned against that recuperative discourse so as to reactivate a residual neocolonial attitude of contempt.

Here intertextuality is not merely generative of textual productivity, far more, it becomes the raw material for the creation and perpetuation of social meanings, in this case patently racist, outside the text. In this way Dabydeen underscores the full significance of reading against all claims for the irrelevance of literature in today's world: his protagonist admits "learn[ing] to read the world through novels" (*Intended* 183–4).

Even the topoi of reading are not contemporary impositions, but can be found to arise out of colonial discourse itself. In Conrad's pre-text, the African fireman has also undergone a sort of education in 'close reading':

> I had to look after the savage who was fireman. He was an improved specimen; he could fire up a vertical boiler. ... A few months of training had done for that really fine chap. He squinted at the steam-gauge and at the water-gauge with an evident effort of intrepidity ... He ought to have been clapping his hands and stamping his feet on the bank, instead of which he was hard at work, a thrall to strange witchcraft, full of improving knowledge. He was useful because he had been instructed; and what he knew was this – that should the water in that transparent thing disappear, the evil spirit inside the boiler would get angry through the greatness of his thirst, and take a terrible vengeance. And so he sweated and fired and watched the glass fearfully. (*Heart of Darkness* 187–8)

In the last analysis, Conrad's fireman is also a reader of the world, interpreting it according to a novel technological paradigm (the gauges), but one that is also generated by its own pre-technological phenotext (the world of witchcraft). What these examples show us is that intertextuality is caught up in processes of interpretation that make social life function, that literally make life go on. It is hardly surprising, therefore, that Dabydeen attributes such importance to the reading of non-canonical postcolonial literatures and in the furthering of "an appreciation of these literatures in secondary schools, thereby reaching a large readership of young minds who are the future's writers, scholars, workers and next-door neighbours".[13]

Story and discourse: encore

What Dabydeen's text dramatizes is not merely the ineluctable presence of intertextuality, but, as in its Conradian pre-text, the constant process of production that generates that intertexuality. As intimated above, I use this notion in order to situate the contestation of cultural meanings, across relationships of intertextuality, as a process of textual production.

Shklovsky's genial distinction between events as chronologically ordered and/or causally connected (*story*) and their artistic ordering in the text on the page (*discourse*), has been extraordinarily productive in spawning contemporary theories of narrative levels. The *story-discourse* pair itself appears to have generated related concepts in a manner resembling its own transformative re-organization and evinces similar zones of free play. Shklovsky's *Theory of Prose* can thus be seen to produce a form of highly marked theoretical intertextuality. The basic division between *story* and *discourse* is analogous to Genette's distinction between *histoire* and *discours/récit*. Genette, like Rimmon-Kenan, supplements these two levels with a further level, that of narration as enunciation. Bal also adds a third level of narration as enunciation, although it already encompasses the words on the page, as does Prince's category of 'narrating' or Stanzel's notion of 'mediation' by the teller or reflector. For Genette and Rimon-Kenan, the enunciative act commences beyond the material text, presumably in the moment of its activation and reception by a reader.[14]

An outsider to the field may be forgiven for feeling utterly confused at this plethora of fine distinctions. However, the manifest lack of consensus regarding the precise point at which *story* shades over into *discourse*, and at which *discourse* in turn modulates into enunciation or reading is significant. This apparent theoretical wrestling ring constitutes a zone of free play that is highly productive and fundamentally resistant to containment.

This free play and attendant lack of agreement gives the critic a mandate to extend the process of text production inherent in the theory of narrative levels beyond the domain of the text itself into that of its reception and debates about its meaning. Arguably, none of the locations proposed by these various theoreticians are in themselves exclusively valid, but that together they go to make up a collective theoretical recognition that what is *discourse* in one context can become *story* (the raw material for a *discourse* located at a superior level of narration) in another context. That *discourse* in turn furnishes the building blocks for a further site of narrative performance. This slippage in the location of *story* and *discourse* embodies the very possibilities of unlimited productivity within a social context already anticipated in the theory of narrative levels. As Lubomír Doležel has suggested, it is "worlds with persons or, better, persons within worlds that generate stories".[15] The narratological debate around fictional worlds and the minds that encode them within stories has increasingly recognized the difficulty of defining the limits of the fictional mind, turning away from an earlier emphasis on the privacy, interiority or inwardness of narrated consciousness.[16] So-called "postclassical" narrative poetics has posited instead a "mind beyond the skin". The question of the "aspectual" construction of the interlocking "storyworlds" that make up the universe of a fiction becomes a debate about the various locations, and their interfaces or connecting frontiers that constitute narration as a process of storyworld construction and reception.[17] Lotman has thus stressed that the very process of cultural creation involves a spatial traversal of various sectors of semiotic space: "Because the semiotic space is transected by numerous boundaries, each message that moves across it must be many times translated and transformed, and the process of generating new information thereby snowballs."[18] Narrative generativity is a process of travel from one fictional location or location of fictionalization to another.

As I have argued above, the Kristevan concept of intertextuality and the notion of narrative levels (i.e. *story* and *discourse*) forged by Shklovsky et al. can be productively placed in apposition so as to give an account of social semiosis. Processes of transmission are enacted and rehearsed in the text, based upon the fact that intertextuality is embedded in respective narrative levels. Intertextuality, therefore, is evidence of the generative history of a text. It is no surprise that Kristeva claims that she forged the concept of intertextuality so as to re-historicize structuralism, that is, to lay bare successive stages of traceable textual productivity.[19] Productive textual processes can be identified within the text's own levels of enunciation, with the aid of the theory of narrative levels. The concept of intertextuality and the concept of narrative levels can be mapped onto each other to obtain a model of textual production which is both diachronic and synchronic in nature. As I suggested in an abstract form above, every instance of narrative *discourse* is constructed out of prior *story*-material; every instance of *discourse* itself can in turn provide the raw material for a superior level of textual production.

Dabydeen's insistant emphasis upon the social activity of reading, underlined by the sometimes subtle, sometimes massive foregrounding of intertextuality in *The Intended*, demands that we pay close attention to the interminable processes of textual production.

Let us follow the successive levels of text production in Dabydeen's novel. The Congo plot, or *story* in the Shklovskian sense, makes up the raw 'story'-material that is worked up into Marlow's *discourse*, itself a genuine instance of spoken storytelling 'discourse', and indeed, a mimetic representation of narrative enunciation: " 'I don't want to bother you much with what happened to me personally,' he began, showing in this remark the weakness of many tellers of tales who seem so often unaware of what their audience would like best to hear ..." (*Heart of Darkness* 141). This yarning 'discourse', however, is merely the *story* that is encompassed by and constitutes the basis for the frame-narrator's on-board *discourse*. His *discourse* in turn becomes the *story* for Conrad's 'narrative *discourse*' in *Heart of Darkness* as a global work. In Dabydeen's *The Intended*, to continue moving outwards, Conrad's fictional *discourse* literally becomes the *story* – the colonial storybook – that the young teenage protagonist is reading for his A-Level exams. The Guyanan boy-immigrant's *story* – that tale of his young life so far – is in turn worked up into the fabric of Dabydeen's narrative voice as *discourse*. To continue this chain of productive transformations, the reader transmutes Dabydeen's *discourse* into the *story* being constructed in the active process of reading. This reading-*discourse* itself can become the *story*-basis for distanced, critical reflection upon the text and its social significance: classroom *discourse*, public-sphere critical debate *discourse*. Here we have moved well beyond the customary boundaries of the *story/discourse* distinction, but in the last analysis, the concept itself demands this sort of infinite extension away from the core story.

A rather looser but analogous process of successive levels of production of meaning can be detected in the text's thematization of reading as an educational practice. Reading (in particular the technique of 'close reading' for theme and imagery) is taught in the protagonist's school but is then transported into the extra-curricula context of the bedsit-debates carried on with Shaz and Joseph. Reading is thereby subject to a process of transformative production. The place of narrative transformation semanticizes the already spatialized debates of the three schoolfriends and their collective appropriations of a set 'pre-text'.

This *story* is in turn transformed within the *discourse* of Dabydeen as writer (and, more distantly, as educator and teacher-trainer). Dabydeen's own *discourse* becomes the *story*-material for students (many of them teacher-trainees) and their debate in the context of university seminars. A further concentric circle of 'transformative textual practice' is constituted by their future professional practice as teachers of English in high schools. Once again, these levels of 'textual practice' as 'productive practice' that potentially run against the grain of the reproduction of hegemonic structures, can be extended indefinitely.

Intertextuality offers a model of text construction in which available 'pre-texts' are used as building blocks for a new text. Furthermore, it also offers a model of reality-construction: texts serve as explanatory templates to deal with emergent social situations. The self-reflexivity of the literary text, by which the text forgrounds its pre-texts and thereby reveals its process of production, is mirrored by movement between *story* and *discourse* levels of the text, that is, between narrative material and process of narrative construction. Intertextuality thus necessarily entails a process of reflection upon the ways in which the reader is implied within processes of social meaning-making. In addition, intertextuality reaches back into the past (into the archive of available texts) and into the future (towards textual and non-textual reactivation and dynamization). It is thus a potentially interminable process. Charles Sanders Peirce coined the term "transuasion" to designate the potentially interminable semiotic process inherent in the sign itself:

> Transuasion in its obsistent aspect, or *Mediation*, will be shown to be subject to two degrees of degeneracy. Genuine mediation is the character of a sign. A *Sign* is anything which is related to a second thing, its *Object*, in respect to a Quality, in such a way as to bring a third thing, its *Interpretant*, into relation to the same Object, and that in such a way as to bring a fourth into relation to that object in the same form, *ad infinitum*. If the series is broken off, the sign, in so far, falls short of the perfect significant character.[20]

Peirce explains "transuasion" as the difference within the sign, a sort of resistance or obstinate difficulty which, far from blocking productivity, spurs it on to creative transformations. Resistance guarantees the productivity of textual semiosis and generates the infinite series of interpretations constituting signification.[21] Here one must think of Joseph's "daft questions" which interrupt the smooth reproduction of hegemonic cultural values via docile readings of canonical texts. Instead, such "daft questions" introduce the possibility of new meanings and novel perceptions of the world. In the context of teaching, understood as the logical extension of this textual productivity, there emerges a situation in which "presentation [is no longer] a (mere) supplement to inquiry" and in which "every pedagogical exposition, just like every reading, adds something to what it transmits."[22]

No less important to the obstinate materiality within the sign than the generativity Peirce focuses upon is the spatial character of this process. Peirce speaks of a "series", but in actual fact the structure he sketches is a triangular one, as Antoine Compagnon's explanatory diagrams demonstrate.[23] It is the interstitial, intersubjective nature of the sign, the space of free play which is always present in its production, which keeps it dynamic. It is in the very nature of language to generate spaces in which language is re-generated, thus creating new spaces of narrativity. The spaces of the sign itself relate it intimately to deiXis, with its reciprocal relations of spatio-lingual reciprocity.

Contamination, association

Space is at the heart of Conrad's, Gide's and Dabydeen's narrative undertakings. Marlow's narration takes place on the deck of a yacht anchored in the Thames estuary, symbolically poised between the darkness hanging over London and the putative darkness of the African continent. The sea forms a continuum, not merely in a symbolic sense but, as Conrad's frame narrator unwittingly points out in some detail, in a very material way – the sea bears the global continuum of imperial exploration, conquest and trade (*Heart of Darkness* 109). Likewise, Gide's narrator and circle of listeners look out across a plain from the vantage point of a village on an outcrop which is compared to an Umbrian hill-town (*L'Immoraliste* 370; *The Immoralist* 5–6). This vantage point anticipates the similarly positioned colonial outposts that Gide would visit in his mid-1920s sojourn in colonial French Equatorial Africa.[24] Though never addressed explicitly, his text thereby contains indices of the colonial empire which provides the enabling framework for Michel's release of his anti-civilizational Nietzschean desires. Conrad's Marlow says as much in metaphorical terms: "how can you imagine what particular region of the first ages a man's untrammelled feet may take him into by the way of solitude – utter solitude without a policeman" (*Heart of Darkness* 206). Finally, the reading-groups of Dabydeen's immigrant youths take place in a South London bedsit, and are thus distanced from the closed ideological circuits of educational reproduction located in the classroom. Space in these narratives is never mere setting in these narratives. Rather, it pervades the very workings of the operations of appropriative intertextuality achieved through the transformative operations of shifting narrative levels. Traditionally, however, narrative theory has been characterized by a focus upon temporality. Space has been regarded as a peripheral and contingent aspect of narrativity:

By a dissymetry whose underlying reasons escape us but which is inscribed in the very structures of the language ... I can very well tell a story without specifying the place where it happens ... nevertheless it is almost impossible for me not to locate the story in time with respect to my narrating act.

[Par une dissymétrie dont les raisons profondes nous échappent, mais qui est inscrite dans les structures mêmes de la language ... je peux fort bien raconter une histoire sans raconter le lieu où elle se passe ... tandis qu'il m'est preseque impossible de ne pas la situer dans le temps par rapport à mon acte narratif.][25]

However, the manner in which Conrad's, Gide's and Dabydeen's narratives generate new narratives, and the way they indicate the spaces in which new narratives can be generated, suggests that space is in fact paramount in literary creation. Far from being contingent and dispensable, space proves to be the very condition of possibility of the act of narration.

In her 1987 Chernobyl novel, *Störfall*, which closes with its narrator reading the opening passages of *Heart of Darkness*, the East German author Christa Wolf is equally concerned with questions of space and the manner in which they impact upon narration. Wolf's narrator, not dissimilarly, thinks of the hypothetical possibility that a nuclear melt-down might bore its way through the centre of the earth "until it reemerges in the antipodes. Transformed, perhaps, but still glowing" (*Accident* 6–7) ["bis er, verwandelt, sicherlich, aber immer noch strahlend, bei den Antipoden wieder herauskäme" (*Störfall* 12)]. The narrator free-associates and remembers childhood message-in-a-bottle games, which involved placing a bottle in the earth, containing a message that, propelled by a solution of salt acid, was to arrive intact to be read by the inhabitants of the Antipodes. The narrator reflects that it did not occur to the children to issue an apology for their intrusion at the other end of the world (*Accident* 6–7/ *Störfall* 12). This short episode points to many of the preoccupations of the novel.

First, the sequence alludes to narration as a medium that bridges gaps, speaks across distance without the certainty of being received. This distance, though at first glance looking like a hindrance to communication, may also be the very condition of its possibility. The theory of spatial narration which we are elaborating here suggests that distance may be the very dimension which is produced by narrative and which in turn generates new narratives.

Secondly, the episode alludes to the global processes by which the West intervenes in the existence of peoples across the globe, disrupting economies, displacing populations, dislocating cultures. It rarely occurs to the West to apologize for centuries of destruction, and when such an apology is demanded, it may be withheld tenaciously (the indigenous people of Australia had to wait until until 2008 for an apology for the havoc wreaked since 1788). Finally, the episode alludes to the ethical problems of communication as a form of 'contamination', just as Conrad's frame narrator is overtaken by a "faint uneasiness inspired by this narrative that seemed to shape itself without human lips in the heavy night-air of the river" (*Heart of Darkness* 173), or Gide's three listeners who are overcome by

a strange feeling of uneasiness. We felt, alas, that by telling his story, Michel had made his actions more legitimate. Our not having known at what point to condemn it in the course of his long explanation seemed almost to make us his accomplices. (*The Immoralist* 211)

[un étrange malaise. Il nous semblait hélas! qu'à nous la raconter, Michel avait rendu son action plus légitime. De ne savoir où la désapprouver, dans la lente explication qu'il nous en donna, nous en faisait presque complices. (*L'Immoraliste* 470)]

For both Marlow and Michel, storytelling may be a way of sharing the blame, a means of communicating it and by the same token, of distributing it to others so as to lessen its burden upon the narrator.

Narrative, like the unsolicited message in a bottle, can constitute an unwelcome intrusion into the life of its recipients, disturbing their comfortable relationships to themselves.[26] Wolf's narration, written under the inauspicious sign of global catastrophe, is an avatar of Conrad's narrative of the proto-globalizing process of Western colonization in the late nineteenth century. Conversely, however, the irruption of a foreign narrative voice within one's own narrative sphere may at the same time constitute a salutary re-vamping of a narrative which has become dangerously monological. Contamination, in such a textual structure, thus becomes a two-way process.

Contamination operates as a diverse thematic and structural principle, from the mobility of the radioactive cloud drifting across Europe, to the manner in which the distant *story* of Conrad's Marlow becomes part of the *discourse* of Wolf's post-Chernobyl narrator:

> I suppose it was thanks to my tiredness that I took from the shelf the thin book by an author who had been urgently recommended to me for a long time but whom I still had not read because of my aversion to seafaring stories: Joseph Conrad. *Heart of Darkness.* ... I tried to picture the Thames estuary as I had once seen it, but the inner image was immediately pushed aside by a description of the evening light across the water which left me wide awake. "The day was ending in a serenity of still and exquisite brilliance" – this is how it starts. I have read it twice. But then the narrator, whose name is Marlow, suddenly spoke the following sentence right to my face: "And this also has been one of the dark places of the earth." (*Accident* 106–7)

> [Meiner Müdigkeit ist es wohl zu verdanken gewesen, dass ich das schmale Buch eines Autors aus dem Regal zog, der mir seit langem dringend empfohlen war, den ich aber, wegen meiner Abneigung für Seegeschichten, immer noch nicht gelesen hatte: Joseph Conrad. *Das Herz der Finsternis.* ... Ich habe versucht, mir die Themsemündung vor Augen zu führen, wie ich sie einmal gesehen hatte, aber das innere Bild ist sofort verdrängt worden durch einen Beschreibung des Abendlichts über dem Wasser, die mich hellwach gemacht hat. "Der Tag ging im stillen Glanz zu Ende", so fängt sie an. Ich habe sie zweimal gelesen. Dann aber hat der Erzähler, der Marlow heißt, plötzlich mir ins Gesicht hinein den Satz gesagt: "Und auch dies ist einmal einer der dunklen Orten der Erde gewesen." (*Störfall* 116)]

The contamination of the narrative levels enacted thus at the end of the text, as the narrator picks up *Heart of Darkness* before going to sleep, is an isomorphism of the duality which has structured the text from the first page on. Such contamination is always presented spatially.

Wolf's text is sewn together out of two spatially distinct but interwoven fabrics. On the one hand, there is a monologue addressed to the anaesthetized brother undergoing brain surgery and on the other, a meditation upon Chernobyl, thousands of kilometres away but suddenly brought close by the drifting radioactive cloud. From the very beginning the constant associative oscillation between the two narrative strands, both of which dramatize distance covered between self and interlocutor, and between here and there, creates a narrative spacing that is relentlessly indexed via prominent typological devices. The respective alternating segments from the two narrative strands are separated by jagged breaks in the text, with randomly spaced indentations reinforcing the impression of a fragmented text. At each juncture, a hyphen signals the cessation of one strand of deixis and the commencement of the other. The hyphen figures the fraying of the edges of the respective textual fabrics – a fraying which creates an interstitial, contaminatory space both separating and linking them.

In this way, the narrative is placed unambiguously within the tradition of the 'constellar' textuality inaugurated by Mallarmé, in which "NOTHING ... WILL HAVE TAKEN PLACE ... BUT THE PLACE" ["RIEN N'AURA EU LIEU ... QUE LE LIEU"].[27] Indeed, very little takes place in Wolf's novel – except the linking of places (the narrator's old farmhouse and the hospital where the brother is undergoing the operation; the rural Altmark region north of Berlin and Ukrainian Chernobyl) via an interior monologue. Wolf's text questions the very notion of linear plot, replacing it by the metonymic linking of contiguous blocks of internal discourse. Association, the ruling principle of metonymy, is the keyword Wolf mentioned when asked by an interviewer about the text:

There's a novel by Aragon that inspired me at the time with its achronological, associative structure. I used that method for the first time in *Christa T.* and realized that in fact I'd found my style. ... I get closer to it when I work associatively, try to become aware of analogies rather than proceeding chronologically, so as to pose myself questions. ... In *Accident* I was was very conscious of that. My aim was to write in the same way that the brain functions. ... I wanted to attempt, via the parallels between my brother's brain operation and the nuclear reactor accident in Chernobyl, to create prose structures as close as possible to the work of the brain. That was the real problem that interested me in the book.

[Es gibt einen Roman von Aragon, der mich damals durch seine nicht chronologische, assoziative Struktur angeregt hat. Bei *Christa T.* habe ich die zum ersten Mal angewendet und gemerkt, dass ich eigentlich zu mir selber finde. ... Ich komme dem näher, wenn ich

assoziiere, versuche, mir Analogien bewusst zu machen, nicht chro-
nologisch vorzugehen und mir bestimmte Fragen zu stellen ... Bei
Störfall war mir das ganz bewusst. Mein Ideal war, so zu schreiben,
wie das Gehirn funktioniert. ... Durch die Parallelität zwischen der
Gehirnoperation meines Bruders und des Kernkraftwerkunglücks in
Tschernobyl wollte ich versuchen, Prosastrukturen zu schaffen, die
der Arbeit des Gehirns am nächsten kommen. Das war das eigentli-
che Problem, das mich an dem Buch interessiert hat.][28]

Association figures in Wolf's description of her avant-garde writing
techniques as a method of connecting separate text sections, embodied
in the dashes which mediate the transitions between the fragmentary
segments of the parallel plot structures.

More broadly, the associative link is the central factor at work in the
creation of association, that is, society. Association is thus not just a
narrative technique for Wolf but, by the same token, and no less significantly, a social, ethical, and finally spatial principle. Wolf's narrative foregrounds the intersubjective character of storytelling. The very
nature of such spatial-deictic undertakings is explored within dialogue,
as indicated by the narrator's telephone engagement (the medium is
not without significance) with her daughter. Meditating upon the self-
destructive impulse in modern human history, the narrator focuses
upon what she calls a sort of blind spot: "Whether in her opinion, one
should nonetheless endeavor to penetrate to our blind spot. In your pro-
fession? she said. Absolutely. But one couldn't do it alone" (*Accident* 93)
["Ob man trotzdem versuchen solle, in unseren blinden Fleck einzudrin-
gen, ihrer Meinung nach. – In deinem Beruf? hat sie gesagt. Unbedingt.
Aber alleine schafft man das nicht" (*Störfall* 103)]. The critical writer,
while attempting to penetrate the hidden, interior truth of humanity,
must remain attuned to the exterior world of readership. The tension
between the voyage inwards (hermeneutic interrogation) and the voyage out (narrative sharing) is also central to Conrad's meta-narrative
musings. Conrad's text eschews an hermeneutical mode placing "the
whole meaning of which ... within the shell of a cracked nut ... inside
like a kernel" and opts rather to invest meaning "not inside like a kernel
but outside, enveloping the tale" (*Heart of Darkness* 138). Wolf's novel
similarly makes narrative an exterior, interstitial matter via the constant oscillation between two associated narrative strands. Associative
narrative is a form of working with language in such a way as to offer an
alternative to the highly developed human capacity for self-destructive
'diss-association'.

The blind spot

Association is the antidote to what Wolf refers to as humanity's illogical death-drive, its "blind spot" ["blinde[r] Fleck"]. The narrator uses this term for the first time in conjunction with the first implicit intertextual allusion to Conrad:

> The blind spot.
>> The heart of darkness.
>> That sounds good, but something in me remains dissatisfied. Where, I thought, would the blind spot have to be situated within me, in my brain – should it be possible to localize it, after all. ...
>> Language. Speaking. It is worth coming back to that. (*Accident* 89–90)

> [Der blinde Fleck.
>> Das Herz der Finsternis.
>> Das hört sich gut an, aber etwas in mir bleibt unzufrieden. Wo, habe ich mir gedacht, müsste der blinde Fleck bei mir, in meinem Gehirn liegen – falls er doch loalisierbar sein sollte. ...
>> Die Sprache. Das Sprechen. Es lohnt sich, darauf zurückzukommen. (*Störfall* 98–9)]

Wolf uses spatial apposition, in other words, the principle of contiguous association, to "localize" the blind spot. The "blind spot" is lined up next to an intertexual marker (the title of Conrad's novella), and triangulated against a third term which interprets the connection between the other two: language, speech, storytelling. The blind spot is thus localized in language itself, epitomized by a linguistic turn of phrase, which in turn is then embedded in language. Wolf employs the processual substantivized verb ("Speaking", "Das Sprechen") to stress that the blind spot lies in language as a practice; the antidote to that practice is equally to be found in language as an associative, triangulating activity. Narrative returns, in an eminently reflexive movement ("It is worth coming back to that", "Es lohnt sich, darauf zurückzukommen"), to its own linguistic fabric so as to get a new purchase upon its own blind spot. Storytelling is precisely that associative activity which allows one, thanks to others' dialogical participation, to gain an alternative perspective on the blind spot of civilization.

Wolf makes it clear that the blind spot is meant not merely as a common-sense humanistic category of analysis, but as one that shares the same fabric as her text itself. Language is that faculty which first demarcated humanity from an earlier community with the natural world. Language constitutes the inaugural medium of 'diss-association'. Language, as that which makes us 'civilized', thus inaugurated a primary "dissociation" or "Abgrenzung" against humans' natural neighbours:

> with the help of language, of all things, did the humans of one horde seem to have dissociated themselves from those of another horde: the one who spoke differently was the other, was not human, was not subject to the murder taboo. ... Language which creates identity but which, at the same time, makes a decisive contribution to the dismantling of the inhibition about killing that member of the species who speaks differently. (*Accident* 82)

> [ausgerechnet mit Hilfe der Sprache scheinen sich dann die Menschen den einen Horde von der anderen Horde abgegrenzt zu haben: Der Anderssprechende war der Fremde, war kein Mensch, unterlag nicht den Tötungstabu. ... Sprache, die Identität schafft, zugleich aber entscheidend dazu beiträgt, die Tötungshemmung gegenüber der anderssprechenden Artgenossen abzubauen. (*Störfall* 90–1)]

In terms which directly echo Conrad, Wolf describes the manner in which language, from the moment of its emergence, has been a highly ambivalent faculty. Language encodes communication but by the same token elides other modes of perception which might have reinforced human community in ways now lost to sight:

> "the brilliance of our most recent evolutionary accretion, the verbal abilities of the left hemisphere, obscures our awareness of the functions of the intuitive right hemisphere, which in our ancestors must have been the principal means of perceiving the world." The Janus face of language ... (*Accident* 82)

> [Die "Brillianz unserer jüngsten evolutionären Errungenschaft, die verbale Fähigkeiten der linken Hemisphäre", verdunkeln also, "wie Sonnenlicht der Sternhimmel, unser Bewusstsein für die Funktion der intuitiven rechten Hemisphäre, die bei unseren Vorfahren das Hauptwerkzeug zur Wahrnehmung der Welt gewesen sein muß." Das Doppelgesicht der Sprache ... (*Störfall* 91)]

Wolf deliberately selects a metaphorics of light and darkness which echoes that of Conrad. Marlow describes Kurtz's speech as "the gift of

expression, the illuminating, the most exalted and the most contempt-
ible, the pulsating stream of light, or the deceitful flow from the heart of
an impenetrable darkness". "No eloquence could have been so withering
to one's belief in mankind as his final burst of sincerity", adds Marlow
(*Heart of Darkness* 203–4, 325). However, whereas Conrad sees language
as somehow external to an evil that it may or may not participate in,
Wolf insists that language itself is implicated in the very denial of co-
humanity which she takes to be the ground of human self-destruction.

To that extent, the solution to that abjured co-humanity lies also
in language itself, and not outside of it. The blind spot must be dealt
with in and by language. If language itself evinces a "Janus face", a
"Doppelgesicht", then language itself must be *doubled* in order to cover
this blind spot. This makes dialogue necessary, which in turn deter-
mines the use to which Wolf puts Conrad's text in the final pages of her
nuclear novella. The conversion of *story* into *discourse* which is enacted
at the end of *Störfall* takes on an ethical dimension. *Story* is not merely
the raw material out of which *discourse* is produced. More fundamentally, *story* is also the indispensable alterity out of which the narrating
subject's full ethical being emerges. The task of the writer necessarily
is, therefore, a metalinguistic task, one that must be carried out with
the help of metapoetic means. It is an exercise in 'self-observation',
'Selbstbeobachtung', to appropriate the idiom of Luhmann, self-distrust
in the narrator's own parlance: "What is nagging me, then? Suspicion,
self-distrust" (*Accident* 90) ["Was ficht mich also an? Mißtrauen ist es,
Selbstverdacht" (*Störfall* 99)]. The writer's mission is to explore the blind
spot, the ambivalence lodged at the very heart of language.

But how best to deal with the blind spot? "Speedy consolation. Our
other eye is said to compensate for this minimal gap in our perception. But who or what can help us fill this gap in our perception which
we inevitably inflict upon ourselves through our special way of holding our own in this world?" (*Accident* 88–9) ["Schneller Trost: Unserer
anderes Auge gleicht diese minimale Lücke in unserer Wahrnehmung
aus. Wer aber, oder was, kann uns helfen, jene Wahrnehmungslücke zu
schließen, welche wir uns durch unsere spezielle Art und Weise, uns
in dieser Welt zu behaupten, unvermeidlich selbst zuziehen müssen?"
(*Störfall* 98)]. The narrator's answer: "Brotherliness – that word was due"
(*Accident* 89) ["Brüderlichkeit – ein Wort, das fällig wäre" (*Störfall* 98)].

This term, "brotherliness", should be understood not as a piece of
old-fashioned sentimentalism but as having clear narrative and spatial
resonances within Wolf's text. It is the dialogue with the brother, fragmented, cast across a great expanse to a figure deep in an anaesthetized

sleep, that provides the model for narrativity. Wolf thereby casts narrativity as a means of empathic imagination that searches out the place of the other, trying to perceive the world from elsewhere than one's own egotistical position. "Brotherliness" refers to a narrative undertaking that seeks to ward off the perils of what Robert Young terms "egology".[29]

> I wished that I could switch off my faculty of imagination. Those who conjure up the dangers above us and themselves must certainly be capable of that, I thought. Or don't they need to switch off anything; do they have a blind spot in their brains in the place of those premonitions which haunt the rest of us? (*Accident* 59)

> [Ich habe mir gewünscht, mein Vorstellungsvermögen abstellen zu können. Diejenigen, die die Gefahren über uns und sich heraufbeschwören, habe ich gedacht, müssen diese Fähigkeit doch besitzen. Oder brauchen sie nichts abzustellen; haben sie, anstelle jener Ahnungen, die uns andere verfolgen, in ihrem Gehirn einen blinden Fleck? (*Störfall* 67)]

If Wolf's task is to probe the blind spot of culture (the heart of darkness which founds language) so as to defend the possibility of a "faculty of imagination" ["Vorstellungsvermögen"], then her metalinguistic undertaking constitutes an implicit rejoinder to Marlow's central query and pessimistic answer: "Do you see him? Do you see the story? Do you see anything? ... We live, as we dream – alone. ..." (*Heart of Darkness* 172). Conrad, despite the tone of doubt, elsewhere insists that the writer's task is "by the power of the written word ... to make you *see*".[30] Wolf concurs with such an undertaking.

Conrad again

In Wolf's narrative, association functions both as a principle of structural fragmentation and, conversely, as a figure of connection of differences across space. Narrative is the linguistic practice which configures such association as a processual activity. Association therefore intersects with the ethical task of narration, that is, to complement an inevitably monofocal perspective upon the world with the multiple perspectives of others' narrations. This multifocal mode of narration is ostended throughout the text as the narrator springs between her two narrative streams of consciousness. But this split narrative is still that of one narrator, albeit a fragemented one. Where, in *Störfall*, is the voice or the eye of the other to be found? Conrad's Marlow, as another narrator, is just such an instance within Wolf's text.

As we near the end of the text, the two principal narrative strands appear to converge with one another. The text's prominently-foregrounded parallel diglossia cedes to a more discrete form of fluid dialogical monologue. This modulation prepares the reader for the embedded diglossia inaugurated in the novel's last two pages by the irruption of Conrad's text. At this point, the zig-zag *discourse*, which none the less remains faithful to the sequential *story* of the progress of that fateful day in April 1986, finally gives way to an intertextual *story-discourse* configuration of the sort familiar to us from Dabydeen's *Intended.*

It is significant that the engagement with Conrad comes only in the final pages of *Störfall*. Exhausted by a day spent mentally following the progress of the brother's operation and anticipating the fallout from the east, the narrator retires to bed with a novel she has never opened before, *Herz der Finsternis* [*Heart of Darkness*]. The openly enacted process of narration is constantly foregrounded as *discourse* by virtue of the fragmentation of the text and is only secondarily identifiable as a *story* by virtue of its loose chronological arrangement. It *terminates* at the *beginning* of a subordinated and embedded text (Conrad's novella in the hands of the narrator) where *story* is constantly marked as *discourse* via its integration to a frame narrative. Where Wolf's 1986 narrator leaves off, Conrad's 1890s narrator is just commencing. This reverses the putatively historical order of the respective narratives. In this way, Wolf can point forward at the very moment of 'going back'. She thus instatiates, temporally, the earlier dictum, "It is worth coming back to that" (*Accident* 89–90) ["Es lohnt sich, darauf zurückzukommen" (*Störfall* 98–9)]. At the same time, however, as the Wolfian narrator's gaze focuses upon the nocturnal private space, Marlow's narrative moves out into the colonial world. Here is *discourse*-construction par excellence as a transhistorical and thus eminently spatial process between narrators whose temporal and geographical positions are rendered mutually interchangeable by the text's own operations.

Wolf's narrator-as-reader begins by appropriating a phrase from Conrad's frame narrative:

I tried to picture the Thames estuary, as I had once seen it, but the inner image was immediately pushed aside by a description of the evening light across the water which left me wide awake.

"The day was ending in a serenity of still and exquisite brilliance".
(*Accident* 106)

[Ich habe versucht, mir die Themsemündung vor Augen zu führen,
wie ich sie einmal gesehen hatte, aber das innere Bild ist sofort ver-
drängt worden durch einen Beschreibung des Abendlichts über dem
Wasser, die mich hellwach gemacht hat. "Der Tag ging im stillen
Glanz zu Ende." (*Störfall* 116)]

Conrad's sentence dispels the reader-narrator's initial indifference. The
citation echoes a phrase from earlier in Wolf's text, "The day remained
flawless up to its final minute" (*Accident* 74) ["Der Tag ist makellos geblie-
ben bis zu seiner letzten Minute" (*Störfall* 82)]. This is not a mimetic
echo, but rather one which is laden with irony. For the clarity of the
day is spoilt by the invisible radioactive cloud – a cloud, paradoxically,
that does *not* obscure the sun as Conrad's metropolitan gloom does.
This paradox picks up Marlow's own ironical treatment of the colonial
rhetoric of light and darkness and transmutes it into a form appropriate
to the nuclear age.

Marlow's persistent efforts to make his hearers "see" ("Do you see
him? Do you see the story? Do you see anything?" – *Heart of Darkness*
172), efforts which by his own account meet with only partial success,
are matched by the eagerness of Wolf's narrator to imagine the scene.
The Wolfian narrator is determined to mobilize the sort of "faculty of
imagination" ["Vorstellungsvermögen"] endowed with such ethical significance by the text, thereby generating an illusion of intimate personal contact between the narrators:

But then the narrator, whose name is Marlow, suddenly spoke the
following sentence right to my face: "And this also has been one of
the dark places of the earth." Finally, after all this time, I once again
felt that pump against my heart which I feel when a writer speaks to
me from the depths of self-experience. (*Accident* 107)

[Dann aber hat der Erzähler, der Marlow heißt, plötzlich mir ins
Gesicht hinein den Satz gesagt: "Und auch dies ist einmal einer
der dunklen Orten der Erde gewesen." Da habe ich endlich einmal
wieder jenen Schlag gegen mein Herz gespürt, den ich nur dann
spüre, wenn ein Schreiber aus der tiefe seiner Selbsterfahrung zu mir
spricht. (*Störfall* 116)]

Wolf's text is concerned not merely to dramatize the experience of reading as a process of immediate communication. This would be tantamount to confining the text to its narrowly descriptive and inevitably illusory dimension. More importantly, in the final pages of Wolf's novella, the author is at pains to stage the encounter of two narrators, just as Conrad's text stages the encounter of several levels of narration. This is a performative rather than a mimetic undertaking, one which builds upon the text's own care to signal that it is a *narration*, not merely a *narrative*.

The text deliberately points out the mediated spatial dimension of this encounter of two narrative processes by the careful choice of a preposition. The dative or indirect *"zu mir* spricht" ("speaks *to me*") creates an audible, tangible interval across which communication occurs. It evokes a much greater gap, for instance, than that of the literal English equivalent, 'speak to'. What comes to the fore in Wolf's "zu mir spricht" is radically opposed to the immediate communication of *'mit'* (i.e., 'with me'). The narator's "zu mir" has something of the echoey quality of 'call to'. The choice of communicative verb, relative preposition and case-determined pronoun in turn highlights the spatial import of Marlow's discourse. The thrust of Marlow's narration is to show up the contaminatory identification of barbarism with supposedly opposed corners of the earth's surface (civilized London and darkest Africa): "And this also has been one of the dark places of the earth" (*Heart of Darkness* 138, cited in *Accident* 107, *Störfall* 116).

Wolf's narrator immediately takes up the challenge of such contaminatory identification. She reiterates, this time without quotation marks, Marlow's claim: "And this also has been one of the dark places of the earth. This also. And also this" (*Accident* 107) ["Und auch dies ist einmal einer der dunklen Orten der Erde gewesen. Dies auch. Und auch dies" (*Störfall* 117)]. The narrator's response is an unmarked re-citation that immediately triggers secondary and tertiary replications of Marlow's discourse. It is as if the space of double narration engenders multiple echoes: those of the reader become writer, and the writer become narrator to subsequent readers – ourselves. The contamination at work is one which eschews geographical distance, thereby blurring the Manichean polarities of civilization and barbarism upon which colonization founded its self-legitimation. At the same time, it is a narrative contamination in which the standpoints of self-and-other are simultaneously condensed (via the erasure of explicit citation) and multiplied (via the dramatization of a reading process that is also taking place 'outside' the text at the moment the narrator reads Conrad 'inside' the text).

The narrator terminates with a laudatory tribute to Marlow's moral courage:

> He set out right into the heart of the blind spot of that culture to which he also belonged, and not in thought alone. Fearlessly into the heart of darkness. And he saw the light which must have led him too, on his way like a "running blaze on a plain, like a flash of lightning in the clouds." (*Accident* 108)

> [Er [Marlow] hat sich, nicht nur in Gedanken, mitten hineingegeben in den blinden Fleck jener Kultur, der er auch angehörte. Unerschrocken ins Herz der Finsternis. Und das Licht, das ja auch ihn begleitet haben muß, hat er gesehen als einen "wandernden Sonnenfleck auf einer Ebene, wie ein Blitz in Wolken". (*Störfall* 118)]

The narrator cites further but, once again, without inverted commas:

> We live in the flicker – may it last as long as the old earth keeps rolling.
> So does this person speak to me. So shy, I could hardly expect to find words such as "hate" and "love" in his works. "Greed" I found, often. Greed, greed, greed ... (*Accident* 108)

> [Wir leben in diesem Aufblitzen – mag es wahren, solange die Erde rollt.
> So redet dieser Mensch zu mir. Wörter wie "Haß" oder "Liebe" würde ich bei ihm kaum finden, so scheu. "Gier" gabe es, häufig. Gier, Gier, Gier – (*Störfall* 118)]

At this point Marlow's text appears to have become her own. Conrad's words (more precisely, Marlow's celebration of the light of civilization – *Heart of Darkness* 139) are taken up as her own commentary. Conrad's *story* has been taken up by Wolf's *discourse*, reorganized by her narrative strategy.

Paradoxically, Conrad's irony appears to have been lost in translation. Some critics wonder whether Wolf has herself not fallen victim to a blind spot of her own by reading Conrad too naively[31] – the light of civilization in Conrad is not without ironic undertones. Marlow's "running blaze on a plain ... a flash of lightning in the clouds" is a mere "flicker", nothing like the idealized "jewels flashing in the night of time" eulogized by the frame narrator. It resembles much more the murderous postscript of Kurtz's espousal of enlightened colonialism, "luminous and terrifying, like a flash of lightning in a serene sky: 'Exterminate all the brutes'" (*Heart of Darkness* 139, 137, 208). Wolf, of course, is not identical with her narrator, but this, perhaps, is not the point. In the dialogue with Conrad that spatializes to an extra degree the narrative process, the overlapping of both narrators' putative blind spots can perhaps function in a manner which is mutually critical.

In the genealogy which connects Conrad's *Heart of Darkness*, Gide's *L'Immoraliste*, Wolf's *Störfall* and Dabydeen's *The Intended*, a series arrested here arbitrarily but susceptible of perhaps infinite extension, we are confronted with a new form of narrative topology. Kristeva terms it "the communicative topology of the subject–addressee connection" ["la topologie communicative ... de la connexion sujet-destinataire"].[32] But this topology is characterized by its tendency to spill over the borders of the dual narrator-narratee relationship. What Kristeva calls "the dialogical space of texts" ["l'espace dialogique des texts"][33] is best described using the rhetorical trope of anadiplosis. This trope refers to the practice of using the last word of one line or clause to begin the next, just as the *story* of one narrative is taken up in the *discourse* of another, only to become *story* in its turn. Anadiplosis as a generative principle creates a textual space full of echoes, somewhat akin to the resonating valley full of bird-calls and childrens' cries Barthes imagines as the place of (inter)textuality.[34] It is a figure that combines continuity and discontinity, a linearity which also encompasses lateral shifts as the very condition of forward movement. It tracks space within the vector of reading itself, making the text an in-between realm of a dialogue of differences. The text stakes out the social ground of its own production, a ground that again and again is marked according to the anchoring gestures of deiXis. But this anchoring is also an avowal of the debt that the text incurs with regard to its readers, both within and without its own boundaries, within its own present and into its own future.

Part II
The Fictions of Space

5
Spatial Amnesia

In Ondaatje's *The English Patient* (1991), the eponymous hero, Almásy, carries with him a copy of Herodotus' *The Histories*. Herodotus is, paradoxically, of particular importance to Almásy because his text appears to be quite unhistorical. In this "guidebook, ancient and modern, of supposed lies", Almásy is constantly discovering "the truth to what had seemed a lie".[1] This apocryphal document appears to contradict one of the underyling principles of modern historiography by proffering lies which transpire to be true, and giving the lie to the ostensible truthfulness of history. Herodotus also perturbs notions of history because he contradicts the other founding principle of modern historiography, namely, that of chronological linearity. Almásy says:

> "I see [Herodotus] more as one of those spare men of the desert who travel from oasis to oasis to oasis, trading legends as if it is the exchange of seeds, consuming everything without suspicion, piecing together a mirage. 'This history of mine,' Herodotus says, 'has from the beginning sought out the supplementary to the main argument.' What you find in him are cul-de-sacs within the sweep of history – how people betray each other for the sake of nations, how people fall in love." (*English Patient* 118–19)

By virtue of "supplementarity", Herodotus' history is more than merely archaic, but also anarchic. Not only does it integrate myth and hearsay to notions of historical fact – it also disrupts the linear "sweep" of history by the nomadism of its author, the "supplementarity" of its plotting, and the dead-end "cul-de-sacs" of its anecdotes. Ondaatje employs Herodotus to dislocate the linear syntax of modern historiography, a technique of which his own narrative makes liberal use. In the interstices of that temporal linearity, he allows spaces to appear, those of the desert, the oasis, the trading place. Ondaatje's text presciently indexes the recent return of space in the human sciences, a return so momentous as to dislodge, or so it has seemed to some at times, the hold of the established paradigms of historigraphical hermeneutics.

The present chapter enacts, on a theoretical level, something similar. It takes up a position analogous to that of Ondaatje and his imagined Herodotus and enquires why space remained for so long beyond the horizon of literary studies, "reified out of time and locality, those factors of human experience of place in which it had been embedded"[2] – the primordial guiding principal of literary criticism for a number of centuries having been time. The reason, it suggests, may be that time is the very medium of modernity, that characteristic by which Europe (more recently including North America) has legitimized its overwhelming subordination of the entire globe for almost five hundred years. In this chapter, I suggest that there has been a long-standing elision of space in narratives of conquest. The purpose of this elision is to obscure the territorial dimensions of Europe's global expansion. Conversely, such an elision of space conceals the profound debt to space underlying territorial mastery. Much postcolonial writing, I argue, exemplifying this with reference (again) to Ondaatje's *English Patient* and to Desai's *The Inheritance of Loss* (2006), seeks to reverse this trend, increasingly laying bare the forgotten substrata of space upon which social existence is built. The chapter concludes by sketching the theoretical notions of deictic activity which will be employed in the rest of Part II as it works from speaker-centred deixis, via self-reflexive deixis, towards spatio-centric deiXis.

The elision of space

From the 1970s in France and somewhat later in the English-speaking academic context there occurred what has come to be called, following the paradigm shift known as 'the linguistic turn', a specific 'spatial turn'. In France this shift in focus was heralded by Lefebvre's *La Production de l'espace* (1974) [Engl. trans. *The Production of Space*, (1991)].[3] In the Anglophone context one might take as significant indices of the emergence of spatial analysis in the humanities Neil Smith's *Uneven Development: Nature, Capital and the Production of Space* (1984) or Edward Soja's *Postmodern Geographies* (1989).[4]

These early works were highly polemical, vociferously rehabilitating spatial studies from a perceived marginality in relation to the historical disciplines. Foucault's dismissive rejection of the previous

of empire, but also in the histories and stories of the literary traditions that were crafted alongside the development of empire.

In the remaining pages of this chapter, I provide a conceptual archaeology of the literary modes that foreground the temporal at the expense of spatiality. This literary form roughly overlaps with realism, and gives pride of place to egocentric deixis. Sabine Bucholz and Manfred Jahn have suggested that there are two main reasons for the elision of the spatial aspect of narrative by aesthetic reflection till very recently. They plausibly posit the weight of influence carried by Lessing's late-eighteenth-century aesthetic theorizations. More interestingly, however, they claim an inherent primacy of the temporal within narrative itself: "It is space, not temporal sequence, which can be radically mini-mised without any obvious loss in 'narrativehood' ... Similarly, a stage can be left wholly bare in a theatre without detracting from the audience's understanding of the enacted events."[14] This echoes Genette's conviction that "the temporal determinations of the narrating instance are manifestly more important than its spatial determinations. ... the narrating place is ... almost never relevant" ["les déterminations temporelles de l'instance narrative sont manifestement plus importantes que ses déterminations spatiales. ... le lieu narratif ... n'est pour ainsi dire jamais pertinent"].[15] Space, then, is apparently quite dispensable within narrative whereas time is not. This assumption is widespread. It has led other narratologists, for instance, to stigmatize texts not susceptible of "story-paraphrase" and therefore "organized according to principles other than chronological" (for example, "some *spatial* ... principle which is relatively or ideally independent of temporality") as "non-narrative" texts.[16]

Yet the very example Bucholz and Jahn select to substantiate what may seem to be a common-sensical claim is misleading. It bears closer attention. They posit that a bare stage embodies the absence of space, revealing temporality as the fundamental dimension of narrative art. Space is equated with the things that fill it it (the props, the set, the actors themselves) rather than recognizing it as a configuration of constitutive relationships which permit the theatrical narrative to *take place*. As avant-garde theatre clearly demonstrates, even a bare stage remains a stage-space. The stage is essentially constituted out of the social interaction of audience and actor. That interaction generates a dividing line which marks out the realm of theatrical fiction. Without that line and the space it creates, however rudimentary or apparently bare it might be, there would be no theatre. In direct contradiction to Bucholz and Jahn, Michael Issacharoff posits that space is the only element that cannot be banished from theatre, while movement, gesture and even dialogue can go, as for instance in Beckett's theatre.[17]

Bucholz and Jahn's second argument thus merely exemplifies the very elision of space they are attempting to explicate. Within this example, as soon as the objects (set, props, etc.) disappear, the framing social dynamics forging space as the fabric of human existence are held to become equally invisible. All their example illustrates is the remarkable tenacity of a temporal paradigm which imperiously gathers up even counter-examples into its own orbit of influence.

It is perhaps then not so insignificant after all that Lessing figures as the other marker of the historical elision of space in narrative. This central theoretician of the German literary *Aufklärung* represents an enlightened notion of literary creation as the work of untrammelled genius. Significantly, that notion of artistic genius emerges at the same period as the unfolding of European colonial expansion. The narrative of the genius' formation (the etymological meaning of the term *Bildungsroman*) is not by chance the direct contemporary of the European narrative of progress – a tale about the collective European "sovereign subject" which comes to age in Enlightenment, a story so convincing as to necessitate being imposed upon the rest of the world.[18] Thus, "the normative claims of a rational project encompassing the whole world, concerned with its destiny as the progressive History of man, translated in the nineteenth century into the idea of a 'civilizing mission' to replace the Christianizing mission that functioned to legitimate conquest and dispossession in early modernity."[19] Lessing's sidelining of space in favour of time may thus be a direct correlative of Europe's calculating downplaying of a brutal process of global expansion in favour of a beatific rhetoric of progress. The egocentric mode of deictic action accurately describes the linguistic agency of a collective subject which sees itself as the centre of the deictic field, and the field itself as the passive domain of its undertakings. This mode of deictic action is self-effacing, and even now consistently privileges temporality as the supposed medium of its agency rather than the more fundamental spatiality of its action.

"A space so big ..."

Kirwan Desai's description, in *The Inheritance of Loss* (2006), of a young Indian girl's return to her native Himalayas encodes a significant counter-discourse of spatio-temporal organization: "Space and sun crashed through the window. Reflections magnified and echoed the light, the river, each adding angles and colours to the other, and Sai became aware of the enormous space she was entering. ... She had a fearful feeling of having entered a space so big it reached both backward and forward."[20] The notion of "a space so big it reached both backward and forward" is of seismic significance in its implications for Western comprehensions of time and space. We generally understand events to 'take place' against a backdrop of setting. We think of their diachronic sequence as being inserted within a synchronic spatial 'context', a sort of 'container'. Such conceptions date from European antiquity, with Lucretius positing that "all nature as it is in itself consists of two things – bodies and the vacant space in which the bodies are situated and through which they move in different directions."[21]

In Desai's text, however, rather than history "taking place" in space as a mere subordinate background, space becomes the primary and over-arching medium of history. Space includes past and present in itself in a manner very similar, for instance, to the spatial conceptions of Australian indigenous cultures, in which the "past does not so much precede the present, as lie contained within it".[22] Here space is the matrix which subsumes history to itself. This idea is so revolutionary because it inverts the entire structure of spatio-temporal understanding upon which European expansion across the globe has been predicated. That structure assumes that temporal progress along the lines of technological development, predicated upon military superiority, can dictate the ineluctable conquest of non-European territories, and the subordination of those spaces to European cultural and economic norms. This process began with the conquest of the Americas and continues today with neoliberal regimes of economic globalization. The colonizing impulse is predicated upon what Mitchell has called "imperial space": the tendency to treat nature as object and resource.[23] The languages of colonization and gobalization most clearly express this form of spatial reference.

The notion of "a space so big it reached both backward and forward" however inverts this hierarchy. Temporal sequence is part and parcel of space, not its imperious master. The archaic imbrication of time and space is an issue we will return to in the final chapters of Part II. The immediate question to be addressed is the unravelling of that imbrication and the consequent privilege of one term over the other. How does the dominance of time over space come about? And which modes of representation allow it to become so potent, thereby serving European global expansion?

A tentative answer to these questions may be found in an essay on urban spaces by the semiotician A. J. Greimas. In a meditation on the significance of space in the urban context, he treats space as the raw material of social and cultural meaning-making. Space resembles the materiality of the signifier (or the visual and phonetic form of the sign); culture in turn resembles the abstraction of the signified (or referent of the sign).[24] Greimas suggests that spatial logic precedes temporal logic in the articulation of social organization:

> Spatial language thus appears, in an initial phase, as the language by means of which a society signifies itself to itself. In order to do this, it operates first of all by exclusion, opposing itself spatially to that which it is not. This fundamental disjunction, which defines that society purely in negative terms, allows the subsequent introduction of internal articulations which enrich its in levels of meaning.
>
> [Le langage spatial apparaît ainsi, dans un premier temps, comme un langage par lequel une société se signifie à elle-même. Pour ce faire, elle opère d'abord par exclusion, en s'opposant spatialement à ce qui n'est pas elle. Cette disjonction fondamentale qui ne la définit que négativement permet d'introduire alors des articulations internes qui l'enrichissent en signification.][25]

Greimas' notion of the spatial sign as a primary means by which a given society marks out its own boundaries and constitutive spaces as the foundation for making sense of itself is probably based, for instance, on anthropological theories about the topographies of pre-literate communities.[26] It may also concur with our own intuitive but often unacknowledged experience, as Stephen Muecke writes: "one lives in a place more than in a time (I feel it is more vital to my sense of self to live in Sydney, for example, than it is to live in 2004, or even 'now')."[27]

Greimas' concept also resonates in interesting ways, however, with the systems theory of the German sociologist Niklas Luhmann. His systems theory claims that any society must begin by drawing a demarcating inside-outside, or system-environment line so as to sift information and elaborate its own particular internal language. Every system must commence with "a difference that makes a difference" so as to be able to establish a filtering mechanism allowing it to determine what external information is relevant for its internal logic.[28] The selective communication between inside and outside clearly assumes a spatial logic. A very simple example would be the way the national boundary allows the elaboration of the concepts of foreignness and citizenship. For Luhmann, this inaugural boundary-marking remains invisible, remaining the unthinkable condition of possibility of society's self-articulation. For Greimas, similarly, once this inaugural boundary-marking has occurred, it tends to be naturalized or even erased: "Over and above all the diachronic transformations inherent to any semiotic system, a contestatory meta-discourse emerges so as to cast into question established human space, a discourse which contradicts space as the signifier of a social signified" ["Par dessus les transformations diachroniques propres à tout système sémiotique, un méta-discours contestataire s'installe pour remettre en question l'espace humain établi, un discours qui nie l'espace comme signifiant d'un signifié social"].[29] The spatial signifier is an active force whose activity is contradicted and erased by subsequent superior discourses.

If this process of spatial marking and subsequent spatial amnesia is to be taken seriously, as Greimas' emphasis upon the diachronic transformations of semiotic systems suggests, then temporal progression appears to be predicated upon the repression or elision of its own spatial foundations. Modernity assumes the forgetting of space, to translate back to the anthropological research Greimas probably alludes to. In the colonial world, the imperial global system certainly chose to elide its own spatial dynamic, presenting spatial conquest as technological and civilizing progress. Greimas' ostensibly neutral description of semiotic processes can thus be read as a highly politicized, albeit displaced and masked analysis of the way modernity as a global undertaking obscures its own territorial ambitions. It is politicized in part because it recuperates a too easily forgotten agency in the repressed element of material space. Greimas' articulation of the spatial sign into its constituent parts (spatial signifier and spatial signified) resists the very elision of the material signifier under scrutiny. For the signifier–signified pair parses these respective elements of the sign as active (signifi*er*) and passive (signifi*ed*). The spatial signifier is an active element whose agency is subsequently hidden from sight. Like Desai's fiction, Greimas' analysis seeks to reverse a chronological process which has insidiously placed chronology in the foreground. Moving back down the conceptual sequence, it recovers an archaic agency of space itself.

This, in a sense, well describes the task that the second part of this book sets itself. It begins, in the following chapter (Chapter 6), with the notion of an "imperial space" assuming a deictic activity firmly centered in the European "origo". It then moves on to examine in Chapters 7 and 8 the post-independence seizure of that "origo" and its transfer away from the European metropolis towards the newly independent nation, by the same token neglecting to transform the "origo" structure of deixis itself. Finally, in Chapters 9 and 10 it reads narratives which re-discover or perpetuate an archaic but ongoing tradition which cedes the "origo" to nature itself, thereby enacting a reciprocal linguistic process of spatial performativity which we term "deiXis".

The elision of space on the one hand and its privileging through the renewed recognition of spatial agency on the other are the two polar extremes of deictic activity within which this book situates its project. Within that compass, however, it enumerates a tripartite model of frequently overlapping deictic modes. That tripartite model, which underpins the argument of the following chapters, demands at least a schematic presentation before proceeding further.

"... to write there"

Let us return once again, this time in conclusion, to a passage from Ondaatje's *The English Patient*. The main setting of the novel is a shell-pocked Renaissance villa somewhere in Tuscany which becomes the domicile of four refugees from the the final battles of the Second World War. One of the fugitives, the young Canadian nurse Hana, wanders the palatial corridors of the half-destroyed villa:

> She walks in front of the shelves in the library, eyes closed, and at random pulls out a book. She finds a clearing between two sections in a book of poetry and begins to write there.
>
> *He says Lahore is an ancient city. London is a recent town compared with Lahore. Well, I come from an even newer country.* (*English Patient* 209)

Significantly, the shattered library is partly open to the outside world (*English Patient* 8), its own architecture thus gesturing at the way the lit-erary archive becomes a site in which new narratives are generated and create connections with other places. The library in Ondaatje's novel is a place no less symbolic of the transmission of literary narrative than the scenes of storytelling discussed in Chapters 3 and 4 above.

And indeed, in this passage from Ondaatje's novel, we find a simi-lar embedding of respective levels of *discourse-* and *story*-narration to that explored in the previous chapters. The most prominent *story* in the passage above is Hana's minute anecdote in italics, a brief tale of geog-raphy comparing the respective ages of London, Lahore and Canada. It is embedded in a *discourse*, that of a transitional moment between the fighting in Italy and the slow return of peace, in a half-ruined villa in Tuscany. Yet that Italian *discourse* is in turn the *story* of a subsequent moment of narration, that of the broadly framing postcolonial world. The postcolonial context is indexed briefly at the every end of the novel by a concluding chapter which sketches the respective Indian and Canadian lives lead by Kip and Hana a few decades later (presumably the 1960s or 1970s). That later *discourse* is also, by extension, the 1990s postcolonial diaspora of which the Sri Lankan-Canadian author Ondaatje himself is a part. These successive levels of *story-discourse* embedding exemplify the manner elaborated above in which the utterance generates a space of its reception, which in turn becomes a site of further transmission.

The text specifically marks the overlap of *story-discourse* embedding by contrasting standard and italicized print. At the seam between the two, the text inserts a deictic marker: "there". That marker is highly ambivalent. Does it refer to the act of textual inscription ("She finds a clearing between two sections in a book of poetry and begins to write **there**")? Or, alternatively, does it refer to the location where the act of writing occurs ("She walks in front of the shelves in the library ... and begins to write **there**")? The former would be an instance of *discourse*-deixis (anchoring in the place of the act of narration, what Chatman has called *discourse*-place), the latter of *story*-deixis (anchoring in the place of what is narrated, Chatman's *story*-place).[30]

It is significant that though Chatman can conceptualize *story*-place, he has nothing further to say about *discourse*-place. Chatman thereby restricts the conceptualization of narrative space to the domain of *story*, that is, of the 'what' of narration. By neglecting the 'how' of narrating, or more precisely, its 'where', he ensures that his narratology remains comfortably in the tradition of a time-fixated narrative theory. This inadequacy has long hampered attempts to deal with discourse-place. Jakob Lothe notes that "While the distinction between 'story time' and 'discourse time' has enabled narrative theory to coin and employ terms such as analepsis, prolepsis, perspective and repetition, that between 'story space' and 'discourse space' has not resulted in a corresponding proliferation of critical concepts."[31] A number of phenomenological approaches to literary space attempt to typologize *story*-places either in terms of atmosphere ("mythical space", "psychic space", "poetic space") or function ("space of action", "space of gaze"), but ignore *discourse*-place.[32] Moretti's *Atlas of the European Novel* builds upon the chiastic distinction between *space in literature* (fictional space) and *literature in space* (historical space); the latter refers only to *story*-space.[33] Barbara Piatti's fine study of "literary geographies", building upon Moretti, springs from a finely nuanced typology of *story*-places ("Handlungsräume") to reading-places ("Leserräume"), skipping the spaces of narrating or story-telling – that is, the *discourse*-places which ought to mediate between them.[34] However, as Carol Clarkson quips, when fiction "oscillate[s] ... between discourses of the typographic and the topographic ... writing about place becomes an interrogation of the place of writing."[35] More soberly, Gerald Prince has suggested that narratology "ought to be more sensitive to the role of context ... in the production of narrative meaning".[36] Filling the conceptual gap to focus on the sites and locations of narrative *discourse* was the task of Part I of this book. Chapters 3 and 4 in particular sought to show that *discourse*-place is of central importance in the generation of narrativity.

Ondaatje's "there" is an ambivalent deictic marker which points towards the way that the "how" and the "what" of writing (the *discourse* and *story* of any narrative) are both inflected by a "where". The dual "wheres" of writing ground and link the various phases of writing as a productive inscriptive process. "Where" can be both the context which allows an act of writing to occur; conversely, it can be the new context produced by an act of narration. The ambivalence of deixis within narrative thus always points towards the manner is which space is both product and producer of cultural action. In the second part of this book it will become clear that space will be principally envisaged as an active producer in its own right – as an agent which is also manifested in the 'givens' of specific places, 'givens' all too easily mistaken for the objects and arenas of human agency.

I have lingered upon this passage from Ondaatje's *The English Patient* because it offers a brief vignette of the ways in which space and literary language interact, focused in the action of deictic language itself. I use this brief passage as a starting point for an overview of the theoretical and conceptual assumptions of the five chapters that follow.

It can hardly be a coincidence that Ondaatje has Hana choose London, Lahore and Canada, as the terms of her comparison. Each of these places is a synecdoche epitomizing, repectively, the metropolitan centre of the colonial world, and two varieties of peripheral outposts: the tropical exploitation colony (such India or Africa) and the temperate settler colony (Canada, Australia, South Africa).[37] The three places are aligned in a rough hierarchy of antiquity or modernity. Between the three of them they instantiate, spatially, very different modes of spatio-temporal marking of geopolitical identity: the pre-colonial (evinced in the antiquity of Lahore), the colonial (characterized by the imperial centrality of London and the then still-extant colonial status of India), and the postcolonial (embodied in Canada as an independent dominion within the British Empire). In their manner of combining space and time, they are examples of what Bakhtin called the literary "chronotope", a device concretizing both temporal and spatial dimensions.[38]

In the chapters that follow, I shall be utilizing numerous examples of colonial and postcolonial writing as chronotopes of a tripartiate organization of literary deixis. I deal first with two modes of deixis in which space is the object of writing, then moving on to a third mode of deixis in which space emerges as the subject of writing. This third mode is the deiXis elucidated in the earlier chapters of this book.

I align these three modes of deictic operation very roughly (for their temporality is often non-sequential and overlapping) with three broad genres of writing of global space: first, the metropolitan writing of colonial space; second, the post-independence celebration of indigenous space; and third, a later postcolonial exploration of the complexities of space and the ways it underlies human community. I suggest that in the metropolitan inscription of colonial space, the Western colonizing subject predominantly describes a space which is implicitly the passive object of European agency. This mode overlaps with what Mitchell has termed "imperial space".[39] In the post-independence mode, the writing of space in general merely mirrors the previous representation of colonial space, making the newly emancipated indigenous peoples the rulers of a still-objectified space – that of the post-independence nation. Only in the third mode does another form of writing emerge, one which acknowledges the debt of writing to the spaces which it portrays, thus opening textuality up to another agency preceding it.

The three forms of deictic action I am presenting here stand in a dialectical relationship with each other. Colonial and post-independence deixis may be understood as standing in an antithetical relationship to one another, paradoxically however mirroring each other in a highly symbiotic manner. Postcolonial deiXis may be conceived as constituting a reaction to their deadlock and a route of escape. However, deiXis does not constitute a neat synthesis, first, because it has always been manifest in the symbolic inscriptions of many societies, and secondly because it also remains perceptible in our own moment. Finally, it also eschews neat closure because at any moment of its manifestation it is always heavily conflicted.

These three phases are also recognizable as being characterized by three temporal models, each with its specific socio-economic and cultural programmes of intervention: that of colonial 'progress', that of post-independence 'development', and that of 'post-developmental' indigenous temporalities of social construction.[40] My concern here is less with the temporalities of progress, development or post-development, though I will focus at some points in my argument on the notions of history implied by various ways of representing global space. Rather, I am more interested in the forms of linguistic-spatial action which go hand in hand with these respective modes and the attendant socio-cultural policies driven by notions of 'progress', 'development', or alternatives to those twin-terms.

Though I have suggested a rough periodization for these modes of deictic activity, I do not wish to suggest that at respective historical periods the corresponding mode of deictic action occurred exclusively. The modes of writing I mark out are here are of course in reality much more blurred, as are the historical periods they characterized. The colonial or postcolonial periods occurred at different moments around the globe, with some colonies attaining independence early in the nineteenth century, and others only very recently; some independent settler colonies such as Australia still contain internal 'colonies' of subaltern indigenous peoples. Following Raymond William's intimation that residual, dominant and emergent forms inhabit any moment of cultural history, it should come as no surprise to discover deictic modes also in impure combinations.[41]

Clearly, deixis in its many varieties informs texts at all times and places. Yet the tripartite quasi-historical model I suggest is relevant for specific cases in sometimes perplexing ways. I detect, for instance, the third form of deictic action (deiXis) in very marked form in Australian indigenous texts, which clearly have not arisen out of any experience of national political independence or its aftermath. The periodizations I model and the corresponding deictic modes I propose are meant rather as conceptual constructs designed to aid us in interpreting the complexity of textual production. They must, therefore, to some extent simplify in order make analysis possible. However, the textual readings themselves will make quite clear how complex the spatial realities dealt with are in fact.

6
Imperial Deixis

The imperial spatial economies which make up our first mode of deictic activity resemble the spatial affront defly executed by one of Conrad's more unpleasant colonial characters in his *Heart of Darkness*: the banal but sinister manager of the Central Station. The manager is constantly irritated by the incessant quarrelling of his subordinates. In order to put a stop to these petty conflicts, "he ordered an immense round table to be made, for which a special house had to be built. This was the station's mess-room. Where he sat was the first place – the rest were nowhere" (*Heart of Darkness* 164).

The manager's method of quelling internecine strife installs a sort of spurious equality which makes his own place central, and all others peripheral. By their negative equality, however, his underlings are relegated to a space which is not merely peripheral but more significantly, non-existent. Just as Marlow's journey to the centre of Africa is articulated within a global logic ("I felt as though, instead of going to the centre of a continent, I were about to set off for the centre of the earth" – *Heart of Darkness* 150), the circular table is symbolic of the globe itself. Conrad's bitingly satirical anecdote thus takes on a synecdochic aspect, describing the colonizers' attitude to the globe in its entirety. Europe is the centre, the rest is nowhere. Conrad thereby anticipates contemporary European discourse and the way, in the words of Mbembe, it assigns to Africa even today "a special unreality such that the continent becomes the very essence of what is null, abolished ... the very expression of that nothing whose special feature is to be nothing at all."[1]

This chapter specifically addresses the workings of this still-potent conception of imperial space. It begins with Naipaul's *A Bend in the River* (1979) by exploring the colonial ideologies of the non-European world as place where space ostensibly eradicates time. This notion of timelessness underwrites the ideologies of the "white man's burden" or the *mission civilisatrice*, while somehow, by the same token, rendering them utterly futile. More importantly however, the notion of timelessness also allows the colonizing gaze to ignore the real processes of production inherent to exploitation while mainting a panoramic gaze over an ostensibly static non-European space. These strategies can be detected operating in texts such as Robert Dunbar's poem *The Cruise: A Prospect of the West Indian Achipelago* (1835), Keats's 'On First Looking into Chapman's Homer' (1816) and Kipling's *Kim* (1901). In contrast, the chapter will conclude by considering alternative perspectives resisting such fantasies of panoramic mastery. Texts such as Césaire's *Cahier d'un retour au pays natal* (1956) [Engl. trans. *Return to My Native Land* (1971)], Jean Rhys' *Wide Sargasso Sea* (1962), Roy's *The God of Small Things* (1997), or Rushdie's *Midnight's Children* (1981) constitute an archive of alternative, contestatory perspectives.

Where the future has come and gone

Conrad's anecdote of the manager's round table is not merely spatial in its import ("the rest were nowhere"), but also evinces a latent temporal assertion: "Where he sat was the first place" (*Heart of Darkness* 164). The ordinal expression "first place" points towards the underlying assumption of temporal progress which legitimized European expansion:

> The line of march will prove, on the whole, to have been from force and cruelty to consent and association, to humanity, rational persuasion ... We have dethroned necessity, in the shape of hunger and fear, by extending the scene from Western Europe to the whole world, so that all shall contribute to the treasure of civilization ...[2]

Expansion was coeval with the march of time and progress itself, so that paradoxically, the further one travelled from Europe, the more one was displaying one's superior civilization. This paradox functioned, of course, according to the differential logic of all signifying systems, that is, by a contrast that produces meaning: "For Enlightenment itself, to assert its superiority as the universal ideal, needs its Other; if it could ever actualise itself in the real world as the truly universal, it would in fact desroy itself."[3] Contact with non-European peoples allowed the European colonizers to perceive themselves as civilized and modern in direct inverse proportion to their own geographical distance from native Europe. That distance, of course, simultaneously indexed the ostensible temporal backwardness of the native peoples: "Going up that river was like travelling back to the earliest beginnings of the world" (*Heart of Darkness* 182).

Just as the subordinate places around the manager's table are not merely peripheral, but "nowhere", so too history has its non-places. In the colonial world, where Europe was the centre of civilization, the colonies were not construed simply as backward or primitive. They were seen more damningly as pre-historic – as outside history. Hegel proclaimed that "Africa forms no historical part of the World; it exhibits no movement or development" ["Afrika ... ist kein geschichtlicher Weltteil, er hat keine Bewegung oder Entwicklung aufzuweisen"].[4] Similarly, in a statement of 1853, Marx commented upon the ambivalences of the British colonization of India, by weighing up the losses and gains to the subcontinent:

> Indian society has no history at all, at least no known history. What we call its history is but the history of its successive intruders who founded their empires on the passive basis of that unresisting and unchanging society. ... England has to fulfil a double mission in India: one destructive, the other regenerating – the annihilation of the old Asiatic society, and the laying of the material foundations of Western society in Asia.[5]

Marx's conclusion is that though British colonization has, manifestly, eradicated much of the indigenous economy (for instance the textile industry) so as to clear markets for British products, it has also introduced some benefits. Among them was the inauguration of history. Only with the arrival of the British, in Marx's view, did India enter the linear temporality of historical dialectics. Or rather, given that India in itself could not be said to have an history proper upon the arrival of the British, it was assimilated into Britain's history. Just as India became an outpost of the empire, so too it became an outpost of British imperial history. To this extent, in Marx's analysis, India continued to be on the margins of history even as it was dragged into the orbit of British imperial history. To be outside of history is to be in a negative space of what Edouard Glissant has called "nonhistory" ["non-histoire"].[6] This is a notion which has been explored most potently in recent times by V. S. Napiaul in his fictions about Africa.

In Naipaul's *A Bend in the River* (1979), the protagonist Salim sets up a trading business in a central African state recently rocked by independence and an ensuing civil war. In a journey inland from his coastal birthplace, a journey that mimics that of Conrad's Marlow, Naipaul's protagonist Salim remarks:

> I got deeper into Africa – the scrub, the desert, the rocky climb up to the mountains. The lakes, the rain in the afternoons ... – as I got deeper I thought, 'But this is madness. I am going in the wrong direction. There can't be anything new at the end of this.'[7]

The refusal of novelty alludes to the motto inscribed over the door of the local *lycée*, "Semper Aliquid Novi" (*A Bend in the River* 40), based on Pliny the Elder's quip, *ex Africa simper aliquid novi*, "there is always something new out of Africa" (*Natural History*, Book 8, Chapter 17). This fragment of European high culture speaks for a progress which, according to Naipaul, post-independence Africa has abandoned. Ferdinand, Salim's protégé from a remote village, is "always dressed as the lycée boy, in white" but, in contradiction of the motto which adorns his school, "offered me nothing in the way of news" (*A Bend in the River* 43). This rejection of novelty in Africa is not restricted merely to persons, but is transferred to the entire continent. To enter Africa is not to move forwards, but rather, to go back into the far past: "I would have to start from the beginning" (*A Bend in the River* 3). For, according to Naipaul, Africa is a space not travelling towards modernity, but slipping back into a primitive and archaic epoch: "You were in a place where the future had come and gone" (*A Bend in the River* 30). This self-cancelling temporality takes Africa out of the linearity of history, throwing it back into the stasis of unalleviated space.

After independence, when the infrastructure of colonialism collapses, the population goes back to its villages – where there is shelter and nourishment still to be found, but where the intense and age-old localism of Africa, Naipaul implies, resurges anew (*A Bend in the River* 5). Africans, he claims, are bogged down in their locality and always have been. The slaves were grateful for their slavery, he suggests, for it offered them a form of protection when out of their tribal territories. Even today, "No-one liked going outside his territory" (*A Bend in the River* 4, 10). Under the new geographical and political conditions, "The country was now too small for its tribal hatreds" (*A Bend in the River* 235). Naipaul imagines in African spatial disputes a fundamental African incapacity to cope with larger spaces than that of the immediate tribal domain. He neglects to identify colonial disruptions of indigenous geography originating from the arbitrary drawing of borders by Western powers, for instance, as causes of modern conflict. For Naipaul, the political strife of post-independence Africa ensues simply from the fact that

Africans cannot manage the new, broader spatial coordinates of the modern world. Whereas Conrad, for instance, records the dislocation caused by imperialism (the natives he portrays have been "[b]rought from all the recesses of the coast in all the legality of time contracts, lost in uncongenial surroundings" – *Heart of Darkness* 156), Naipaul claims that this fear of other spaces is something essential, inborn, only generic to Africans.

The concrete inability to deal with spaces other than the immediately local has a cultural concomitant, which is the finitude of African culture. The reason for this is that African culture is specific, not universal. Naipaul's Africans are "buried so deep in their lives that they [are] not able to stand back" (*A Bend in the River* 18). Salim wonders whether his young protégé Ferdinand "even had an idea of Africa; or whether the idea of Africa had come to him ... at school, from the atlas" (*A Bend in the River* 54). Without the aid of Western culture, Africans cannot see their own culture from outside, cannot objectify, cannot reflect upon it. Irony, for instance, the fundamental form of double consciousness, is unknown to them (*A Bend in the River* 49). Only with the help of another culture can Africans enter modernity – not unlike the trading-woman Zabeth hooking her dugout onto a steamer so as to piggyback its momentum (*A Bend in the River* 8). Salim describes this cultural piggyback process with reference to his own coastal homeland, and the postage stamp which suddenly allows him to see that community from outside:

> Without the stamp of the dhow I might have taken the dhows for granted. As it was, I learned to look at them. Whenever I saw them tied up at the waterfront I thought of them as something peculiar to our region, quaint, something the foreigner would remark upon, something not quite modern, and certainly not like the liners and cargo ships that berthed in their own modern docks.
>
> So from an early age I developed the habit of looking, detaching myself from a familiar scene and trying to consider it as from a distance. It was from this habit of looking that the idea came to me that as a community we had fallen behind. And that was the beginning of my insecurity. (*A Bend in the River* 17)

The postage stamp, a synecdoche of international communication, bearing an icon of premodernity, condenses a complex ideological operation. Postcolonial critique would understand this operation as the colonized people's internalization of the gaze of the colonizer, producing a permanent sense of self-denigration: "It was from this habit of looking that the idea came to me that ... we had fallen behind." Naipaul, by contrast, inteprets this operation as the salutary arrival of universal culture that rescues the colonial subject from the restrictions of the particular. The West allows one to attain distance with regard to one's environment.

Exile and deracination, within this ultra-conservative perspective, are not the result of the immense forces of economic disruption triggered by global capitalism in its merchant, trading and imperialistic phases, but the necessary costs of a redemptive disruption. Dislocation frees the colonized subject from being bogged down in the particular and qualifies him for the universal. Salim is saved by his loss of roots – and this is the basis for his much-ruminated difference from the Africans around him. In a significant phrase, Salim boasts, "I knew that there was something that separated me from Ferdinand and from the life of the bush around me" (*A Bend in the River* 48). Africans, by contrast, are trapped in Africanness by virtue of being trapped in Africa.

Salim is rescued from this fate. He laments that he has no sense of home: "I will inherit no house, and no house that I have built will now pass to my children"; "I had been homesick for months. But home was hardly a place I could return to. Home was something in my head. It was something I had lost" (*A Bend in the River* 123, 124). Though Salim and his kin are the deracinated offspring of modernism and of the disruptions of postcolonialism, by the same token, according to Naipaul, their homelessness forces them to travel, and thus to generalize. Western culture is a gain to be paid for by the loss of traditional culture: "There could be no going back; there was nothing to go back to. We had become what the world outside had made us; we had to live in the world as it existed" (*A Bend in the River* 285). The outside world is the future, and its action upon the community is conceived of as saving it from retardedness. To go back in the sense of a return to an intact homeland, to an intact traditional culture, is explicitly couched in the diachronic language of regression. In contrast, progression can be entertained as the painful but necessary gift of the West and its surgical interventions into the non-West. Thus Salim advocates the hard-nosed approach of the novel's opening lines: "The world is as it is; men who are nothing, and who allow themselves to become nothing, have no place in it" (*A Bend in the River* 3). When Salim speaks of the world, he does not just mean "life" – he genuinely means the world, which in turn means the universal reach of Western culture. Not to embrace that universal is to fall out of "becoming", to be nothing.

In economic terms, "becoming" has meant 'development', and more recently, 'structural adjustment'. Africa has failed to respond to these imperatives in the manner imagined by the West, and in recent years has increasingly been isolated from global economic processes.[8] There is a global hierarchy of cultures in which the universal is that of the West, with its time-line of linear progress. Anywhere which does not participate in that universal falls into the particular, which in turn is caught in the stasis of non-history. The West travels, the rest of the world stays put. Naipaul's neo-con philosophy of history is also a philosophy of space which merely naturalizes what has been institutionalized around the globe by contemporary migration and refugee regimes: the West benefits from universal mobility, while non-Westerners (Africans, Arabs, South Americans, Asians, East-Europeans) face barriers to migration everywhere.

Naipaul essentializes the inertia of Africa. The dictator of his imaginary African country attempts to create a modern, dynamic Africa, realized in the Domain outside the town. But this effort of cultural renewal cannot change the fact, precisely, that Africa cannot change: "He was creating modern Africa. He was creating a miracle that would astound the rest of the world. He was by-passing real Africa, the difficult Africa of bush and villages, creating something that would match anything that existed in other countries" (*A Bend in the River* 116). The new Domain represents an attempt to establish the far-away, the other-of-Africa, within Africa itself. It is thus fundamentally oxymoronic, and fundamentally in denial of the brute realities of African life, which, inevitably, finally get the upper hand: "All around, the life of dugout and creek and village continued; in the bars in the town the foreign builders and artisans drank and made easy jokes about the country" (*A Bend in the River* 117). These, for Naipaul, are not mere fictions, for they derive from his journalism about contemporary Africa, in particular Mbotu's Congo, a "country trapped and static": "The inherited modern state is being dismantled, but it isn't important that the state should work. The bush works; the bush has always been self-sufficient."[9] The state is the heritage of colonialism, the gift of universal culture, which, after independence and the ungrateful refusal of the legacy of the West, cannot but be overhauled again by the static, particular Space which is Africa: the Bush as non-place.

The retreat of imperialism does not merely leave Africa with the debris of cultures disrupted by colonization. More insidiously, it allows Africa's true nature (in all the senses of the term, because Africa is primarily nature rather than culture) to re-emerge: "You felt the land taking you back to something familiar, something you had known at some time but had forgotten or ignored, but which was always there" (*A Bend in the River* 9–10). There is a core of primitivism which subsists under the veneer of the civilization installed by colonial powers and lost after the second revolution and independence. One character pontificates: "This isn't property. This is just bush. This *has always been* bush" (*A Bend in the River* 25–6; emphasis added). If from the African perspective, property (European possession, *territoire*) reverts to being nature (*terre*), from the colonial point of view – that of Naipaul – civilization recedes, revealing that it has never had any real purchase on African primitivism.

Africa cannot elude its own localism, and thus cannot traverse the interval to the universal validity of Western culture, and into the flow of history. Naipaul's spatial racism is posited upon a absolute spatio-cultural apartness. Distinct regimes of culture are hypostatized in their universal and local status (Europe and Africa respectively). The only possible salvation is to leave the local for the universal – a jump which denies any commonality between the two regimes:

> They had begun to rot. I was like them. Unless I acted now, my fate would be like theirs. ... I decided to rejoin the world, to break out of the narrow geography of the town. ... I wrote to Nazruddin that I was coming to London for a visit. (*A Bend in the River* 266)

Naipaul's ultra-conservative, neo-Orientalist opinions have considerable sway in Europe, not least because of the cultural status cemented by the award of the Nobel Prize in 2001. Edward Said has described Naipaul's work as "the most virulent example of colonial reassessment that emerged in the post-1960s, post-Vietnam atmosphere".[10] Kirwan Desai has one of her characters comment explicitly on the author of *A Bend in the River*: " 'I think he's strange. Stuck in the past. He has not progressed. Colonial neurosis, he's never freed himself from it' " (*The Inheritance of Loss* 46). And Derek Walcott has mocked, "I see these islands and I feel to bawl, | 'area of darkness' with V. S. Nightfall."[11] By bowdlerizing Naipaul's name, his authorial trademark, Walcott can imply that the benighted, atavistic stasis that Naipaul attributes to the erstwhile colonial world is merely an attribute of his own gloomy persona.

Doreen Massey has commented upon the way in which "other places, peoples, cultures ... are deprived of histories. Immobilised, they await ... our, or global capital's ... arrival. They lie there on space, in place, without their own trajectories."[12] Reducing the colonial world to mere static space outside the mobility of time has a clear ideological function. It makes of the non-European world a *tabula rasa* awaiting progress, civilization, technology. Into the temporal vacuum of Africa or Asia, time will come, salutary and redemptive. The temporal emptiness of the ahistorical world is a concomitant of the *terra nullius* of imperial law, and serves the same purpose: the legitimization of European colonization. The evacuation of temporality allows the colonizer with his imported progress to persuade himself that there is no necessity of engaging with a local history or trajectory of civilization. The "timeless land" may simply be conquered.

Panoramic deixis

Where there is no history, eventless space is assumed to be curiously vacant. The assumption of atemporality permits the unimpeded establishment of a spatial mode of representation in which European perception operates as an absolute and unquestionable perceptual centre or "origo". The European gaze is the central norm around which everything else is organized. This centrality of the conquering gaze is given literal concrete expression in a nineteenth-century poem by Robert Dunbar, *The Cruise* (1835) – and significantly subtitled *A Prospect of the West Indian Achipelago*. In one important passage, the speaker surveys a Caribbean island from the peak which dominates it:

> The summit gain'd, how glorious the reward! –
> Bursts on the eye, and thrills upon the heart,
> Reality more bright than dream of bard,
> Or triumphs of Lorraine's creative art:
> The land lies stretch'd like an illuminated chart,
> The sea one glistening sheet of silver shines;
> And the sun's fires such dazzling radiance dart,
> That each far isle, that in the glare reclines,
> Quivers, like leafy gold, in undulating lines.
> White peasant-villages embower'd in trees,
> And garden'd mansions, dot the wide-spread map;
>
> While o'er them, to the east's undying breeze,
> The princely palm unfolds his feather'd cap:
> Plenty lies cradl'd in the isle's soft lap;
> Canes clothe with waving wealth the smiling land;
> The rural powers their hands exulting clap;
> Havens, with dark hulls speck'd, indent the strand,
> And towns, and bristling forts, emboss the silver sand.[13]

The poem opens with the moment of arrival at the summit, presenting the viewer with the panoramic view of the island: "The summit gain'd, how glorious the reward!" A more concrete exemplification of the deictic "origo", with its attendant sense of colonial possessiveness, could not be imagined. It epitomizes the colonizer's typical gaze from "above or at the centre of things, yet apart from them so that the organization and classification of things takes place according to the writer's own system of value."[14]

But who speaks here? Who is the viewer, the possessor of "the eye" and "the heart"? The depersonalized "origo" of the gaze from above is a position which is left all but blank. In this way, the reader can insert her- or himself seamlessly into that position of masterful scopic command, barely noticing what has happened. "The images of landstrip, horizon and sky seem anonymous, impersonal", Meaghan Morris writes regarding contemporary landscape portrayals in the same tradition; "all trace of the photographer's presence is effaced. Yet for that reason, subjectivity dominates here; any one of I/you/all of us can take her place and assume that vision. This is the timeless land, 'our' land, laid out ahead alluringly for acts of possession to come."[15] As disembodied in our purely mental activity of reading as the poem's speaker, we slip imperceptibly into the viewing position we are offered. Identification functions so smoothly because it goes unnoticed – and it goes unnoticed because it remains textually unmarked.

But the curious emptiness of the viewing position serves another purpose. In the elision of the viewer's position it replicates the functioning of Western perspective representation, which arranges the viewed landscape according to a radiating zone of straight lines emanating from the viewer's stance. The position of the viewer, however, is invisible.[16] It is indicated only by "the eye", but that marking is held in check by couching the viewing in a passive mode: "Bursts on the eye". The act of viewing as a form of agency is not mentioned. Its almost complete invisibility allows it to become natural and normative. There is no need to mention a mode of viewing which is coeval with the shape of reality itself. In its very invisibility, the power of this way of seeing is most effective, because it is hidden behind the ontological self-assurance of that which is natural, taken for granted.

Dunbar's reiterated allusions to cartography corroborate this interpretation. Maps are in fact a highly selective and distorting mode of representation. They reduce three-dimensional space to the two dimensional surface of the paper. At a certain magnitude of scale they necessarily flatten out the multiaxial curvature of the earth's surface into the even surface of the map, a problem first dealt with by Mercator and his famous projection. Their symbols are highly conventionalized, sometimes gesturing towards a residual iconicity (a crenelated square may denote a castle), sometimes towards indexicality (as in the crossed swords indicating a battlefield), sometimes totally symbolic (a circle or stands for a town or city, with its colour telling us whether it is a national or regional capital). Maps are not realist representations. They are only taken to be so because their mode of portrayal of the world has been endowed with normativity by virtue of their crucial role in the Western dominance of the globe.[17] Maps were instrumental in aiding the exploration, the conquest and the parcelling-up of the non-Western world. That role gave them the epistemological power conveyed by association with an economic regime of virtually uncontested global hegemony.

Thus the simile "The land lies stretch'd like an illuminated chart" conceals the fact that a chart probably helped to conquer this land and to administer its division into segments possessed by European plantation owners. The chart is not a mere accidental metaphor to adorn the narrator's portrayal, it is that which has rendered that gaze possible – not merely in this particular locality, but indeed in the very specificity of its scopic command. When we are told, "White peasant-villages embower'd in trees, | And garden'd mansions, dot the wide-spread map", the map is not a mere background for the topography of mastery and subordination. Rather, to think chiastically, that mastery and subordination has been installed by the utilization of navigational charts, military maps, cadaster books.

The viewer's position above the island thus encodes a distinctive European mode of seeing which lays out the landscape before the viewer but by the same token removes the viewer as such from that landscape. As Edgerton points out, the "fixed view-point [of perspectival representation] is elevated and distant, completely out of plastic or sensory reach of the depicted [landscape]."[18] There is no viewer's body to be seen in the view itself. The pure disembodied gaze of the viewer is betrayed only by the adjectival participle "gain'd", which makes climbing and gazing cognates of the entire exploratory and capitalist processes. Gain is a synonym of profit. Climbing and gazing are forms of work which do not appear as such because the bodily labour involved is elided – just as in the rest of the poem the bodily labour involved in the cutting of cane, the loading of ships, the building of houses, the manning of fortresses, is consistently elided.

There are no slaves in this poem, only "peasants", whose implied rootedness in the land (borne out by the quasi-European "peasant-villages") belies the brutal displacement inherent in the slavery system. The past participle "gain'd" reflects the completedness of a process ("gain" as the accumulation of profit) which requires no further comment because it can be seen from the vantage point of detached superiority. The spatial-visual code of altitude translates a temporal code of completed process and finished product. As in many forms of pastoral, the perfection of 'the work' displaces the untidiness of 'work'.

Thus the disembodied viewing position from above the island embodies the cultural egocentricity of the standard accounts of deixis. It may even reveal some of the historical processes which have contributed to the normativity of that spatial egocentricity. Just as the maps alluded to in the poem have been instrumental in establishing the colonial system, so too the deictic mode of linguistic marking which imposes upon the world a Eurocentric view of space may be part of the historical process of conquest. The egocentricity of Western deixis may have inserted the mentality of conquest within the very fabric of language itself.

"Silent, upon a peak …"

To understand the way in which egocentric deixis may have helped to structure the mentality of empire, it is helpful to examine the history of deixis in English in its literary manifestations. Egocentric deixis emerges both in the colonies and at home as an index of a double but interdependent economic revolution, that of colonialism–capitalism. Let us begin with domestic developments.

Before the Romantic period, deictic marking in poetry, if it occurs at all, is manifest only in a very vague and general form. Only from the Romantic period onwards, Bruhn has suggested, does deixis occur in literary texts in intensified and concrete form.[19] He argues that as the distance between narrator and narratee increases, and the concrete situation of enunciation fades away (e.g. that of publicly recited poetry) to be replaced by purely internalized reception (e.g. poetry read by an isolated reader) deictic markers become more frequent, serving to mobilize imaginary spatial schemata: "Where there is no shared perceptual, interpersonal or memorial field of reference … deixis must be construed with reference to conceptual-linguistics schemata"; "the more difficult it is to construe deixis, the more foregrounded and salient its operations become".[20] "The importance of such deictics in poetry can scarcely be overestimated", notes Culler: "Such deictics are not determined by an actual situation of utterance but operate at some distance from it. … The deictics do not refer to an external context but force us to construct a fictional situation of utterance."[21] Bruhn focuses upon "Keats's use of deixis to foreground the situation-of-discourse as the represented situation".[22] Indeed, the dieictic strategies of a Keats increasingly blur the levels between the level of *story* (the spatial situation whose description is buttressed by the use of deixis) and the level of the *discourse* (the use of deixis to refer to the act of narration itself). Keats' poetry, notes Lachman, "undermine[s] mimesis by displacing the reader's interest from the event to its staging (and consequently to its perception and reconstruction)."[23] The poem itself becomes a 'shifter', much like the deictic markers whose emergent salience it evinces.

These changes in the uses of deixis may appear to be far removed from the culturally egocentric implementation of deixis in a colonial context. However, such shifts were intimately related to the changing socio-economic fabric of the metropolis, which in turn was always closely connected to the colonial economic system.[24] It can plausibly be suggested that the intensified use of deixis to mark an imagined spatial framework of enunciation was a compensatory strategy betraying the way in which nature receded from everyday human existence in the wake of industrialization. Raymond Williams remarks that

> one of the decisive transformations, in the relations between country and city, occurred [in the English context] very early and with a thoroughness which is still in some ways unapproached. The Industrial Revolution not only transformed both city and country; it was based upon a highly developed agrarian capitalism, with a very early disappearance of the traditional peasantry.[25]

As urban and agricultural industrialization increasingly encroached upon rural contexts, propelling the rural exodus and contributing to an expanding urban industrial proletariat, nature emerged as a reified literary object. Literary nature did not reflect real nature so much as index something which had to be signified in language because it was increasingly inaccessible. At an earlier period when nature as a part of everyday experience was ubiquitous, it had remained unmarked. 'Real' nature did not need to be described, because it was all-pervasive. However, as nature became increasingly marginalized by growing industrial and technological influences upon everyday life, it needed more and more to be rescued by the literary imagination.

Dorothy Wordsworth's odd turn of phrase "nature (though we mark her not)" in the poem 'Floating Island' neatly summarizes within a poetical artefact the 'production' of nature in the wake of the Industrial

Revolution.[26] The awkward phrasing expresses humans' inattention to nature in such a manner as to underline that inattention and make it the object of attention. By the same token, inattention is bracketed off in the same way that it tends to bracket off nature. This apparently trivial parenthesis thus enacts the very boundary which has to be "marked" to make "nature" a visible cultural entity. The brackets perform the retreat of nature caused by industrialization, the very pre-condition of the spurious 'naturalness' of 'Nature'. The parenthetical "(though we mark her not)" thus enacts the forgetting of the loss of nature which generates Nature so as to remind us of that loss. In line with this paradoxical development, the post-Romantic prevalence of spatial deixis (another form of spatial "marking") could be seen as one further index of the receding presence of an erstwhile natural environment.

Bruhn also stresses that the prevalence of deixis as elements of imaginary spatial schemata is an index of the increasing isolation of the reader. In the absence of a common context of enunciation, an "utterance ... delivered at increasing removes from the hearer's/reader's immediate perceptual field ... becomes more and more difficult to construe, and the question, *'What ...'* is cognitively reframed ... as the more primitive question *'Where?'* ".[27] The isolation of the individual under capitalism appears to have accelerated the usage of spatial deixis. Capitalism constructed the subject as a monad within a competitive market. The subject was driven less by the community ethos of a traditional society and its collective bonds than by the fragmenting, reifying urge to accumulate wealth, or simply by the self-interested pursuit of bare economic and material survival. Romanticism foregrounded individual aesthetic consciousness as a redemptive alternative to capitalism's gross materialist pragmatism. By virtue of its choice of the individual as the site of redemption, however, this strategy was entirely a product of the very tendency it attempted to combat. The imaginary deixis of the Romantic poem reinforced that individualism by folding the described situation (the poetic *story*) back into a self-reflexive situation of narration (the poetic *discourse*). The self-reflexive loop performed by the detached, imaginary deixis of Romanticism thus founded a contestatory individualism that in no way questioned the subjective premises of individualizing capitalism.

The contribution of industrial capitalism to individual, egocentred deixis translates chiastically into the contribution of individual, egocentred deixis to the colonial economy as the motor of global capitalism. The translation is underpinned by material relations of economic transfer: the metropolitan industrial economy was intimately linked into the colonial raw-materials economies of sugar, tea, coffee, wool and cotton. The Atlantic triangle of trade, which carried slaves from Africa to the Caribbean and the Americas, raw products from the Americas to Britain, and finished commodities back to the colonies, linked Europe and the non-European world in an emerging global economy. The credit systems which buttressed the Atlantic triangle and buffered its liquidity fluctuations further increased the profit margins and reached right into the heart of the metropolis and its domestic economy.[28] The rising prevalence of deixis as a symptom of the increasing dislocation of space in the metropolis went hand in hand with the crucial role of egocentric deixis in the colonial context as a template for the subjective modality of off-shore capitalism, that is, colonialism.

Such connections are evinced in a poem such as Keats's 'On First Looking into Chapman's Homer'.[29] The poetic speaker feels "Like stout Cortez when with eagle eyes | He star'd at the Pacific – and all his men | Look'd at each other with a wild surmise – | Silent, upon a peak in Darien" (lines 11–14). This poem connects 'real' acts of reading with 'imagined' exploits of conquest. It creates an analogy between the act of "looking into" a literary classic, the imaginary realms it opens up, and the masterful colonial gaze (the view afforded from a peak in the region of Darién, today's East Panama) exactly replicating that of Dunbar's *Prospect*. Reading is shown here to provide an imaginative protocol for the manner in which the colonial subject inserts himself into the dominated colonial landscape.

The imaginative act of reading is coeval with an imaginative act of seeing, which projects a future profitability on the landscape: "the eye scanning prospects in the spatial sense knows itself to be looking at prospects in the temporal sense – possibilities of a Eurocolonial future coded as resources to be developed, surpluses to be traded, towns to be built."[30] In this way, Keats enacts the manner in which literary diction creates the founding conditions for a mindset of territorial possession: "Oft of one wide expanse had I been told | That deep-brow'd Homer ruled as his demesne" (lines 5–6). Patently, Homer does not really rule the Mediterranean. However, he does provide an explicitly literary analogy with the help of which future imperial rulers can articulate their more tangible oceanic hegemony while occluding their status as hegemons.

The poem labours to prevent the real business of colonial conquest from contaminating its imaginary evocation. This is the condition of possibility, paradoxically, for the literary template functioning as the bearer of the colonial mentality. Against the background of analogies between a reading subject ("I heard Chapman speak out loud and bold", line 8) and the imperial gaze ("Then I felt like some watcher", line 9), the poem carefully relegates financial gain and exploratory, conquering gaze to its respective inaugural and concluding lines. Only the opening line alludes, in displaced form, to the metropolitan demand for bullion: "Much have I travell'd in the realms of gold" (line 1). Such allusions are only permissible because they are removed as far as possible within the sonnet's limited dimensions from the person of gold-greedy Cortez.

In a sense the poem itself is, in its own words, "Silent upon" the motivation for its concluding spatial reference, "a peak in Darien" (line 14). The speaker-centred enunciation of this poem accompanies the construction of a Eurocentric spatial system. That system, in turn, masks the normalization of the commanding view of non-European space under the guise of aesthetic experience. Keats's poem models the establishment of the poetic "I" and its spatial situation as the normative epistemological apparatus necessary for the more material processes of colonial exploitation.

Astride the colonial cannon

Let us cast a brief glance at one more instance of this marking of the European cultural "origo" in its colonial manifestation. The opening passage of Kipling's *Kim* (1901) presents a vignette of this mode of hege-monic force:

> [Kim] sat ... astride the gun Zam-Zammah on her brick platform outside the old Ajaib-Gher – the Wonder-House, as the natives call the Lahore Museum. Who hold Zam-Zammanh, that 'fire-breathing dragon', hold the Punjab, for the great green-bronze piece is always first of the conqueror's loot.
>
> There was some justification for Kim – he had kicked Lala Dinannath's boy off the trunnions – since the English held the Punjab and Kim was English.[31]

The cannon stands in front of the museum in Lahore. It is reduced to a mere metonymy of erstwhile panoramic military-economic command. Its brick platform gestures rather lamely to a prior emplacement, per-haps a fortress or another position with a favourable arc of fire. This weapon no longer serves its direct purpose in warfare, but has been relegated to the symbolic status of exhibit or curio. It points towards culture as the continuation of warfare by other means.

This de-militarization notwithstanding, Kim's boyish – but mani-festly phallic – possession of the artillery piece is none the less derived from his status as "A Sahib and a son of a Sahib" (*Kim* 139). The merely symbolic role now devolved to the cannon in the maintenance of colonial hegemony is not inappropriate to Kim's ambivalent position within the colonial apparatus. He is halfway between childhood and adulthood, between native and European culture. He can never under-stand his part in the Great Game from outside, as it were, but remains embedded within the everyday fabric of events. Only the lama attains a global view of his place in the grander scheme of things (*Kim* 337), and that view is couched in the language of mysticism rather than the language of colonial geo-politics. The displaced position of the cannon therefore fully corresponds to Kim's own position within the colonial system. He is an actor in its machinations, but one invested with only limited knowledge of his place. Only the text's overriding extradiegetic narratorial instance can offer access at a higher level than that of the individual character's circumscribed experience.

To that extent, Kim himself embodies the masking of the colonial order, while by the same token, the disembodied extradiegetic narrator fills the position of silently active egocentric deixis. As Said observes, Kipling "is writing not just from the dominating viewpoint of a white man in a colonial possession, but from the perspective of a massive colonial system whose economy, functioning and history had acquired the status of a virtual fact of nature."[32] What Said calls "the dominating viewpoint of a white man in a colonial possession" and "the perspective of a massive colonial system" are the concrete concomitants of egocen-tric deixis as an underlying textual principle.

In a sense, Kipling's cannon, shifting from one master to another, from one site to another, but finally guaranteeing spatial command via the apparently anodine workings of 'culture', provides a neat allegory of speaker-centred colonial deixis itself. The cannon is akin to a deictic 'shifter', being implemented in many different contexts. It provides a site for the speaking subject to position himself at the nexus between dis-course and the situation of enunciation. In the very relationships which are intrinsically configured by this mode of deictic activity, colonial superiority is reiterated and reinforced with every successive speech act.

However, Ondaatje, in *The English Patient*, has Hana, in one of her sporadic marginal scribblings in tomes from the library, register an objection: "She pulls down the copy of *Kim* from the library shelf and, standing against the piano, begins to write into the flyleaf in its last pages: *He says the gun – the Zam-Zammah cannon is still there outside the museum in Lahore. There were* two *guns ... The other gun was lost during a battle crossing in the Chenab River"* (*English Patient* 118). What of the other cannon? Can it somehow be retrieved? It is time now to shift our gaze to the other side of the colonial divide, out of reach of the colonial arc of fire indexed by the showcased cannon. Let us now attend to alternative perspectives beyond the limiting purview of the colonial gaze.

The other side

These "origo"-based literary panoramas or their displaced avatars make possible the extra-literary workings of a deictic activity which rendered possible and reflected the mentality of colonization. Yet they would be vociferously contested from the outset. In his classic *Cahier d'un retour au pays natal* [*Return to My Native Land*] (1956), the great poet of *negritude* Aimé Césaire explicitly rejected the panoramic view of Western industrial superiority: "I heard rising from the other side of disaster a river of turtle-doves and savanna clovers which I carry deep inside myself, at inverse depth to the twentieth storey of the most insolent buildings" ["j'entendais monter de l'autre côté du désastre, un fleuve de tourterelles et de trèfles de savane que je porte toujours dans mes profondeurs à hauteur inverse du vingtième étage des maisons les plus insolentes"].[33] The disaster to which Césaire refers is the disaster of colonization, an event explicitly spatialized here so as to redeem its oppressive singularity and inevitability. That event was indeed a spatial disaster, encompassing the deportations of slavery and the destruction of indigenous economies and their environmental basis. But it is also a disaster of narrative, one that must be rectified, at least in part, in narrative. Those corrective narratives offer points of view directly opposed to the panoramic views from the skyscrapers of the West.

Not dissimilarly, Jean Rhys has a character in her *Wide Sargasso Sea* (1962) enjoin the protagonist to "listen to the other side".[34] "The other side" is a topos of anti-colonial thought which questions the exclusive validity of the European origin and its deictic activity. In opposition to that singular, all encompassing view, it demands a multiplicity of stories documenting the elided sectors of the panoramic landscape: the experiences of indigenous peoples (as in Henry Reynolds's path-breaking *The Other Side of the Frontier*),[35] the lives of slaves on the plantations. Thus Edouard Glissant proposes a corrective to the exclusive European "origo" by allowing "The implosion of ... the converging histories of our peoples [which] relieves us of the linear, hierarchical vision of a single History that would run its unique course" ["L'irruption à elle-même de l'histoire ... de nos peuples, convergentes [qui] nous débarrasse de la vision linéaire et hiérarchisée d'une Histoire qui courrait son fil"].[36] Far from being a place of "non-history" and "non-story" waiting in its pristine, virginal emptiness to be inscribed by the deictic activity of the West, the non-European world is a place in its own right whose agency never ceases to resist the incursions of the invaders.

There is not a single space of European activity (Keats's "one wide expanse") ruled by a single European "origo", now situated in the metropolitan centre, now surveying the colonial periphery from peaks and outposts. Rather, there are many heterogenous, overlapping spaces each with its own narrative and mode of deixis. Foucault once observed, in a conversation with a Japanese interviewer, that "European space is not space in its entirety ... we experience space in a series of polymorphous spaces ... there is not a single history ... there are several histories, several durations, several speeds, tangled up with each other" ["l'espace européen n'est pas l'espace dans son entier ... on vit dans une série d'espaces polymorphes ... il n'y a pas qu'une seule histoire ... il y en a plusieurs, plusieurs temps, plusieurs durées, plusieurs vitesses, qui s'enchevêtrent les unes avec les autres"]. He then went on to define the very notion of the event in such a way as to deconstruct chronological, linear dating: "An event is not a segment of time, in reality it is an intersection of two durations, two evolutions, two lines of history" ["Un événement, ce n'est pas un segment de temps, c'est au fond l'intersection entre eux durées, deux vitesses, deux évolutions, deux lignes d'histoire"].[37]

This notion of plural and often incommensurable histories rupturing the spurious singularity of Western linear history is commonly performed in postcolonial writing. Arundhati Roy's *The God of Small Things* (1997) explicitly addresses this issue by opening with an epigraph taken from John Berger: "Never again will a single story be told as if it's the only one."[38] In Roy's novel, "History" is a malevolent force of indigenous, native tradition – the caste system with its repressive sanctions – which survives within postcolonial modernity. History, capitalized by Roy, does not merely run counter to the Western history of emancipation invoked, for instance, by Marxism (and indexed loosely by the Marxist Naxalite activists who people the novel – *The God of Small Things* 64–9). It is intertwined with that same history and infiltrates it, with the various characters appealing to these differing modes of history for their own purposes. These multiple strands of history are condensed only in a single site, that of the History House. It was once the residence of a Sahib who went native, thereby overturning the European narrative of the white man's burden; later it is the place where Amma's paravan (untouchable) lover Velutha is beaten comatose by the police who take on the role of the punishing his caste transgression; subsequently it becomes part of an elaborate "heritage" hotel and resort for foreign tourists (*The God of Small Things* 52–3, 304–12, 126). "History" is thus, turn by turn, the unstable narrative of Western civilization in its ostensibly ineluctable penetration to the four corners of the globe, the oppressive force of native tradition which can only be maintained by co-opted state coercion, and neocolonial history-kitsch offered on a global tourism market. The History House captures and stores each of these modes of historical logic, sedimenting them successively within its own spatialized historicity.

The pluralization and spatialization of history is likewise instantiated in Saleem Sinai, the narrator of Rushdie's *Midnight's Children* (1981). He begins his tale by observing, "there are so many stories to tell; too many, such an excess of intertwined lives events miracles places rumours ... I have been a swallower of lives; and to know me, just the one of me, you'll have to swallow the lot as well. Consumed multitudes are jostling and shoving inside me."[39] This process reaches its logical conclusion in Rushdie's fiction when Saleem, the pathetic and parodic Subject of the Story, a literary concomitant of the Subject of History increasingly problematized in postwar European societies,[40] is assimilated into the postcolonial collective actor of the emergent non-Western nation. Saleem is swallowed up by the "the crowd without boundaries", becoming "a broken creature spilling pieces of itself into the street, because I have been so-many too-many persons, life unlike syntax allows one more than three ... it is the privilege and the curse of midnight's children ... to forsake privacy and be sucked into the annihilating whirlpool of the multitudes" (*Midnight's Children* 462, 463). Rushdie's novel creates a bewildering collage in which various versions of history butt up against one another: Western-influenced narratives in the political mode of progressivist linear emancipation and esoteric religious narratives barely accessible to a European reader (*Midnight's Children* 194). Here Rushdie the literary artist performs the expansion of the linear historical sequence, described in theoretical terms by Foucault, in which "the relationships between different series" ["les rapports entre différentes series"] are supplemented by other sequences "so as thus to constitute series of series, or 'tables' " ["pour constituer ainsi des séries des series, ou des 'tableaux' "].[41]

In the following chapters, however, we will see that the "excess of intertwined lives events ... places" (*Midnight's Children* 9) mobilized by Rushdie as an onslaught upon European egocentric deixis only becomes predominant in postcolonial literary production after a series of false starts. In the immediate post-independence period, the mode of writing which foregrounds egocentric deixis is appropriated by postcolonial writers without its fundamental mode of representation being contested. What results is a Trojan horse which from the outset smuggles imperial space into the postcolonial compound.

7
Self-reflexive Deixis and the Aporias of the Nation

Sometime around 1948, J. E. Clare McFarlane, minister of finance in Jamaica, wrote a poem entitled 'On National Vanity'. Neither the poet nor the poem are well known. But McFarlane's rather stilted verse deserves attention for it accurately gives a measure of its time. The poem presciently launches a critique of the nation-building gathering momentum across the erstwhile imperial and colonial world.

> Slowly we learn; the oft repeated line
> Lingers a little moment and is gone;
> Nation on nation follows, sun on sun.[1]

McFarlane's poem opens by addressing the aporetic nature of repetition. Paradoxically, as he seems to point out, repetition does not ensure perpetuity. Repetition is essentially backward-looking, it moves forward sluggishly ("lingers") but eschews innovation and therefore contradicts the very notion of futurity. Repeating the national pattern handed down from the colonial mother country to the newly independent scions, McFarlane intimates, merely inaugurates a succession of shortlived and unstable avatars of the nation.

The present chapter suggests that one of the reasons for the debacle of post-independence nationalisms was that they were built upon the same deictic ground as that of colonial deixis. The transfer of the imperial "origo" from the European metropolis to the newly independent nations was problematic because it neglected to transform the "origo" structure of deixis itself. The ill-omened repetition of metropolitan deixis in the erstwhile colonies is explored in readings of Achebe's *Things Fall Apart* (1958) and Ngũgĩ wa Thiong'o's *A Grain of Wheat* (1967/1986). In the latter novel, however, an intimation that the self-reflexive national mode of deixis may be plagued by insoluble problems is already in evidence.

"The oft repeated line"

The opening of McFarlane's poem bears reiteration. It commences upon a clearly pedagogical tenor:

> Slowly we learn; the oft repeated line
> Lingers a little moment and is gone;
> Nation on nation follows, sun on sun.

Bhabha has coined the term of "nationalist pedagogy" to describe the role of rhetoric in inculcating the notion of the nation in the hearts and minds of its citizens.[2] McFarlanes's poem is aware of such pedagogy, probably in quite pedestrian manifestations, and deliberately intervenes with its own less docile didactic intention.

The poem ostentatiously foregrounds the "oft repeated line". The rote-learning of hundreds of lines of Latin (and Greek) poetry formed the stock pedagogical method of Britain's elite educational system in the nineteenth and twentieth centuries. Rote-learning was the standard fare of the public school education from which a sizeable proportion of Britain's elite went to a career in the colonial civil service.[3] The poetry of the Roman Empire, internalized via repetition, furnished the rhetoric of the latter-day British *imperium*.

By focusing upon "the oft repeated line", the poem goes to the heart of the rhetoric of empire. It immediately highlights the manner in which language marks the ground upon which empire is built. Symbolic linguistic and rhetorical practices regulate the material practices of geographical mastery. But the line of poetry, whether in the rhetoric of empire imbibed by its administrators, or, self-reflexively, in the sceptical anti-imperial stance of the poem itself, is flimsy. It works by repetition, and only by repetition. McFarlane's poem evinces a non-theoretical but no less effective awareness of the performative aspect of language. In its focus upon the "oft repeated line" it displays a remarkable sensitivity to the role of iteration in the generation of ideology and its sheen of naturalness. The "petrifying mound" of the nation, its apparent rock-solidity, is merely the result of discursive sedimentation: "a set of repeated acts within a highly rigid regulatory frame that congeal over time to produce an appearance of substance, a natural sort of being".[4] That sedimentation can equally easily be eroded, the poem shows, by any competing discourse mouthing the same platitudes: "Last come, shall mount our withered vanities, | Topmost to sit".

The "oft repeated line" in question, however, may denote more than the rhetorical line of poetry and by extension of imperial discourse in general. It may equally denote the lines by which the borders of nations are fixed upon maps. Such lines were patently contingent: in the colonial context, they often ran at loggerheads to natural contours or indigenous community demarcations. Yet their contingency became fact by virtue of the colonial power which, buttressed by military force, could impose and maintain them on the ground. One index of the potency of that symbolic and material power was that the borders of the erstwhile colonies, forged in the process of imperial conquest, frequently furnished templates for the post-independence nations.

The post-independence nations were fraught constructs, shackled by a number of burdens inherited from the colonial era. Basil Davidson has enumerated some of these inauspicious legacies, beginning with "the territorial awkwardness of the state formed by colonial partition and 'transferred' to African hands". Another factor was "the contradiction between continued state dictatorship and the expectations of state democracy". Finally, there was "the contradiction between the interests of the few and the interests of the many: in general terms, between the city and the countryside". These combined factors resulted in the "destruction of the accountability of the state upon which the nation was supposedly built", at the latest by the 1980s, though the nation's credibility was undergoing a process of erosion long before.[5]

Frantz Fanon, for instance, writing at the beginning of the 1960s, was still committed to national consciousness as "the all-embracing crystallization of the innermost hopes of the whole people ... the immediate and most obvious result of the mobilization of the people" ["la cristallisation coordonée des aspirations les plus intimes de l'ensemble du peuple ... le produit immédiat le plus palpable de la mobilisation populaire"]. But his formulations were embedded in sentences warning that the national spirit might become "an empty shell, a crude and fragile travesty" ["une forme sans contenu, fragile, grossière"]. Already, Fanon predicted a situation in which "the nation is passed over for the race, and the tribe is preferred to the state. These are the cracks in the edifice which show the process of retrogression that is so harmful to national effort and national unity" ["on passe de la nation à l'ethnie, de l'état au tribu. Ce sont ces lézardes qui rendent compte des retours en arrière, si penibles et si préjuciables à l'essor national, à l'unité nationale"].[6] Fanon's polemic was largely directed at a postcolonial middle-class elite which continued to identify with metropolitan culture and sought its own material betterment at the cost of the rural masses. The increasing gap between the urban elite and the peasant masses whose standard of living often remained unchanged after independence created major rifts in the putative unity of national liberation projects.[7] Fanon concluded, "The moment for a fresh national crisis is not far off" ["L'heure d'une nouvelle crise nationale n'est pas loin"].[8] A quarter of a century later, Fanon's predictions remain forceful: "the African state ... exists ... for itself and for the bourgeoise which has taken control of it. The people are elsewhere and define themselves by a sub-or trans-state identity."[9]

The predicament of the post-independence nation was a spatial one. Its contours were the result of imperial divisions dictated from Europe, creating ethnic conflicts which in some cases the colonial powers had deliberately exacerbated; at the same time, these nations were the geographical and political receptacles for economies which were were too small as units of economic organization to compete with the rapidly emerging system of transnational neocolonialism with its global reach.[10] That system had existed in incipient form from the earliest days of colonization; decolonization was part of the process by which the global system of colonial exchange was overhauled by more efficient transnational economic networks.[11] Thus, from the colonial moment onwards, as Stuart Hall has pointed out, national "power relations were *always* displaced and decentred by another set of vectors – the transverse linkages between and across nation-state frontiers and the *global/local* inter-relationships which cannot be read off against a nation-state template."[12]

Neil Lazarus has rightly observed that by and large, postcolonial theorists have tended to deal with nationalism via

> a culturalist emphasis on nationalism[s] as *a mode of representation* ... to the extent they tend to involve the attempt to secure consent for their claims to representativeness. ... All nationalisms are therefore appropriative, since they all claim unisonance, and since these claims necessarily involve speaking for – and therefore silencing – others.[13]

Bhabha, the foremost representative of this line of thought, typically privileges "the *vox populi*: to a relatively unspoken tradition of the people of the pagus – colonials, postcolonials, migrants, minorities – wandering peoples who will not be contained within the *Heim* of the national culture and its unisonant discourse, but are themselves the marks of a shifting boundary that alienates the frontiers of the modern nation."[14] Material and spatial factors, albeit notionally acknowledged, are subsumed here to voice, discourse and psychoanalytic thematics indexed by the lexeme *Heim*. Much postcolonial critique of national discourse, fixated upon representation and its discontents, has thus neglected other pressing matters such as the material (and thus spatial) fabric of the national construct.[15]

These critiques notwithstanding, even if the aporia of postcolonial nations were never exclusively a question of representation, they were at least in part a matter symbolic claims and counterclaims. It is certainly manifestly apparent, for instance, that from the 1960s onwards, many African writers were less and less committed to the nation as a symbolic platform for African emancipatory aspirations.[16]

In this respect, McFarlane's poem is remarkably prescient. At the very moment of incipient postcolonial national independence, the fatal iteration of national rhetoric is dissected and targeted as an inflexible and flawed model of independence:

> in our pride
> We strain towards the petrifying mound
> To sit above our fellows, and we ride
> The slow and luckless toiler to the ground.

The clumsy national edifice is imagined as a beast of burden collapsing under the weight of its isolating, reifying, pre-independence ballast.

The educative task the poem undertakes is significant for its historical context, that of the great wave of decolonization following in the wake of World War II. The poem consciously refers to the demise of empire as a world-historical, indeed almost cosmic process: "With empire's dust fate builds her great design". However, that moment of decolonization, paradoxically, was a moment in which the divisive heritage of colonization was adopted by the newly-independent nations in the very form of their nationhood:

> But we are blind and see not; in our pride
> We strain towards the petrifying mound
> To sit above our fellows.

The substantive "mound" is quickly overhauled by the verbal "mount":

> Fools we are for our pains; whom we despise,
> Last come, shall mount our withered vanities,
> Topmost to sit upon the vast decay
> Of time and temporal things.

The apparent solidity of the noun "mount" is revealed as merely the ephemeral result of a process. The "vast decay | Of time and temporal things" lays bare the real character of spatial entities such as the nation. The nation is a time-bound entity. Much and all as national rhetoric attempts to construct a long and noble tradition, the nation remains something which is made – and potentially unmade.

The "ground" figures here only as a marker of destruction ("we ride | The slow and luckless toiler to the ground"). It is that place where the living body of the community is destroyed by the form imposed upon it, that of the imperialist legacy of nationhood. Yet the "ground" may also signify something which pre-dates both the colonial carving-up of space and the post-independence perpetuation of that slice of land. "Ground" may subsist beneath and beyond the fraught structures of nationhood, re-emerging in their demise as an alternative paradigm for postcolonial community. This chapter investigates the dialectical tension between a negation of postcolonial nationhood and the shadowy re-appearance of something more fundamental which has never been quite erased by the nation: ground.

National narratives and self-referencing space

How is that ground manifest, if only in residual form, in post-independence literature? A brief glance at the final chapter of Achebe's classic *Things Fall Apart* (1958) may elucidate the difficulties this mode of writing encountered in its task of national self-definition, and the ambivalent place it assigned to indigenous space. Achebe's novel famously concludes with the District Commissioner ruminating on the significance of the events he has witnessed in the broader context of the colonization of West Africa. What the reader has encountered as a novel-length narrative is reduced to a chapter, no, to a paragraph, in an imperialist chronical:

> The Commissioner went away. ... As he walked back to the court he thought about that book. Every day brought him some new material. The story of this man who had killed a messenger and hanged himself would make interesting reading. One could almost write a whole chapter on him. Perhaps not a whole chapter but a reasonable paragraph, at any rate. There was so much else to include, and one must be firm in cutting out details. He had already chosen the title of the book, after much thought: *The Pacification of the Primitive Tribes of the Lower Niger.*[17]

Achebe's novel reverses the sequence of imperial temporality. It restores the hidden narrative suppressed by the self-celebratory narrative of conquest or "pacification" which concludes the novel. It re-establishes the pre-history of colonialism as a story in its own right. Prior to the civilization marked, for instance, by Westminster legal procedure and localized in the court, there are other equally sophisticated structures of indigenous civil society which the novel portrays. Yet such a fictional project is hampered by a number of factors.

Achebe's final chapter seals the demise of autonomous indigenous society. Even though he makes indigenous civilization sequentially prior to colonization, the culminating point of the novel and its teleologically determining moment is that of defeat. Despite Achebe's effort to award indigenous history the lion's share of his narrative energy, it is none the less imperialism's narrative elimination of that history which literally has the final word.

Achebe's project came soon after release from a colonial yoke which nonetheless, in 1958, appeared to still be firmly in place, albeit in virtual form. Achebe's fictional restoration of pre-colonization society to narrative visibility is bound to colonization and is caught in an oppositional deadlock with colonization. The same must be said of the concluding spatial marking of the novel. If Achebe's opening pages mention "the nine villages and beyond ... from Umuofia to Mbaino", these too are finally subsumed into the English appellation of "the Lower Niger" (*Things Fall Apart* 3, 148). Achebe's modern, post-independence Nigerian national identity attempts to appeal to indigenous spatialities, indexed via specific place names. However, the ultimate defining framework within which that national identity is constructed is that of colonial geographical discourse, in turn perpetuated in the name of the new nation. The post-independence nation foregrounds indigenous culture, eschewing European derivation, as does Achebe's act of setting local place-names in the very first lines of the text. Yet the national project which fosters such self-definition appears to owe its very existence to an enduring colonial discourse of territorial conquest.

The nationalist phase of post-independence spatial triumphalism built upon the necessary unity of the liberation movements, celebrating the purported unanimity of the emergent nation. This phase hypostatized a national indigenous space, ironically forgetting that this self-same space had been defined, in many cases, in the moment of colonization. That putatively indigenous space was therefore in many ways as dislocated from the spatial realities of everyday life as colonialism had been: "the new rulers were themselves Africans ... But there was a great gulf between them and the mass of ordinary men and women in the villages and in their fields, for whom life went on much as it had before, except that the District Commissioner now had a black face."[18]

The post-independence moment can be seen as being characterized by a broadly dominant mode of deictic action. During the first wave of post-independence self-definition, the new nations took themselves, and not Europe, as the measure of self-definition. This self-reflexive mode of deictic action, though no longer grounded in an external norm (Europe), none the less remained inherently egocentric, albeit under the aegis of what one might term 'afrocentrism' (otherwise conceptualized as 'negritude'). Mbembe has acerbically characterized this attitude as the assumption that "the African [or colonial subject in general] possesses a self-referring structure that makes him or her close to 'being human'."[19] Paradoxically, these self-reflexive deictic actions were grounded in a self-confidence which was inherently oppositional, but by the same token deeply indebted to the very colonial structures it eschewed.

This mode of deictic action can be seen to be modelled in a particularly prominent manner in literary texts belonging to this historical context. Following the colonial mode of standard deixis, I suggest that the post-independence era ushered in a mode of self-reflexive deixis evinced in a specific form of literary textuality. That literary mode is one which Joseph Frank subsumed to the concept of "spatial form", which "in its simplest sense designates the technique by which novelists subvert the chronological sequence inherent in narrative".[20] In spatial form, Frank explains, "the customary order of combination [linear syntax] is overlaid by an order based on 'equivalence' – that is, by a 'space-logic' which runs counter to the linear temporality of syntactical structure."[21] This "space logic" does not genuinely break free of temporality, for it merely reverses the traditional time–space hierarchy to make "time an aspect of space".[22]

Such "space-logic" may be taken as an analogy for the deep structure of post-independence writing. "Space-logic" is defined exclusively by its resistance to linearity. If linear narrative tends to be referential (that is, oriented towards the context) in its functioning, the subversion of linearity results in an intensification of self-referentiality (that is, oriented towards the text itself). This merely reactive, self-referential spatiality furnishes a structural analogy with the self-referential privileging of indigenous cultural space over against the erstwhile dominance of teleologies of European modernity derived from the colonial metropolis. Such a spatiality, however, is impoverished by its reactive structure. It cannot do justice to the positive complexity of indigenous spatial experience because the very terms of its opposition are dictated by the distorting influence of that which it strives to dislodge.

I am not suggesting that the post-independence literatures were highly self-referential in their manifest textual form. Achebe's novel makes only two very cursory gestures at metatextuality. First, its title is drawn from Yeat's apocalyptic poem 'The Second Coming', ironically pointing up colonial expansion as the nemesis of and not the transmitter of civilization it claimed to be.[23] Secondly, the novel concludes with a book-within-the-book, encompassing within its own storytelling the discourse of colonialism just as the discourse of colonialism had long enclosed native discourse. These are its sole concessions to anti-naturalist metatextuality. The "spatial form" of post-independence fiction lies not so much in its stylistic features, as in its inherently oppositional (but ultimately reiterative) stance.

The "spatial form" of post-independence literatures resided in a rejection of the imposed hierarchies of 'modernizing' imperialism and a re-assertion of cultural content emergent out of the post-independence national space itself. The cultural self-reflexivity of post-independence writing is to be found primarily at the level of its content (a shift of perspective to that of indigenous narrators, the prevalence of nativist motifs, and so forth), and is paradoxically countermanded by its realist tenor. "It was the same order of things that had led to disorder in the first place", Nadine Gordimer acerbically comments on a British military intervention in her imaginary post-independence Africa as it subsides into civil war.[24] Yet her comment might equally apply to the very form, realist and stylistically settled, in which her novel about the aporias of independence is couched. Conversely, it might plausibly be suggested that its self-determining indigenous content is a reaction to a cultural hegemony whose residual manifestation continued to be the form from which it could not yet escape, that of realism. In the same way, post-independence self-definition was a reaction within a broader political form, that of the nation, itself in turn a residual effect of colonial expansion. The 'form' of the nation was manifest in the territorial borders inherited from the imperial powers' division of the conquered territories, and in the political and institutional structures left behind by the colonial administrations.

The clasp that locks the fictional form to the political superstructure is the ascendant hegemony of the realist novel in the high age of European national self-definition. The novel, as "the only symbolic form that could represent [the nation-state]", constituted a form of "national allegory".[25] The naturalist novel was the form given by the European nineteenth-century – the very period which had shaped the colonial world by a process of military occupation and economic exploitation. The premises of the naturalist novel (objective knowledge of an empirically measurable world surveyed from the vantage point of a heterodiegetic narrator) were not dissimilar to the premises which governed imperial aspirations to global control, underpinned by confidence in an extensive and sophisticated machine for producing empirical knowledge of the Orient.

The spatial paradigm which was typical of that novel was one of objectivized "Faustian space".[26] George Eliot exemplified the heterodeigetic position of panoramic spatial control when she wrote that "our old-fashioned country life had many different aspects, as all life must have when it is spread over a various surface and breathed on variously by multitudinous currents, from the winds of heaven to the thoughts of men."[27] "Different aspects" are gathered up in the homogenizing medium of "all life – spread over a ... surface". This spatial paradigm acknowledged the multiplicity of space only to subsume it, as a unified domain, to the all-encompassing view of an external narrative instance. This space was unified because it was graspable by the narrator's knowledge. Kipling's observation that "the English held the Punjab" (*Kim* 49) is the devolved attribution of the novelist's own superior hold upon the imagined territory.

How much of this spatial scheme was questioned by the epistemology underpinning post-independence self-determination? The postcolonial nations defined themselves as non-European. They cast off the moorings of a European historical tradition ("nos ancêtres les Gaullois") and launched themselves into independent nationhood on the basis of a self-referential invocation of their own native traditions. This gesture of nation-building very much resembles the internal logic of "spatial form" in fiction. Yet, just as "spatial form" appeared to neglect the real complexity of lived space because it was conditional upon rescinding temporality, so the postcolonial nation, fixated upon casting off the trappings of the colonial machine, remained as distanced from the fabric of indigenous existence as the erstwhile colonial apparatus it replaced. The negative self-reflexivity of the nation, like the negative self-reflexivity of modernist "spatial form", could not endure. Both, in the course of time, would cede to a stronger sense of more complex modes of referentiality and spatial grounding.

Generic spaces, greedy residues

Yet did the national paradigm in the post-independence really remain at arm's length from the dynamics of lived space? A reading of Ngũgĩ wa Thiong'o's *A Grain of Wheat* (1967/1986) will show that this was not entirely the case. Rather, any text that confronted those complex dynamics of space, however strong its commitment to realist form and post-independence self-definition, inevitably began to reveal the aporias of the national paradigm.[28]

Ngũgĩ's novel is centrally concerned with the history of land: with appropriation by the British during the colonial period in the land-consolidation process, with confiscation during the Emergency, with questions of subsistence – and with the prospect of the return of land after Uhuru, independence. Ngũgĩ's novel intervenes in spatial history: "People started singing ... Again they recreated history, giving it life through the words and voices: land alienation, ... taxation, conscription of labour into the whiteman's land" (*A Grain of Wheat* 214). Even in this single anecdote, however, the novel indexes a tension within its own textual economy. The *discourse* of its narration of a historical period – the Emergency, the dawn of Uhuru – remains sober and factual. In contrast, the *story* references a collective oral mode of history which reworks historical event and interweaves it with music, song, and, patently, forms of communitarian libidinal energy. The text unwittingly points to the generic rifts which would later fracture the corpus of post-colonial African literature.

The realist mode in which the novel is framed, making it one of the classics of immediate post-independence naturalist literature, has been seen as a problem by later critics and writers. Appiah has famously commented upon the transition from postcolonial realist writing to post-colonial postmodernist fiction. This coincides, he claims, with a sense of disappointment regarding the results of decolonization.[29] The rejection of novelistic naturalism is the fictional correlative of the sober re-assessment of the achievements and failures of the post-independence nation as a basis for the transformation of the living conditions of its citizens.[30] Postcolonial novels written in a postmodern style sought to "delegitimize not only the form of realism but the content of nationalism".[31] But what does the realist novel as a generic paradigm have to do with geographical, territorial, spatial questions?

The post-independence nations in Africa inherited a set of administrative structures, an economic infrastructure and a geographical territory which were all the fruits of the colonial period. The nation was the political expression of a set of spatial and geographical assumptions at the heart of Western culture since the Enlightenment. In particular, the nation embodied a specifically modern "disenchantment of the world" ["Entzauberung der Welt"] and attendant "emptying of space".[32] The nation was the bearer of a mode of spatial organization in which nature lost its sanctity to become a utilitarian resource at the disposal of man. Indices of this nexus of control, rationalism, and "disenchantment" can be detected in Ngũgĩ's evocation of the dual arrival of colonialism and Christianity: "The few who were converted ... trod on sacred places to show that no harm could reach those protected by the hand of the Lord" (*A Grain of Wheat* 11). Like the external position of the hetero-deiegetic narrator and the reading position it creates in its wake, the colonial viewpoint and its territorial mode of operation set itself at great distance from the spatial fabric of the terrain.

Not only the narrative world structure of realism was thus clearly a Western construct. In addition, the narrative progression set within that framework, that of the European novel of education or maturation, reaching its peak in the *Bildungsroman*, lent itself ideally to the paradigm of Western adulthood as opposed to Oriental childishness.[33] The *Bildungsroman* was the fictive codification of a developmental teleology which informed the "white man's burden" or the *mission civilisatrice* legitimizing imperial expansion. Indeed, such narrative structures were conveyed as normative by the colonial school system. The centrality of the progressivist teleological paradigm of narrative was clearly maintained in the post-independence national paradigm, and would only be abandoned in the 1970s.

This model of development was at the centre of the realist post-independence novel. In Ngũgĩ's earlier *Weep Not, Child* (1964), the protagonist is "sustained by his love for, and belief in education and his own role when the time came". Njoroge is convinced that "[o]nly education could make something out of this wreckage. He became more faithful to his studies. He would one day use all his learning to fight the white man."[34] It is significant that the name of Njoroge is taken up by Vassanji in a later novel (to which we will turn shortly) to discredit the progressivist role of education, particularly in connection with the question of land and its restitution to the indigenous population.

The issue of land would also be recast, however, by the demise of realist writing, roughly about the same time as developmental models were being re-assessed as models for national growth in African nations. The spatial paradigm which corresponded to the developmental novel envisaged a progression from territory to nation. The development from territory to nation reposed upon a shift, in more abstract terms, from land as unmarked nature ("The largest half of Africa [is] one enormous blank" wrote Henry Morton Stanley in 1877[35]) to land as marked culture: "The unformedness of colonial space is the geographic metaphor of the savage mind; both consciousness and space form the childlike innocence which is the natural surface of imperial inscription."[36] The territory-to-nation paradigm ignored the prior markings of nature-as-always-already-culture, relegating the precolonial space to the realm of nature. By extension, it assumed that the contingent demarcations imposed by Western nations at summits such as the Berlin conference were indices of developmental maturation and as such could be maintained after independence as viable spatial frameworks for a post-independence inter-ethnic *socius*.

But the developmental paradigm of space was part and parcel of a colonial manipulation of indigenous societies, as indexed by the coupling of political repression and topoi of modernization. Significantly, the Kenyans detained during the Emergency find themselves enlisted in the service of development: "The detainees worked on a new irrigation scheme on the Mweya plains in Embu. They were converting the new plains into rice-growing fields" (*A Grain of Wheat* 240). This brief scenario exemplifies the manner in which a colonized people is harnessed for the utilitarian, developmentalist re-working of the space that had once been their own.

Ngũgĩ's *A Grain of Wheat* certainly inherits the empiricist paradigm of colonialism. Land has been taken away, land must be given back. The battle-cry "The soil belongs to Kenyan people" implicitly countermands a prior moment of expropriation (*A Grain of Wheat* 96). This symmetrical, binary formula simply replicates the agency of the colonial era within the counterpoised agency of the postcolonial era. In both cases the land is a rationalized given to be transferred to new or old owners. Only rarely is the land registered in the tenor of myth, allowing it to regain its own agency under the aura of sanctity.[37]

The problematic character of this empiricist paradigm of representation of land is registered in two ways. Both are significant because they will continue to echo in later postcolonial novels. The first problematic aspect of the empiricist paradigm is that it merely perpetuates the cycle of violence inaugurated with the original expropriation by the white settlers: "Surely enough blood had already been shed: why add more guilt to the land" (*A Grain of Wheat* 176). The second problematic aspect of the empiricist paradigm is that it may not achieve the results it aspires to. The novel harbours a sneaking suspicion, well-founded as it will later transpire, that perhaps land may not be returned to its rightful owners: "Would Uhuru bring the land back into African hands? And would that make a difference to the small man in the village?"; "The Party must never betray the Movement. The Party must never betray

Uhuru. It must never sell Kenya back to the Enemy. Tomorrow we shall ask: Where is the land?" (*A Grain of Wheat* 204, 217). This scepticism is already confirmed well before the end of the novel. Gikonyo's plans to buy up the land of a departing white settler, Burton, with some other farmers. However, the very post-independence local MP Gikonyo consults about a loan advises him to bide his time and pre-empts the bid, buying Burton's land himself (*A Grain of Wheat* 58–9, 61–2, 164).

The failure of the empiricist spatial paradigm underlying independence was widespread in East Africa. In Zimbabwe, Mamdami has written, it is not the transition to independence but rather the more recent dispossessions of white farmers from 2000 onwards that "the people ... are likely to remember ... as the end of the colonial era". Mugabe's dispossession of white farmers marked the first real rectification of a state of injustice left untouched by the transition to independence:

> Though widespread grievance over the theft of land – a process begun in 1889 and completed in the 1950s – fuelled the guerrilla struggle against the regime of Ian Smith, the matter was never properly addressed when Britain came back into the picture to effect a constitutional transition to independence under majority rule. Southern Rhodesia became Zimbabwe in 1980, but the social realities of the newly independent state remained embedded in an earlier historical period: some six thousand white farmers owned 15.5 million hectares of prime land, 39 per cent of the land in the country, while about 4.5 million farmers (a million households) in "communal areas" were left to subsist on 16.4 million hectares of the most arid land, to which they'd been removed or confined by colonial rule.[38]

The question, "Where is the land?" (*A Grain of Wheat* 217) is an interrogative deictic. It implicitly demands an answer containing the deictics 'here', 'there'. But in its interrogative form it registers the aporetic nature of a spatial deixis which posits the owner of land as the anchor of spatial reference. That anchoring of spatial language in the rhetoric of ownership ("Gikonyo's secret ambition was to own a piece of land where he could settle his mother" – *A Grain of Wheat* 73) betrays the legacy of an imperialist mode of spatial rationalism: "Very good timber. Why else do you think the white people appropriated that land to themselves?" (*A Grain of Wheat* 73). This spatial rationalism fundamentally orients the narrative and taints its very mode of narration even in an era which hopes to have put off the shackles of colonization.

In his classic founding text of *négritude*, Césaire dreamed of a form of spatial belonging which reposed upon "this most essential country, restored to my utmost greed" ["ce plus essentiel pays resitué à ma gourmandise"].[39] Césaire's rhetoric invokes a form of spatial belonging which has remained unchanged despite the ravages of colonialism and which can be rediscovered, intact ("restored", "resitué") once independence has cleared away the false façade of Western civilization. The self-reflexivity of the post-independence paradigm is indexed by the bodily tenor of "greed"/"gourmandise". It is the self-confidence of the new citizen which allows an autochthon gesture of naming without reference to the discarded European paradigm. Yet the strange undertone of greed somehow unsettles this narrative of recuperated spatial essentialism. To what extent does the essentialism upon which the rhetoric of restoration or restitution is predicated carry within it associated aporia? Essentialism, one suspects, merely drags in its wake a new avatar of imperial greed sanctioned by the self-celebrations of national independence. This notion is the burden of the fictions which will be read in the following chapter.

8
Critiques of National Narratives

A white settler woman in nineteenth-century colonial Victoria is ostensibly kidnapped by the natives of Gippsland. A group of self-appointed rescuers band together in a search-party and, fuelled by public moral outrage and the self-righteousness of racial superiority, set out to find the white woman's whereabouts. However, what the rescuers in Liam Davison's *The White Woman* (1994) actually discover is evidence of massacres perpetrated by the white settlers against the indigenous people. The white woman, whether she exists or not, gives the settlers a legitimizing pretext allowing them to push forward their expansion in the most brutal manner possible. The narrator of Davison's novel comments,

> I can see now why [the natives] didn't come straight out and deny they ever had her. It was us, you see? It was exactly what we wanted. And if they had her and were to give her up ... What then? I can see it now, for what it's worth ... our own stories came spinning back on us the way we'd always told them, as if they knew all along it was our own voices we wanted so much to hear.'[1]

The narratives of rescue have no purchase upon reality. They are merely tales told by a group of carbine-carrying colonial crusaders to convince themelves of their moral fortitude.

Such tales primarily foreground their own mode of placing themselves in an alien landscape, just as the belligerent settlers seize as much native land as they can take and hold with their superior firepower. This self-referential logic reaches its acme when the search-party, discarding the indigenous names of its native guides, baptizes them anew: "They answered to whatever you called: Jacky-Jacky, One-Eye, Bill-Boy,

Friday" (*White Woman* 94). The leader of the party even bestows his own name: "Yes, Mr DeVilliers. The conceit of the man, the untempered self-absorbtion – to replicate himself out there … Better than naming rivers or a mountain range … it was as if he'd brought himself into the world and could exercise his will twice over" (*White Woman* 95). This colonial narrative names neither the bush, nor the landscape, nor the natives. It merely denotes, albeit in masked manner, its own invasion project, a project which underwrites the founding of the colony, and in due course, of the nation which follows.[2]

This myopic and self-serving autoreflexivity is perhaps endemic to national rhetoric. The chapter analyses such self-reflexive deictic structures in two phases. It begins by defining the characteristics of self-reflexive deictics with reference to Davison's portrayal of a settler colony soon to attain national independence. Subsequently, it scrutinizes the consequences of such self-reflexive deixis, namely, the perpetuation of colonial structures beyond their political demise. The chapter instantiates the disturbing continuities between pre- and post-independence spatial regimes with reference to Fanon and Kourouma's *Les Soleils des independences* [*The Suns of the Independences*] (1970). A closing examination of Wicomb's *David's Story* (2000) and Vassanji's *The In-Between World of Vikram Lall* (2003) shows how these tragic continuities have contributed to the contemporary discrediting of national independence paradigms. Such narratives point the way however to an alternative form of spatial marking that we have baptized as deiXis.

Self-reflexive naming

The self-referential mode of linguistic engagement with the new country has been investigated at length by Paul Carter in his *Road to Botany Bay*.[3] Carter claims that the names given to features of the Australian landscape by the early colonial explorers were bound up in a logic of difference: Australia did not resemble what these transplanted Europeans expected to find. Thus typically Antipodean place-names such as "Mount Disappointment" (named thus because the explorers Hume and Hovell could not make out the sea, sixty kilometres away, from its peak when they climbed it in 1824) could index the explorer's sense of frustration at constantly deflated expectations of geography, flora, fauna.

Strictly speaking, such names did not describe the landscape itself. Rather, these appellations indexed the journey within whose monotony the physical object, or rather, its discovery, was an important punctuation mark. The place-name "faithfully preserved the traveller's sense of facts, not as discrete objects, but as horizons increasingly inscribed with spatial meanings, defined not in terms of objective qualities, but as directional pointers articulating and punctuating the explorer's destiny" (*Road to Botany Bay* 16). The place-name was not referential so much as systemic in its functioning: "What mattered was that the name described a conceptual place: whether it described a physical object was unimportant" (*Road to Botany Bay* 51). Place-names are self-referential, they annotate their own moment of naming, rather than the object they henceforth cling to. Carter states programmatically, "the charm of exploring lies not in discovery, but in the act of exploring" (*Road to Botany Bay* 81) – the same thing might be said of the charm of naming.

Carter constantly stresses the intentional nature of naming. To name is to set a place within a structure of experience which is oriented by the vector of travel: "In fact, phenomena enter the traveller's narrative only in so far as they align themselves with the direction of his desire" (*Road to Botany Bay* 77). This makes the process of Antipodean travel resolutely egocentric in its deictic functioning: "names preceded places. The spatial effect was to render 'yonder' central" (*Road to Botany Bay* 137), that is, to draw it into the orbit of the settler's self-centred world of experience. Carter praises this so-called "spatial history" enacted by settlers. This is hardly surprising, as the immigrant narrative the author explores models his own trajectory of expatriation and settlement.[4] Carter's book is also an auto-reflexive deictic act which references, more than anything else, its own self-positioning in an Antipodean landscape of intelligentsia and academia.

Yet Carter also acknowledges deep aporia informing this egocentricity. He notes, for instance, that the settlers' failure to incorporate Aboriginal names into their language "is one reason why English here continues to float, as it were, off the ground and why, despite its ability to name isolated objects, its poetic power to evoke the living space remains patchy" (*Road to Botany Bay* 136–7). This critique is not merely an observation about the geographical alienation experienced by the first settlers. In Carter's opinion, this malaise in the white settler poetics of place lingers on into the contemporary period. The current Australian nation remains caught up in what Carter calls "the lie of the land". The nation is founded upon a self-reflexive and thus non-referential mode of naming and experiencing, an alienated poetics which is removed from the ground: "we walk on the ground as we drive on the road; that is, we move over and above the ground. Many layers come between us and the granular earth ... We live in our places off the ground."[5]

This spatial alienation is evinced in the very strategies by which set-tlers ostensibly place themselves in the unfamiliar landscape. Carter exemplifies the linguistic positioning of the settler mentality by pro-viding a sample of paradigmatic spatial statements, one of them explic-itly deictic: "The tree is there", "That house is where I live". He claims that this pair, configured according to a "subject–predicate" structure, mobilizes "the creation of a place where meanings can accrue": "The predicate brings the I/here into being" (*Road to Botany Bay* 138). The proximal/distal relationships of this form of settler deixis are clearly egocentric. The bush is marginal in relationship to the house, the cen-tral icon of pioneer or settler identity. Curiously, the "here" which one would expect as a counterpart to the "there" is elided, apparently slid under the central term of the house. This elision would appear to cor-roborate Carter's theory of a "floating" geographical denotation. The settler's lack of connection to the occupied territory engenders a disem-bodied, dislocated deixis. There is a deep aporia at the heart of settler deixis, a mode of spatial marking which is self-reflexive in such a way as to elide its own destructive grounding. The argument of this chapter is that the self-reflexive deixis which underlies the settler mapping of place works to undermine the post-independence rhetoric of nationalist identity.

The instances of self-reflexive national deixis analysed here and in the previous chapter quite clearly belong to two quite distinct political contexts. The foundational gestures by which a settler nation legitimizes its own uneasy sense of guilt about its violent past need to be differenti-ated from the post-independence celebrations of nations newly liberated from their exploitation-colony status and drawing upon rejuvenated native traditions. Yet the nations which are thus called into existence, and the spatial contours which are thereby constituted, are similarly ungrounded. Both forms of national self-definition employ a rhetoric of place-naming endowed with similar structural features. Their deictic strategies are, essentially, self-reflexive, betraying in advance the aporia which will never cease to unsettle them.

Continuity of rupture

A central problem in the self-constitution of the post-independence nation is that it inherits the ungrounded deictic marking which was instituted under the colonial reign. The post-independence nation per-petuates, across the apparent caesura of independence, a problematic relationship to its own territorial ground which is essentially colonial.

Ashcroft, Griffiths and Tiffin comment rather sceptically that "the term 'colonial' has been used for the period before independence and a term indicating national writing, such as 'modern Canadian writing' or 'recent West Indian literature' has been employed to distinguish the period after independence."[6] In this version of literary history, "national writing" emerges against the background of a clear political rupture. Yet in spatial terms, it appears more accurate to say that it evinces a disturbing continuity with the colonial period – a continuity which merely preserves a more fundamental rupture, namely, between the body politic and its rhetoric of (national) naming, and the body of the land.

It is instructive, in this respect, to compare two narratives of the colonial city pre- and post-independence. Fanon's classic description of the colonial city, dating from 1961, reveals a Manichean spatial configuration of the urban space, resolutely divided between white and black:

> The colonial world is a world divided into compartments ... cut in two. ... The zone where the native lives is not complementary to the zone inhabited by the settlers. The two zones are opposed, but not in the service of a higher unity. Obedient to the rules of pure Aristotelian logic, they both follow the principle of reciprocal exclusivity. ... The settler's town is a strongly-built town, all made of stone and steel. It's a brightly-lit town; the streets are covered with asphalt ... The settler's town is a well-fed town, an easy-going town; its belly is always full of good things. The settler's town is a town of white people, foreigners.
>
> The town belonging to the colonized people, or at least the native town, the Negro village, the medina, the reservation, is a place of ill fame, people by men of evil repute. ... It is a world without spaciousness; men live there on top of each other, and their huts are built one on top of the other. The native town is a hungry town, starved of bread, of meat, of shoes, of coal, of light. ... The look that the native turns upon the settler's town is a look of lust, of envy ... there is no native who does not dream at least once a day of setting himself up in the settler's place.

> [Le monde colonial est un monde compartimenté ... un monde coupé en deux. ... La zone habitée par les colonisées n'est pas complémentaire de la zone habitée par les colons. Ces deux zones s'opposent, mais non au service d'une unité supérieure. Régies par une logique purement aristotélicienne, elles obéissent au principe d'exclusion réciproque ... La ville du colon est une ville en dur, toute de pierre et

de fer. C'est une ville illuminée, asphaltée … La ville du colon est une ville repue, paresseuse, son ventre est plein de bonnes choses à l'état permanent. La ville du colon est une ville de blancs, d'étrangers.

La ville du colonisé, ou du moins la ville indigène, le village nègre, la médina, la réserve, est un lieu mal famé, peuplé d'hommes mal famés. … C'est un monde sans intervalles, les hommes y sont les uns sur les autres, les cases les unes sur les autres. La ville du colonisé est une ville affamée, affamée de pain, de viande, de chaussures, de charbon, de lumière. … Le regard que le colonisé jette sur la ville du colon est un regard de luxure, un regard d'envie. … il n'y a pas un colonisé qui ne rêve au moins une fois par jour de s'installer à la place du colon.]⁷

This description has its own spatial history. Fanon's essays on the Algerian revolution, published in 1959, before the achievement of independence, stressed the Manichean urban structure as an element within the anticolonial war.⁸ Thus the 1961 text already points towards a neo-colonial continuity in the configuration of urban divisions. A description of the colonial city offered by the West African novelist Kourouma, dated precisely a decade later, reinforces this impression via its preservation of exactly the same Manichean structure. In his significantly entitled *Les Soleils des independences* [*The Suns of the Independences*] (1970) Kourouma's colonial city is no less divided than before:

The street, one of the most frequented in the black quarter of the capital, was teeming with people. On the right, towards the sea, clouds were piling up, crowding the horizon and the buildings together. On the left, the summits of the skyscrapers of the white quarter provoked other clouds gathering and expanding part of the sky. … The sun, already harassed by the scraps of cloud in the west, had stopped shining on the black quarter so as to concentrate on the white buildings of the white city. Damnation! Bastardy! The Negro is damnation! The buildings, bridges, roads over there, all built by black hands, were inhabited by and belonged to the whites. The independences had changed nothing there!

[La rue, une des plus passantes du quartier nègre de la capitale, grouillait. A droite, du côté de la mer, les nuages poussaient et rapprochaient horizon et maisons. A gauche les cimes des gratte-ciel du quartier des Blancs provoquaient d'autres nuages qui s'assemblaient et gonflaient une partie du ciel. … le soleil, déjà harcelé par les bouts de nuages de l'ouest, avait cessé de briller sur le quartier nègre pour se concentrer sur les blancs immeubles de la ville blanche. Damnation! bâtardise! le nègre est damnation! les immeubles, les ponts, les routes de là-bas, tous bâtis par des doigts nègres, étaient habités et appartenaient à des Toubabs. Les Indépendances n'y pouvaient rien!][9]

The narrative perspective has shifted in the intervening ten years: "over there", "là-bas" is the white quarter, while the implicit here, the proximal pole of narrative deixis, is the indigenous quarter. Its deictic centrality is unmarked, as is its ethnic character. The native quarter has become the unmarked norm, but by the same token, the deictic marking of the white quarter ("over there", "là-bas") signals that it continues to constitute the object of envy and desire as in Fanon's divided world.

Kourouma rather quirkily pluralizes "the independences", "les indépendances". He gestures thereby at the numerous transitions to independence which had been achieved in the once-colonized world in the twenty-five years preceding his moment of writing. In this manner he claims for his tale of a fictional post-independence African country a much broader relevance. The pluralization leaves space for a multiplicity of specific modes of independence, one of which is described in the novel. Fiction of course possesses the paradoxical capacity to describe a specific, local context, while making that specificity stand for more general trends. The synecdochic capacity of fiction thus simultaneously preserves and surmounts a contextual anchoring – and a deictic indexicality – which is at the heart of its undertaking.[10]

The other element of the title, "the suns", "les soleils", is a temporal metonymy (the sun denotes a day) which, similarly pluralized, refers to the post-independence period. Yet, by virtue of its spatial significance (one part of the town is in shadow, the other in bright sunlight), this solar metonymy allows one to gauge the discrepancies of post-independence neocolonialism. The common conceit of 'the sun shining' on the one city rather than the other is mobilized in service of an implicit critique of neocolonialism in its urban manifestation.

The deictic work done by the "over there"/"là-bas" is simply to establish a reversed perspective in contrast to the pre-independence period. The cultural "origo" has been shifted from the white city to the indigenous city, but political and economic power, that is, spatial power, remains firmly rooted in the white city. The spatial deictic anchoring of 'here' and 'there' evinces a shift, while the temporal deictic marking of 'then' and 'now' belies any significant change. Stasis itself is marked as an abstract deictic: "The independences had changed nothing *there*!" ["Les Indépendances n'y pouvaient rien!"] Merely shifting the focus of egocentric deixis, these texts demonstrate, is part and parcel to the insidious spatio-economic continuities of neocolonialism.

In the last sections of this chapter I move forward to a later phase of writing, namely to what may be termed a post-nationalist tenor in post-colonial fiction. In recent works such as Wicomb's *David's Story* (2000) or Vassanji's *The In-Between World of Vikram Lall* (2003), the nation is laid bare as a spatial organization whose aporias have become all too evident. The nation grounded upon egocentric deixis has lost its legitimacy as the framework for post-independence identity. To that extent, these narratives point the way to an alternative form of spatial marking that we have baptized as deiXis.

The search for a homeland

David Dadzo, the central protagonist of Zoë Wicomb's *David's Story* (2000), is in search of a homeland.[11] The place is South Africa, the time the early 1990s as the ANC reorganizes in preparation for the imminent dismantling of apartheid. A historical caesura not dissimilar to that of national independence is on the horizon, and spatial consciousness is likewise undergoing significant transformations.

Yet the re-assessment of spatial consciousness that David Dadzo embarks upon is primarily reactive rather than creative. David, a cell-leader in the movement's military wing, is disoriented by the transition to a post-conflict stance. Above all, the cessation of 'hostilities' shows up the illegitimacy of many of the ANC's own practices. In particular, the novel focuses upon human rights abuses and patriarchal hierarchies within the organization. David himself appears to have been a victim of torture in an ANC punishment camp in Angola, following upon his contacts with the South African government intelligence while on a posting in Scotland: "Others have lost their limbs, but nothing untoward has happened to Comrade Dadzo. Only there were deep scars on the soles of his feet ..." (*David's Story* 11). And Dulcie, another ANC military cell-leader for whom David has an unavowed but obviously recip-rocated passion, is apparently subject to ongoing torture in her own home. This torture occurs during regular nocturnal visits by masked rapists, and seems to be carried out in retribution for Dulcie's insubordi-nation as a women member of the organization (*David's Story* 80–2). In times of peace, these abuses can no longer be reconciled with a rhetoric of emancipation by the erstwhile logic of necessary retaliation.

These difficult adjustments provoke a crisis of legitimization in David's hitherto duty-obsessed identity. As a form of compensation for these aporias, he embarks upon a historical study of his own people, the indigenous coloured Griqua minority.[12] His research concerns the reasons why the Griqua voluntarily accepted exile into a forerunner of the homelands: "It is the later, Namaqualand trek that interests him, the agitation for a Griqua homeland in the Western Cape, which culminated in a strip of godforsaken desert that the chief nevertheless believed would flourish with their labour. How had Le Fleur come to be converted to separate homelands before the Nationalists ever dreamt up that idea?" (*David's Story* 77–8). Wicomb's novel thus projects onto the plane of spatial belonging the ambient interrogations of politico-ethical conduct. The enquiry that David pursues is clearly a refracted version of his own implicit dilemma: namely, the awful suspicion that an ostensibly emancipatory practice may ultimately end up replicating the oppressive practices of the apartheid system to which it is opposed. "Can it be, [David] asks, can it be that he does not know the truth? Or worse, that it stares him in the face, the truth which he cannot bear? And is truth not what he has been pursuing all these years of trouble and strife and dallying with death – the grand struggle for freedom?" (*David's Story* 116). The narrative dramatizes "a disturbance at the very time of liberation" (*David's Story* 177) all the more acute for the fact that the ANC would subsequently become the ruling party in the new post-apartheid South Africa, a nation predicated upon the rectification of the injustices of the past.[13]

David's attempt to unravel the riddle of Le Fleur's espousal of a homeland *avant la lettre* offers no resolution to his ethical conundrum. As an investigation into the textual construction of spatially constituted identities, the narrative cannot but be riven by all the aporias of writing as a multiple site of deferred meaning and repressed trauma. It is hardly surprising then, that the frame narrator David engages to help him tell his own story and that of his ancestors never tires of pointing up their respective evasions and duplicities:

> What became clear as the lightning flashed across the window was that these texts were no cause for fear and anxiety, that David, having come from the meeting wild-eyed and trembling, was using the Griqua material to displace that of which he could not speak. (*David's Story* 134)

Clearly, David's historical researches merely beg the questions they address by displacing them to the domain of spatial identity. David's search for the past is located in a specific place, the Griqua homeland

and its regional capital Kokstad. A trip to Kokstad produces no tangible historical knowledge of the sort David yearns for.

On the contrary, the trip to the ostensible place of ethnic origin merely plunges him into further turmoil when he discovers in his hotel room an internal ANC hit-list featuring his own name and that of Dulcie. In a confused attempt to rescue her, David crosses her name from the list. Paradoxically, in so doing he symbolically erases her identity, thereby imitating the very proleptic annihilation of the named victims which is the function of a hit-list. Kokstad, far from affording a place for a new and alternative identity construction, merely becomes the scene of a perpetuation of the ANC's own imitation of apartheid methods of repression at the very moment when those methods are being abolished as state practice. The tragic perpetuation of neocolonial practices into the postcolonial moment, overlaid upon a spatial template, is once again enacted by the literary text.

Kokstad does not offer David an alternative place for identity, grounded in a minority history. Rather, Kokstad concretizes spatially within the regressive impulse his fascination with a mythical past predicated upon separateness. To that extent, the town merely becomes the site where the perpetuation of the fantasized racial purity upon which South African nationhood itself was posited is textually dramatized. The Griqua homeland established by Le Fleur, the historical leader whose diaries David wishes to read in the Kokstad archives, is a forerunner of the later Nationalist concept of the homelands. These distinct ethnic territories offered a parody of the nation, based upon the principle of racial separation, so as to relegate the native peoples to impoverished enclaves from which cheap immigrant labour could be extracted. Le Fleur imitates the perverted premises of the very apartheid system which exploits his Griqua community: "Here, good people, is the solution for God's stepchildren: absolute separation. From white and from black. ... Let us work together as one nation in our own homeland, where, through work and work and more hard work, we can uplift ourselves" (*David's Story* 161). Le Fleur's wife, always a fount of commonsense at the side of her increasingly mad husband, is fundamentally sceptical about nationhood: "what an unhealthy and accommodating business the idea of nation was, she thought" (*David's Story* 63).

Thus the vitiated historical quest for a homeland is refracted through a more recently sullied struggle for liberation and the emancipatory but troubled narrative of an emergent post-apartheid society: "[Dulcie] has done nothing less than ... fighting for freedom and justice – even though these words have now become difficult. ... Uttering such tarnished words makes them sound at best foolish, at worst, false" (*David's*

Story 179). The narrations of spaces of belonging now and then are flawed. Likewise, the spaces that are narrated are fallacious, imaginary, contaminated by the corrupt fictions that construct them, just as the discrete spaces of South Africa, Angola and Scotland constantly interfere with each other's narratives. David repeatedly discovers South African place-names in the Scotland from which they were originally borrowed, so that during a secret ANC-sponsored visit to Glasgow, "the city began to haunt him with its history of elsewhere" (*David's Story* 188); the hotel waiter in Kokstad, where he searches for his own ethnic past, may be one of his former torturers in the Angolan Camp Quatro – and, significantly, this recognition is triggered by a memory of a painting seen in Glasgow (*David's Story* 195).

The palimpsest of past and present narrations of space and spaces of narration merely echo each other. David's futile excusions to Kokstad merely replicate those of earlier compromised Griqua leadership: "the young Andries disappeared from time to time, roamed the hills in search of ancestral history" (*David's Story* 89). Even worse, the real spaces of South Africa are compromised: "[David] has developed an agoraphobia of sorts since his return from Kokstad and will sit outside even in bad weather" (*David's Story* 200). This alienation of contemporary space even contaminates the realm of the frame-narrator, a ghost-writer David has engaged to help him make sense of his own story. She too finds herself the target of harassment, presumably because her transcription of David's narrative threatens make public a darker side of the ANC's fight for liberation.

Soon after the collaboration is ended by David's mysterious death, a bullet destroys the narrator's computer, deleting the text. She asks herself, "Is this no longer my property?" (*David's Story* 212). The question refers to her text, but also to the privacy of her Cape Town house and its garden, violated by the carefully aimed bullet. It also refers obliquely to south Africa itself – no longer the property of its inhabitants as apartheid comes to an end, though whether the "my" refers to white (no longer dominant), coloured or black inhabitants (not yet compensated for their losses) cannot be decided. Or does it simply signal the end of landscape as "property" sanctioned by a historical narrative? Perhaps Wicomb's text gestures towards a new form of relationship to the land that eschews historically legitimized possession and the separateness that founds nationhood, albeit without having the naivety to posit this new relationship too hastily in the emergent South Africa.

"I do not acknowledge this scrambled thing as mine" are the penultimate words of the text (*David's Story* 213). This ending is intertextual (it echoes Shakespeare's Prospero in the final lines of *The Tempest*) and polysemic, referring as much to the aporias of Griqua historiography as portrayed in the narrative as to the ruins of the narrator's text. It may express a refusal of responsibility for an intractable historiographical geography – or alternatively, a renunciation of the ill-fated will to ownership predicated upon scission which underlay apartheid and its tragic consequences still reverberating in the national present. The nation, Wicomb's narrative suggests, even that newly constituted entity posited upon truth and reconciliation, is a "scrambled thing" which cannot escape the legacy of its colonial origins.

Wicomb's text is resolutely sceptical about the possibilities of constructing a homeland around the notion of the nation,[14] or on the paradigm of the walled garden. Her novel makes no attempt to propose alternatives. Yet this pessimism is not unanimous across the board in postcolonial writing. As we move towards our final chapters and their explorations of the creative possibilities of postcolonial deiXis, it may be worth taking a look at another African text, one that imagines, albeit as an incomplete project, a possible form of post-national deixis. M. G. Vassanj's corrosively satirical but also celebratory *The In-Between World of Vikram Lall* (2003) presents both sceptical and affirmative perspectives on the relationship between postcolonial space and its linguistic representation.[15]

Probable and improbable spaces

Vassanji's text works with two forms of space whose relationship to one another is one of chiastic inversion. On the one hand, the text posits the impossibility of constructing the standard paradigm of national liberation for Kenya, complicating liberation narratives by counter-narratives of corruption and blood-guilt so ubiquitous as to envelop the entire nation. On the other, it suggests that a highly improbable paradigm of rootedness in the landscape may emerge out of the diasporic history of Kenya. These two spatial narratives are inverted mirror images of each other. The first is widespread but declared impossible. The second is generally thought to be impossible, but, it transpires, is widespread.

Let us begin, in examining Vassanji's dismantling of the standard narrative of liberation, with the fundamental questioning of the national space of Kenya itself. The novel is in the very most traditional sense a historical narrative. The lives of its protagonists are constantly benchmarked by references to historical events: the coronation of Queen Elizabeth II, the Mau Mau uprising, Kenyan independence, the secession of Ian Smith's Rhodesia, the expulsion of writers such as Ngũgĩ, the end of the Cold War, and so on. Far from offering a triumphant narrative of emergent postcolonial nation-building, however, the narrative marks the history of Kenyan independence with a number of disturbing continuities. Two examples may suffice. The police officers remain the same under the British and under independence: the brutal Lieutenant Soames, responsible for the torture of innocent suspects during the Mau Mau uprising (*In-Between World* 37,109, 156), returns after independence as CI Soames (*In-Between World* 256–7), making a final appearance as the manager of a private security company, SecuriKen, in the fully deregulated and corruption-ridden 'failed-state' of the final chapters (*In-Between World* 391). Pre- and post-independence Kenya are thus, the novel suggests, fundamentally identical policed spaces. The label 'Kenya' points to a perpetuation of colonial and neocolonial structures of coercion. The historical aspect of the novel thus confirms the teleological force of a colonial order that is still operative today: "History, so powerful an instrument in Europe's construction of world reality, not only records 'the past' but outlines a trajectory which takes in the future."[16]

A second aspect of the novel more closely related to the novel's preoccupation with the politics of space is the continuity of colonial and postcolonial regimes of land management. The text relates in some detail the machinations of the British to exacerbate precolonial rivalries between different ethnic groups such as the Kikuyu and the Masai, implemented for instance in the expulsion of the Kikuyu during the Emergency (*In-Between World* 40, 73). The Mau Mau freedom fighters expect to be rewarded for their long struggle by the return of their traditional lands. This expectation of post-independence is bitterly disappointed, for land merely passes from a departing colonial elite to a rising indigenous elite. The landless remain landless:

> "Don't you see whose got the prime property now, the lion's share of the Kenya Highlands previously owned by the whites? Why, it's the Old Man [Kenyatta] and his cronies, some of whom even collaborated with the British. Who's getting fat on the land? Mau Mau are now languishing in prison – because they dare to ask, Where is the land we fought for?" (*In-Between World* 215)

> All those who had collaborated with the colonial police were now in all the high posts and had taken for themselves the *best land* and opportunities. (*In-Between World* 301; my emphasis)

This aspect of the novel is one of the many sites where Vassanji implicitly enters a dialogue with his Kenyan antecedent Ngũgĩ. Here Vassanji confirms, with the advantage of several decades of hindsight, Ngũgĩ's earlier intimations that the redistribution of land in the newly independent nation might prove to be a fraught business.

The narrative of ongoing territorial dispossession ("You stole the country from us! All of you!" – *In-Between World* 265), though significant within the novel's narrative economy, is only one of two principal sites where the rhetoric of independence is deconstructed. The other location of that task is the ubiquitous corruption and attendant violence which takes up much of the space in the second half of the narrative.

It is at this point that an alternative mode of spatial positioning begins to appear, albeit initially only in negative form. In this respect, the eponymous Vikram's ongoing incapacity to take up a moral position of a sort demanded by the politics of post-independence Africa is exemplary. This inability is couched in spatial terms: "Politics confused me; large abstract ideas bewildered me; and – what was definitely incorrect in newly independent Africa – I had no clear sense of the antagonists, of the right *side* and the wrong *side*" (*In-Between World* 210; my emphasis). By the same token, however, Vikram's moral neutrality perfectly equips him for the role of middleman or facilitator in all manner of transactions – "the guilty one in the middle, the perilous in-between … I was simply an intermediary between donors and beneficiaries" (*In-Between World* 303, 315). This facet of the text is not merely about the corruption rife in post-independence Africa, but is also fundamentally connected to issues of place. Can a mere middleman, one of these "wily Asians who were not really African" (*In-Between World* 311) secure only by virtue of their utilitarian role under the new dispensation of Nativism, make claims to some genuine form of African identity? How does the middleman find a place in Africa that is not constantly negated?

Vassanji implies that it is precisely this indefinable position which may furnish an alternative form of belonging in the ruins of a discredited nationalism. The text embodies this poorly defined position by setting at the heart of the action two doomed cross-racial loves: that of the narrator for the white girl Annie who dies in a Mau Mau massacre, and that of the narrator's sister Deepa and his friend Njoroge. Despite the tragic failures of both of these relationships, they posit as a hypothesis an alternative African model of social cohesion. This alternative would throw off the constricting equation of place and ethnicity, eschewing likewise the concomitant modes of exclusion, the "Black chauvinism and reverse racism [which] were the order of the day against Asians" (*In-Between World* 276).

In contrast, this model of social cohesion posits an African *socius* grounded in a rapport with place that disregards the conflicting demands of ethnic rootedness on the one land or or diasporic uprootedness on the other: "how desperately I loved this country that somehow could not quite accept me" (*In-Between World* 354). Clearly, this mode of spatial belonging is contradictory (love confronts non-acceptance) and intensely painful. Yet the novel persists in positing, at least as an unfulfilled, utopian future, a non-organic form of African belonging.

The possibility of an interethnic love is always grounded in descriptions of place. The friendship and love between Vikram and Annie and Vikram's sister Deepa and their friend Njoroge emerges in a banal shopping mall in 1950s Nakuru (*In-Between World* 5–7). It is not by chance that the first groundings asserted by the novel build upon an artificial environment arising out of the transformations wrought by colonization. The novel does not posit some Nativist, organic base in the land as the pedestal for belonging. Rather, it awards primacy to a site which is social and commercial in its nature. This by no means precludes the narrator's love of Kenya's natural beauty, which is frequently mentioned in the novel. But it is only later, and as a derivative index of a non-natural form of belonging, that text will reference the natural world.

In this way, the novel disowns the apparently self-evident, natural copula linking Africa and Africans. It dismantles Nativist, self-referential deixis, and thereby opens up the possibility of a non-natural but wider relationship to the land. The emergent and contingent connection to the land is not a given, but emerges out of a reciprocal and constructed rapport. Between belonging (what once might have been in India, and what Africans ostensibly can claim about Africa) and exile (Vikram ends up in Canada, just as his forefathers ended up in Africa) there is 'non-belonging' – a form of belonging which is constructed rather than organic, affiliative rather than filiative.[17]

Significantly, Vassanji's African-Indian characters have no monopoly on such modes of affiliation. White settler indigeneity of the sort apparently felt by the Rhodesians Vikram meets in London apparently functions no differently: "They both loved Rhodesia and did not support Ian Smith's unilateral declaration of independence ... there was an affinity between these two Rhodesians and myself in a way there wasn't between them and the people of their race in England" (*In-Between World* 347). Such gestures allow Vassanji to endow his project with a broader, paradigmatic relevance for the postcolonial context.

Non-belonging

The non-natural, constructed nature of this relationship ('non-belonging') to place is figured quite literally in this novel. Vassanji's African-Indian protagonist experiences a rapport with the land as a result of the railway construction work undertaken by previous generations of Indian labour migrants to Africa, among them his own grandfather:

> We have been Africans for three generations ... Family legend has it that one of the rails on the railway line just outside the Nakuru station has engraved upon it my paternal grandfather's name, Anand Lal Peshwari, in Punjabi script ... The railway running from Mombasa to Kampala, proud "Permanent Way" of the British and "Gateway to the African Jewel", was our claim to the land. (*In-Between World* 16)

The construction of the railway is a project of continental dimensions. By virtue of its immense reach, the African railway system becomes a metonymy of the reciprocal construction of African physical space and of African social identities: "We have been Africans for three generations ... The railway ... was our claim to the land." These spatialized identities are never simply given, nor permanent, but remain perennially performative. They must be re-inscribed and re-enacted by future generations. Rather pithily, the novel revels in the narrator's boyish fascination for steam railways and chooses that topos as the location for this performative reaffirmation of 'non-belonging'. Railway travel affords a sense of spatial belonging based upon a direct rapport which takes the forefathers' act of building the railway as its spatial template. Recounting a childhood journey from Nakuru to Nairobi, the narrator extols:

> That scene outside the train window I can conjure up any time of the day or night; I would see, feel, and experience it in similar ways so frequently in my life; in some quintessential way it defines me. ... this, all around me, was mine, where I belonged with my heart and soul. (*In-Between World* 121)

Even in Vikram's Canadian exile, the railway provides a guiding motif: "I feel strongly the stir of the forest inside me; I hear the call of the red earth, and the silent plains of the Rift Valley through which runs the railway that my people built ..." (*In-Between World* 405). The train is so important a motif for the narrator because it embodies a participative mode of access to something built by his own immediate forefathers. The railways afford a performative involvement in the country via the structure literally laid down across the land by them. The train, "a living, micro-cultural, micro-political system in motion" not unlike Gilroy's Black-Atlantic ship,[18] is a chronotope of a new, affilitiative mode of spatial identity-formation.

The train in turn affords a concrete framework – that of compartment and window – for viewing the country. That is, the train compartment and window furnish a position for constructing a selective perception of the natural world. As framing instances, they 'ground' the perceiver in that natural world and at the same time offer her or him a place to view it from. The system is reciprocal and circular, eschewing any origin, always assuming that apparently inaugural acts of building or writing are predicated upon a permanently deferred prior spatial text or context. This non-organic, non-Nativist 'non-belonging' is thus revealed to be a never-ending process of dialogue between subject and space. Both subject and space are performative and textualized, and manifestly non-organic. The train as a vehicle of movement eschews any notion of rootedness: "If we rethink culture ... in terms of travel, then the organic, naturalizing bias of the term culture – seen as a rooted body that grows, lives, dies, etc. – is questioned. Constructed and disputed historicities, sites of displacement, interference, and interaction, come more sharply into view."[19] And the view of Africa is the view from the window of a train.

The Indian indentured labourers of previous generations embark upon a process of affiliation which engenders a constructed relationship with the land, with "what had become beloved Africa" (*In-Between World* 17). That relationship is processual. This process is continued by the boy Vikram travelling to Nairobi, and perpetuated by the man he grows into when he is commissioned to audit the newly-nationalized Kenyan sector of the erstwhile colonial East African Railways. His task is to explore the railway network and audit scrapped locomotives, old rolling stock, abandoned stations, mouldering records. This involves travelling the entire length of the country, thereby re-enacting yet again the family's relationship to the land:

> We had come full circle, from my grandfather laying down rails at the inception of the railway to myself, assistant auditor and inspector on the line in independent Kenya. No other job could have thrilled me so much. ... The country was mine to explore, on this mysterious metal highway stretching from the coast into its interior, its iron

rails reaching to diverse, far-flung and strange places. (*In-Between World* 276–7)

The in-between notion of 'non-belonging', neither ethnic belonging nor exile, emerges thus out of the eponymous in-between-ness of the traveller protagonist, himself an avatar of his diasporic labourer forefathers. The narrator observes that "[i]n that intermediate state, between place and place, one life and another life, perhaps there was also a kinship with my own inner nature" (*In-Between World* 282). The inherited in-between-ness of the Asian in Africa ("I ... prefer my place in the middle ... This is easy, being an Asian, it is my natural place" – *In-Between World* 333), neither white nor black ("my skin annoyingly 'medium' – *In-Between World* 27), belonging neither to the colonial rulers nor to the indigenous colonized, ideally suited to the middleman's facilitator position in the incessant machinations of corruption, is the privileged position from which to construct a new, mediated relationship with the land.

DeiXis

There is one marginal *locus* in Vassanji's novel which particularly embodies the text's shift of focus. The text configures a transition from flawed national narratives to new versions of belonging via a change in the connotations of the space of the forest. Both within the individual childhood narrative and within collective narratives of Kenyan national liberation, the forest stands as a recognized topos of the Mau Mau and their violent contribution to the attainment of independence.[20] The forest is the place where the Mau Mau fighters responsible for the death of Vikram's childhood friend Annie hide out. One night the narrator follows his Uncle Mahesh, only to discover that he is aiding and abetting the terrorists: "he was trotting off into the forest with supplies at his back. And I knew what the jungle portended. ... I dared not venture inside that dark wood, follow that trail that could only lead to oblivion" (*In-Between World* 143). This Dantesque forest is a space from which the post-independence nation is forged, but which already proleptically contaminates its ostensibly emancipatory project with the stains of bloodshed. The inaugural violence which paves the way to post-independence nationhood also vitiates the nascent cross-racial love between Annie and Vikram, thereby prefiguring the ethnic purity upon which the new nation is predicated.

Later in the novel, however, the semantic coding of the forest changes. During his railway peregrinations, Vikram comes to know an elderly couple, a white woman Janice and her African husband Mungai, living in a secluded railway settlement called Jamieson. The place is named after Janice's first husband, slaughtered years before in a Mau Mau massacre. Despite the trauma, she stays on in Kenya, eking out a living on the land with Mungai. Jamieson, a small branch station on the Indian-built African railways, carrying a European name, becomes a *locus classicus* of Vassanji's affiliative belonging: "I wanted to be able to return one day to this simple primitiveness. ... It is the forest, in whose shadow we are, that owns us" (*In-Between World* 423). The forest, "in whose shadow we are", indexes an alternative site of spatio-existential belonging emerging out of and in spite of the debacle of independence.

Affiliative belonging is not a natural given reposing upon native or organic ethnicity. It is contingent and constructed, emerging out of historical processes in which an attachment to a place is forged. By the same token, however, it is not purely the result of human intention or action. The landscape, though now the site of contingent modes of connection, is no less an actor in this narrative of slowly accumulated bonds to the environment: "the forest ... owns us". In a sense, the Canadian exile from which Vikram conducts his frame narration, the *discourse*-here-and-now in which he recounts his life, merely reinforces the contingency of his African identity. Exile becomes a guarantor of belonging: "One more thing for which I am grateful to this hideaway is that it has brought me in touch with the sky and the earth, and through them, with myself" (*In-Between World* 386). Access to personal identity appears to be mediated across the rupture of exile just as access to topographical identity is mediated via the non-natural interval of a contingent relationship to place.[21]

Subjective identity is generated by place; place, in turn, stripped of any trace of "blood and soil" naturalness, is endowed with spatial agency: "this hideaway ... has brought me in touch with the sky and the earth, and through them, with myself". This agency becomes part of a reciprocal interaction out of which spatial identity emerges, for which we have coined the term 'deiXis'. If we think of 'Kenya' as a deictic marker of a national space, this novel demands that we relinquish the bankrupt model of self-reflexive national deixis. The text demands we adopt more complex, multimodal notions of geographical deixis, founded upon a consciousness of reciprocity and ontological indebtedness. To such reciprocity we now turn in the two concluding chapters.

9
DeiXis and Loss

"Let the ground rise up to resist us, let it prove porous, spongy, rough, irregular – let it assert its native title, its right to maintain its traditional surfaces – and instantly our engineering instinct is to wipe it out; to lay our foundations on rationally apprehensible level ground", writes Paul Carter in his essay *The Lie of the Land*.[1] The title of his book is polysemic, harbouring several layers of possible meaning. The "lie of the land" refers to those contours and elevations which civilization inevitably tries to even out and erase in the interests of speed and convenience. As a consequence, the "lie of the land" may also denote the supine character of territory thus reduced to utilitarian docility. Finally, the "lie of the land" signifies, in metalinguistic terms, the myth which claims that this cultivated landscape may be regarded as "natural". The "lie of the land" conceals the unnatural nature of nature itself. All these meanings, increasingly tending towards the negative pole of mendacity, gather around a landscape that has become a mere theatre for staging human agency.

This repression of nature is given expression in the concept of the road in various postcolonial literary traditions. The Nigerian poet Femi Fatoba has written, "In America | The highway runs too fast | For men to feel the ground underneath".[2] The personification of the highway via the verb "runs" explains how that construction itself has usurped human beings and displaced their prior relationship to the ground. A similar instance of usurpation can be found in a quirky semi-fictional, semi-theoretical volume by Stephen Muecke. One of the book's many narrative voices tells a story

> about when you went up to the Top End on some ex-Canberra project. In Darwin you were charmed by one of the local men, he was from an outlying community.

"Good place is it?" you asked, referring to his home country.
"Ooh, very good place, you should come out there to visit us."
"Is there a road out there, is it a good road?"
This puzzled him a bit.
"Road? No road ... NO ROAD. Bitumen all the way. Bitumen aaall the way."[3]

At first glance this negation is paradoxical. Is not a metalled highway the very epitome of a good road? No longer a mere dirt track, the bitumen highway cannot be washed away in the wet season or rendered unpassable by floods. Apparently, however, for this indigenous man from a remote outback community, a road and a highway are diametrically contradictory terms. Perhaps the hardened macadam surface obscures the true road. Bitumen covers over the natural element through which one travels – the land itself, which, in indigenous culture, is the medium of travelling-storytelling. In modernity, however, there is no road, merely a highway separating the travelling from the ground.

This chapter reads texts in which space as a medium of human existence re-emerges (albeit primarily in negative form) in its own right – invested anew with forms of agency which make it an active partner of human beings. In the previous two chapters, we interrogated a selection of texts from the colonial and postcolonial modes of writing which privileged egocentric models of deixis. Their centres were the European and the post-independence collective actors respectively. Even in the self-reflexive model which characterized the post-independence moment, deixis continued to be anchored in human actorship. Alternatively, however, there emerged in the postcolonial nations a more thoroughly integrated sense of spatial fabric which often explicitly rejected the space of the nation in favour of other spaces, ethnic, natural, religious. This alternative sense of space stressed a more practicable dialogue between the natural environment, human practice, cultural traditions and political institutions and processes, to which we shall turn in the two concluding chapters of the book. In the first instance, we will address examples of deiXis where it appears as a residue of something lost, deducible more by its absence than its presence. Texts such as Naipaul's *The Enigma of Arrival* (1987), Warner's *Indigo* (1992) or Chamoiseau's *Solibo Magnifique* (1988) appear only able to apprehend this mode of deictic intimacy and reciprocity in an elegiac tenor, registering the loss of such cultural legacies. The positive, active mode of spatial marking exemplified in deiXis, and referenced briefly by Glissant's *Mahogany* (1987) will be addressed in the final chapter of the book.

It is important to stress that I am not setting up a temporal teleology, in which egocentric deixis, self-reflexive deixis and finally deiXis – in its negative and positive manifestations – succeed one another in a neat succession. Granted, I have roughly aligned these three modes with the colonial, post-independence and postcolonial periods. But these periods themselves are quite non-synchronous across the world, with a number of settler colonies (in South America, for instance) reaching independence before other colonies (in Africa) were even conquered. Even more paradoxically, in some erstwhile colonies such as Australia political independence from the imperial motherland went hand in hand with ongoing internal colonization of the indigenous popula-tion. It has been argued by a number of theorists that the 'post'colonial mode itself existed from the moment of colonization onwards as a form of resistance.[4] Thus egocentric and self-reflexive deixis, and what we term deiXis, may inhabit all the periods we have evoked in a form of asynchronous simultaneity. These respective modes of deictic action, jostling alongside each other, become more or less salient depending on the respective pressures and constraints of the historical moment in question. In Ngũgĩ's *A Grain of Wheat*, to take an example discussed above, a hybrid mode of imperial or empirical and self-reflexive deixis is predominant – with deiXis figured in proleptic form on the margins of the text.

DeiXis as a mode of spatial marking endures before, during and after periods in which egocentric or self-referential deixis are hegemonic. In similar manner to the broader cultural trends described by Amilcar Cabral, deiXis would survive as a residual substrate within linguistic practices: "with certain exceptions, the *period of colonization* was not long enough, at least in Africa, for there to be a significant degree of destruction or damage of the most important facets of the culture and traditions of the subject people."[5] This goes equally for spatial modes of representation.

Lost sanctity

In some postcolonial writing cast in an elegiac tenor, deiXis is a mode of linguistic action more honoured in the breach than the fulfilment of its potential. It comes as no surprise, then, to find that V. S. Naipaul pro-vides a first instantiation of negative deiXis. As a writer whose presenta-tion of postcolonial societies is overwhelmingly condemnatory, Naipaul registers something akin to deiXis but can only cast it in a mode analo-gous to his allusions to the indigenous people of the Caribbean: that is, as a cultural form erased by colonization and irretrievable in the ruins that, for him, are postcolonial societies.

It is significant that Naipaul indexes an "aboriginal" landscape in his magisterial novel of post-imperial space, colonial and metropolitan alike, entitled *The Enigma of Arrival* (1987). Referring to his native Trinidad, the narrator states that "[t]he landscape which, when I was a child, still retained some of its aboriginal, pre-discovery features, was to be irrevocably altered, and the people with it."[6] In this account of postcolonial spatial transformation, the indigenous people are already evacuated from the landscape, leaving behind their name as a reified attribute of the physical world itself. Naipaul's turn of phrase already registers a late phase of that process of obliteration of successive landscapes. By virtue of his judiciously neutral tone, however, Naipaul succeeds in implying that the process of remaking space is cyclical and natural. The erasure of an earlier spatial fabric is portrayed as an inevitable process of change. In this way, Naipaul depoliticizes the brutal manner in which an imperial landscape is produced out of the preconquest environment.

Naipaul can execute this sleight of hand so deftly because the opening sections of the book, telling of the narrator's long stay in a small rural community in Wiltshire, present change as part of metropolitan reality as well. Spatial change, it would seem, belongs to the normative English frame of reference, thus rendering such transformations elsewhere (for instance, in the colonial world) customary, if regrettable.

A more thoroughgoing postcolonial critique of spatial transformation in the English countryside would however, dislocate that normative frame of reference. On the contrary, an analysis of the world economic system would recognize the English condition as an interdependent sector of the the ubiquitous colonial economic order, rather than seeing the colonies as a peripheral area within the empire. Such a critique would situate those alterations of the English landscape within a wider global transformation driven in large part by the colonial process. Indeed, the narrator obliquely concedes this: "The estate had been enormous ... It had been created in part by the wealth of empire" (*Enigma of Arrival* 56). The decay of the estate itself is a late spinoff from the demise of the imperial economic system, with its cheap raw materials and its market for surplus domestic production, upon which the estate would have depended.[7]

The narrator's very presence in Wiltshire and the apprehension he gains of rural England are predicated upon the end of the imperial order: "Fifty years ago there would have been no room for me on the estate; even now my presence was a little unlikely" (*Enigma of Arrival* 55). Yet, typically for Naipaul, these colonial traces are simultaneously conceded and disavowed:

> But more than accident had brought me there. Or rather, in the series of accidents that had brought me to the manor cottage, with a view of the manor church, there was a clear historical line. The migration, within the British Empire, from India to Trinidad had given me the English language as my own, and a particular kind of education. ... The history I carried with me, together with the self-awareness that had come with my education and ambition, had sent me into the world with a sense of glory dead. ... My meditations in the manor were not of imperial decline. Rather, I wondered at the historical chain that had brought us together. (*Enigma of Arrival* 55)

Naipaul's notion of history acknowledges empire as tradition, but elides it as contingent history. His construction of links between the colonies and the metropolis are presented as concrete fact. Immediately, however, they are pressed into a model of universal history which eschews an analysis of the destructive effects of colonization as an embodiment of imperial power relations. Spatial change results in an individualized sense of melancholy but not in a critique of colonial and neocolonial inequalities.

Naipaul conceives of spatial transformation as a universal phenomenon. It is universal because, within the narrative syntax of the novel, it occurs first in England, only later being described as part of the narrator's Caribbean youth. This narrative sequence is not neutral. It suggests an ontological priority, making England the norm and the colonial world the derivative version of that norm. If change can happen in England, then it is only logical that it happens elsewhere. The very syntax of Naipaul's spatial logic is neocolonial in its structure, artfully depoliticizing the global and imperial dynamic of the phenomena he describes. It follows, therefore, that he can provide no alternative to spatial change as a phenomenon understood as an inevitable and universal process of loss.

Naipaul's narrator records the progressive reduction of the English landscape to a mere object of human labour: "The land, for the new workers, was merely a thing to be worked. And with their machines they worked it as though they intended to turn all the irregularities of nature into straight lines or graded curves" (*Enigma of Arrival* 59–60). The contours of the landscape are pressed into the mould of economic productivity. That productivity is expressed via a geometrical or topo-graphical metaphor. The metaphor conveys the reduction of natural place to functionalist space. Elsewhere, another conceit translates this repressive functionalism. The flinty ground must be flattened so as to render it fit for agriculture: "the point of the roller was to press down the 'Wiltshire flints' into the ground, so that when the time came the grass could be cut without damage to the cutting machine ... The flints of Wiltshire and the downs of my daily walk were given an importance and malignity I had never attached to them" (*Enigma of Arrival* 60). The point could hardly be pressed home more heavily. Wiltshire as a tangible spatial reality is ground into submission by modern mechanized agri-cultural production. The earth emerges here with a degree of agency – but it is an agency which can only be coded negatively ("malignity"), foregrounded only in its resistance to technological rationality.

Spatial history as the path of technological progress appears to elimi-nate an earlier sense of place in which the natural world was on a par with its human inhabitants. However, it is only in the moment of its dis-appearance, in the prospect of "the earth stripped of sanctity" (*Enigma of Arrival* 62), that Naipaul can suggest the active presence of the spa-tial matrix of human existence. It is a negative form of agency because the positive agency it gestures towards is one which belongs to the lost antiquity of an England past. Paradoxically, it is only the passing of old England in its peripheral manifestation (colonial Empire) which allows the narrator to gain access to the central manifestation of that same Englishness (the rural landscape) – now equally subject to demise. What he finds can only be found by him because its passing away makes room for him as finder: "Fifty years ago there would have been no room for me on the estate" (*Enigma of Arrival* 55). In the narrator's present, Englishness only becomes tangible in the moment of its historical loss, just as in the imperial past, Englishness only became tangible in the loss of homeliness experienced in the colonies ("'Englishness' ... [was] itself a belated 'effect' which emerge[d] as a consequence of contact with alien cultures").[8] It is hardly surprising, then, that the English nature which is passing as Empire has also passed can only be envisaged in a moment of negative contrast. Gordimer's *A Guest of Honour* (1970) indexes this sense of negative spatio-temporal contrast by setting its opening with a moment of split consciousness between a beautiful Wiltshire valley, which makes the novel an intertext of Naipaul's *Enigma*, and Africa. The Wiltshire where the ex-colonial officer Bray settles temporarily between two stays in pre- and post-independent Africa is a mere counterfoil to the main theatre of war. England, "this house, this life in Wiltshire",

is no longer "the definitive one, in the end", but has become a derivative of the colony, a place from which to "come back to us" (*A Guest of
Honour* 11, 7). Gordimer, writing from outside the England she imagines
here, makes explicit what in Naipaul will remain implicit. In a sense,
the English-ground can only be encoded as a 'not-here', just as it has
always been defined in relation to a colonial 'not-there'. What emerges
in Naipaul's bleak vision of the countryside is a negative deiXis.

The entire narrative is predicated upon the loss of that which it scrutinizes. The deictics of what one might call Naipaul's post-imperial pastoral is inherently an empty deictics. That emptiness is not merely a
function of the in-built roving flexibility of deixis. Rather, the referent
itself is empty – the place of Englishness indexed by the deictic pointing
is already gone by the time the narrator points at it. It is not by chance
that the narration is resolutely in the mode of the past perfect. By the
time the narrator notices the absence of Jack's father-in-law, for instance,
the old man has been dead some time. The England the narrator discovers is one which is marked from the outset by its ephemerality.

It is only when the narrator remembers the cows of his childhood that
he can envisage a positive version of sanctity: "We were at the very end
of the old Aryan cow-worship" (*Enigma of Arrival* 91). It is that legacy of
traditional Indian reverence for the cow that enables a bleak view of the
"disenchantment of the world"[9] in its English manifestation: "But these
animals on the downs ... were without the sanctity, the constant attention of men, which as a child I thought cows craved. ... No sanctity at
birth, and none at death; just the covered van" (*Enigma of Arrival* 91).
Even the sanctity still residually available in the narrator's Trinidadian
childhood, however, is marked by its liminal, penultimate temporality.
By the end of the narrative this sense of the sacred has been lost in the
ex-colonies. The narrator returns home after years of absence for his sister's funeral, only to discover a postcolonial society which has changed
as rapidly as the metropolitan society he has been observing so intently.
Even this residual sanctity, however, has been lost in Trinidad:

> We were immemorially people of the countryside, far from the courts
> of princes, living according to rituals we didn't always understand and
> yet were unwilling to dishonour because that would cut us off from
> the past, the sacred earth, the gods. Those earth rites went far back.
> They would always have been partly mysterious. But we couldn't sur-
> render to them now. We had become self-aware. Forty years before ...
> we would have felt ourselves to be more whole, more in tune with the
> land and the spirit of the earth. (*Enigma of Arrival* 384)

The once-available sense of the sanctity of the earth can only be evoked, as in much of the novel's narration, in the past-perfect, as a had-been. The here-and-now of contemporary modernity is characterized by an almost Marcusian one-dimensionality.[10]

> We had made ourselves anew. The world we had found ourselves in ... was one we had partly made for ourselves, and had longed for, when we had longed for money and the end of distress; we couldn't go back. There was no ship of antique shape to take us back. We had come out of the nightmare; and there was nowhere else to go. (*Enigma of Arrival* 385)

For the narrator, this means that no return to the colonies is possible. The grim reality of contemporary Britain, itself stripped of the aura once ascribed to it, is his final destination. This "disenchanted" deixis is one that points, in a purely negative manner, to the mode of deiXis that we will investigate in the next chapter.

This negative deixis is given expression in the ekphrasis (or textual gloss on an image) indexed by the title of the novel, *The Enigma of Arrival*. The title alludes to a painting by Chiricco, to which a lengthy commentary is devoted (*Enigma of Arrival* 105–7). That ekphrasis culminates in the bleak statement spoken to the imagined traveller of the painting: "There. You are there. Your journey's over" (*Enigma of Arrival* 188). The deictic marker "there" indexes a stasis which is that of modernity as an irreversibly completed project (*pace* Habermas).[11] In its completion there emerges a curious sense of depletion. Existential and axiological poverty appear to replace the material poverty (and perceived cultural poverty) which the immigrants had once fled. Above all, the stasis of definitive arrival is accompanied by a paradoxical lack of connection to a place from which there is no escape.

Dulé's ladder

Let us turn to another instance of the deictic marker "there". In Marina Warner's novel *Indigo* (1992) "there" is also a negative deictic. Warner's re-imagination of the Shakespearean *Tempest* recreates the world of Sycorax and narrates the demise of this wise woman of the islands. Sycorax's hut is incinerated by the English settlers and she only survives badly burned and permanently disabled: "The revolving of the world came to an end, space and time collapsed to a point, and the point was *there*, where the tatters of Sycorax's pagne adhered to her flesh and burned her."[12] Like Achebe's *Things Fall Apart*, Warner's novel explores the moment of "disaster" ending the harmonious precolonial order.[13] In that erstwhile, now-abolished harmony, "the past abided, rolling into the present, an ocean swelling and falling back, then returning again" (*Indigo* 95). This interplay of spatio-temporal flows is disrupted, and that disruption is signalled by the dot, the punctuation mark which punctures a continuity and reduces it to a singularity. The impoverished deictic mode that remains gestures towards a disconnected coordinate stripped of its prior matrix of reciprocity and interplay. In this narrative, egocentric, colonial deixis emerges from an event in which a complex and interconnected world is destroyed by violent invasion.

In Warner's narrative this process of spatio-temporal reduction accompanying colonization is heralded even before the arrival of English settlers on Sycorax's island. In the character of Dulé, Warner references the slave trade, a parallel catastrophe intimately connected with Caribbean colonization. Dulé is the baby that Sycorax is able to rescue from the womb of a drowned slave woman who had been tossed off a slave ship and washed up on the beach. Sycorax adopts and raises him, but he remains marked by his sense of having no origins:

> Dulé developed an idea of the past that was foreign to the people among whom Sycorax had been born and raised; it was a lost country for him which he wanted to rediscover … Dulé apprehended that he was born in a place that the ocean never brought back to lay at his feet, even in fragments, a shell here, a pebble there: something lay far, far beneath him, and he could not dive deep enough to retrieve it. (*Indigo* 95)

The deictic mode by which Dulé articulates the tension between "here" (place of exile) and "there" (his putative place of belonging) is indexed by shells and pebbles: isolated, fragmented objects whose hard singularity, like that of "space and time collapsed to a point" (*Indigo* 131–2), embodies the absence of a homeliness which can only ever be known in abeyance. Significantly, Dulé will become a seafarer, paddling his boat around the archipelago of the novel's islands, eventually launching a seaborne attack on the English settlers. But he will never reach that mysterious "lost country", just as the *négritude* and Rastafrianism prefigured by Dulé's nostalgia would never recapture the mythical Africa they posited.

Warner renders this mode of negative deixis by a remarkable conceit, that of the ladder:

> Dulé knew that at the very moment of his emergence something inalienably his had been drowned alongside the body of his mother, and had been irretrievably lost to him, and he had formed his vision of a ladder, spanning one isolated phenomenon of space-time to another. He sensed that he and his friends had forfeited a way of life, and so history presented itself to them as a linear continuum. (*Indigo* 121–2)

The notion of the ladder embodies the sense of history which expresses the slave experience: "time as a straight line that can be interrupted, even broken" (*Indigo* 121), a chain of singular events connected to but separated from each other by ruptures which replicate the originary moment of disaster. The ladder of history forms a linear quasi-continuum modelled on writing. Such a mode of inscription is predicated upon gaps and ruptures, for they allow the elements of the sequence to make sense. It is absence which drives this concept of history. That loss is modelled according to the syntagmatic axis of writing, with its intervals and spaces, and according to the paradigmatic axis, along which any word expels another – just as the sign inevitably replaces and displaces the thing itself. It is significant that Dulé has drawn on his hand "a map of the country of his birth so he should not forget, though he had never known a word of his people's language, since he had been born of water, before speech. But he had pieced together a story from others like himself whom he had encountered" (*Indigo* 115). The map translates into the two dimensions of drawing the biaxial process of writing, expelling at the very moment of representation the place represented. Travelling with the body of the explorer it is a 'shifter', that grammatical element which has no content and thus can be employed in any specific context – like the deictic marker itself, the "here" that can index everywhere. Dulé's map and ladder are both egocentric because they index himself, cut off from his past and origin, and self-reflexive because they index the process by which he marks that tragic sense of dispossession.

Dulé becomes a master of acrobatics, his favourite trick being to balance at the top of a real ladder. He boasts: " 'I'll throw a ladder between ... Between earth and sky, of course! ... Between the time now and the time I can't remember' " (*Indigo* 96). Dulé's ladder and the tricks he performs upon it dramatize the dilemma of a negative deixis, pointing to the ground it stands upon yet swaying in the air, arriving nowhere with its upper end. The vertiginous freedom of the upper reaches of the ladder betrays the groundlessness of its stance on an earth it is only arbitrarily in contact with.

The text suggests an alternative to Dulé's ladder. Long after Sycorax has died and been buried, she continues to hear the petitions that the islanders nail to the ancient saman tree above her resting place (*Indigo* 210–11). The present cannot hear the past, but the past continues to hear the present, thus perpetuating the indigenous islanders' notion of time as a continuum that "did not swallow up individuals, or snatch their own stories away from them ... but folded them deeper into the pleats and folds of ... existence" (*Indigo* 122). This concept of a time which is not linear and segmented, but folded and pleated, spills over into a manifestly spatialized temporality (one repressed in modern conscious, albeit omnipresent, until our recent digital past, in the spatial representation of time in time-lines, sun-dials, clocks, or metaphors such as the river). The past is not separate from the present, but underlies the present, nourishing it and manifesting itself in the antiquated fig tree where Sycorax once resided. The tree and the vertical axis of wise woman to islanders constitute an alternative vertical axis which rebuts the negative axis embodied in Dulé's ladder. This axis is made of the solidity of earth, not of the flimsiness of air. It points to another form of deixis, one which is grounded in a notion of place not yet stripped of its sanctity.

Trees have varying symbolic valencies in Caribbean literature. Some are of gloomy portent, such as the tamarind tree in Patrick Chamoiseau's *Solibo Magnifique* (1988). The tamarind is the meeting point for a group of listeners who gather to participate dialogically in the oral traditions of which Solibo is the respected elderly custodian.[14] Solibo dies under the tree, choking on his words, thereby symbolizing the end of a tradition of oral literature endangered in modern culture. The police seek for a scapegoat among the listeners, torturing several of them and provoking a suicide. The "orature"-testimony composed by the narrator, also named Chamoiseau, indicts the coercive culture and the culture of coercion that have brought about the demise of orality which occurs under the tamarind. At the same time, however, Chamoiseau's "orature" of written "cric crac" dialogism (*Solibo Magnifique* 233, 235), which verbalizes the space of narrative exchange localized under the tree, attempts "to incorporate into his [text] elements derived from the oral traditions which stress and are part of community".[15]

Other trees in Caribbean fiction promise more. In Edouard Glissant's *Mahogany* (1987), the mahogany and ebony trees at the centre of the narrative are witnesses to the fugitive existence of the maroons, escaped slaves who lived in the jungle.[16] Their evasive, secret pathways, circling around the trees, forged a new relationship with place constructed in the wake of the catastrophe of slavery but capable of redeeming its suffering via a novel sense of place. As the title of *Mahogany* indicates from the outset, it is "le mahogoni qui est au principe de cette histoire" ["the mahogany tree which is the principle underlying this history/story"] (*Mahogany* 14). Paradoxically, the tree (paradigmatic for the singularity of rootedness) epitomizes histories whose forms are rhizomatic rather than radixmatic: "C'est qu'il épelle la forêt, dont il multiplie partout la profondeur" ["The reason is that it reads/deciphers the forest, whose depths it multiplies everywhere"] (*Mahogany* 13). The first part of Glissant's gnomic explanation ("it reads/deciphers the forest") is elucidated by the second ("whose depths it multiplies everywhere"). The tree performs a function somewhat akin to Jakobson's definition of the poetic function as that which "projects the principle of equivalence from the axis of selection into the axis of combination".[17] Glissant's mahogany projects connectivity from the (paradigmatic) axis of rootedness, of depth, onto the (syntagmatic) axis of expanse, of geographical space, of sylvan co-existence of the maroon and the jungle which habours her or him. The tree's own connection to place is linked to the spaces around it by virtue of its own ramifications, both branches and roots. Glissant elaborates elsewhere: "Submarine roots ... floating free ... extending in all directions in our world through its network of branches" ["Dans les racines sous-marines ... dérivées ... prolongées dans tous sens de notre univers par leur réseau de branches"].[18] Rather than the singularity of an "axle-tree"[19] embodying the post-catastrophe "point" of negative deixis, Glissant's mahogany gestures to the generously all-embracing, reciprocal deiXis to which we now turn in our concluding chapter.

10
DeiXis Rediscovered

Child's Play, a short 1982 novel by the Australian writer David Malouf, explores the paradoxical relationship between a Great Author and the terrorist who is planning his assassination. Paradoxically, this hostile connection conceals the terrorist's intimate knowledge of the great man's life and works. The novella explores the interdependence which underpins even the most deadly relationship. The terrorist develops an intimate rapport to the Great Writers he is to liquidate. His narrative effectively usurps the works of the Great Writer – works which we can never access except via the terrorist's own commentary. Yet little by little, as he studies the texts of his intended victim, the assassin finds himself integrated to them as if he too were merely a character in a book:

> Once again I am lost in admiration. ... Am I to step in and break the patter, to act, as it were, against 'nature'? Or am I part of the natural order of his life? ... in entering so completely into his world ... I am fitting myself to become at last one of his characters, the one whose role it is to bring all that fictive creation down about his ears and to present him with his end.[1]

Dependence and determination work both ways, whether in relation to the writer or to writing. The terrorist threatens the existence of the Great Author, yet without the latter as victim of his crime, the narrative of the assassination could not come to being. This "language murder" is equally dependent upon the conservative vocabulary of social order it seeks to overturn, and upon the media in which it will be reported as *"mindless violence* and *anarchy"* (*Child's Play* 91).

Any act of writing is dependent upon the pre-existing linguistic ground it re-inscribes, just as the Great Writer, the terrorist admits "has also, and so long ago that it quite scares me, both understood and accounted for me" (*Child's Play* 54). In this manner, Malouf's Writer-terrorist couple may offer an analogy of deiXis and of the way space underpins the language which describes it.

In the following readings of Malouf's *An Imaginary Life* (1978), *Child's Play* (1982) and *Remembering Babylon* (1993), this chapter begins its exploration of deiXis on a fraught note – that of violence. In this way it attempts to register the negative historical processes clearly indexed in the previous chapter by writers such as Naipaul, Warner, Chamoiseau or Glissant. Within that sober framework, it subsequently moves on towards more positive presentations of a poetics reposing upon deiXis as a reciprocal form of spatial representation, beginning with readings of E. M. Forster's *A Passage to India* (1924), Ondaatje's *English Patient* (1991) and Wright's *Carpentaria* (2006). The chapter concludes by listening to Australian indigenous storytellers, Kim Scott and Hazel Brown in *Kayang & Me* (2005) and Bill Neidjie in *Story About Feeling* (1989). The oral narratives passed on by these storytellers embody a contemporary deiXis which evinces the respectful acknowledgement of the spaces of the natural environment as the indispensable other upon whom human existence is dependent.

Threshold

The opening of Malouf's *Child's Play* approaches this vital nexus of dependence, independence and inter-dependence by addressing the spatial anchorage of writing. Before going into hiding to prepare the assassination plot, the terrorist returns for what may possibly be the last time to a place of personal significance, an abandoned farmhouse near his birthplace:

> I had known the place as a child and had always loved it. It stands on a slight rise looking back into the valley, an unusual view that suggests that before there was a farm the site might have had other, darker uses. ... what attracted me to the place were the markings on its marble doorstep. A single stone, deep sunk and hollowed with footsteps, it might once, my father suggested, have been an Etruscan altar. (*Child's Play* 1)

The threshold is place of exchange. Once it was an altar, a place of exchange between man and the gods, sacred and profane, the mundane and the transcendent. It is a also a place of writing as exchange between paternal and filial instances – between a regime of authority which denies or regulates legibility, and a contestation which suggests an alternative order of reading, intimate, non-visual, haptic:

> The doorstep was smaller than I had remembered, but the markings, two rows of them, were still there, cut so deep you could read them with your fingers, and I had the sudden clear recollection in doing so in the bright sunlight of the first time I had tried it as a child. The script, my father insisted, was indecipherable. But I had been convinced that the stone stood in a unique relationship to me and that if I shut my eyes and traced the letters with my fingers the darkness itself would reveal their meaning. (*Child's Play* 2)

Malouf is interested in the threshold as a place of sacrifice (it will be replicated by the steps of the cathedral where the assassination takes place – *Child's Play* 140). Clearly the sacrifice re-enacts social boundaries and the manner in which inaugural violence is expelled from ordered society, or in which an inaugural lawlessness is banished from the rule of law. Giorgio Agamben has recently explored the figure of *homo sacer* who marks, within the polis, its constitutive exterior: "The life ... of the sacred man ... [is] a threshold of indistinction and of passage between ... exclusion and inclusion ... [the sacred man] dwells paradoxically in both [the city and outside it] while belonging to neither."[2] The threshold is thus endowed with significance as the site of the violent inscriptions which found society as a meaningful space.

For a writer such as Malouf who in later novels such as *Remembering Babylon* (1993) has explicitly addressed the genocide which inaugurated Australian settler society, the notion of *homo sacer* takes on a gruesome significance. The hybrid, border-crossing Gemmy of *Remembering Babylon* is a ship's boy who grows up with an indigenous tribe after being shipwrecked on the Queensland coast. He rejoins white society only to be lynched by the members of the small Scots settlement at the edge of the unexplored wilderness, and later killed in one of the many frontier massacres of the early colonial period.[3] Thus the notion of the sacrifice located at the interstices of society and its exterior – mapped literally onto the settlement/bush opposition which embodies the colonial frontier – becomes part of the collective guilt of contemporary Australian society which Malouf, perhaps misguidedly, attempts to palliate via the cathartic medium of fiction.[4] *Child's Play* offers an earlier avatar of this fraught undertaking.

What may compensate for the worrying desire to integrate sacrifice into a mythic notion of "the oneness of things" (*Child's Play* 90) or of "all the outline of the vast continent ... in touch now with its other life" (*Remembering Babylon* 200) is the more challenging notion of writing itself as a threshold site of exchange between culture and nature, between language and its ground. The writing which the narrator of *Child's Play* remembers tracing with his fingertips is engraved into the stone – between stone and air, between ground and world. The writing is both of the ground and not of it, readable and unreadable. Malouf suggests that such writing can only be accessed by making room in our adult (and by extension modern) world for modes of reading which preserve a more immediate and visceral relationship to place and environment. Malouf does not divulge the meaning of the threshold inscriptions. Of greater significance is the location they occupy and their mute spatial language. In their liminal position they block access to but by the same token point the way to the natural world, to the ground under our feet and to a mode of 'being at home' in the world.

The implicit sacrificial aspect of Malouf's threshold inscriptions is not to be underestimated. It allows us to weigh up against the violence which may reside at the very heart of mimetic representation itself (posited, for instance, by the work of René Girard[5]) an alternative form of non-mimetic spatial marking. Rather than a founding act of sacrifice marking the boundaries of society like a ritual scarification, that non-mimetic marking would point to an intimate, reciprocal interdependence of writing and locality. In place of a violent dialectic of inclusion and exclusion, according to which that which is excluded inaugurates and perpetuates the very possibility of the bounded space of the polis, this mode of deiXis would stress the transitional, fluid connections severed by the walls of the city. Likewise, its non-mimetic character would restore lost traces of the reciprocal relationship between writing and space obliterated by mimesis and its imposition of 'description' over above the 'described'.

A further reason why it may be important to register the presence of violence within the work of deixis is the way in which it strikes a sober note within what might otherwise becomes a celebratory notion of alternative belonging.[6] The 'being at home' indexed by what we have called deiXis is not a cosy complacency. From the outset, it is never immune from violence even if its own founding principle is one of reciprocity. Writing of natural disasters described in Bengali women's discourse, Rukmini Bhaya Nair has described the uses of deictics as strategies within a "tabula rasa world" in which "infinite imaginative possibilities are opened up. ... Yet the situation is far from being one of painless make-believe." In this context of tragic loss "primary narrators ... use deictic references to the devastated scene around them as gestures of witness".[7] DeiXis emerges in the midst of violence, even as it contradicts it. It is unclear how Malouf himself evaluates this violence. Do the bullets striking home at the piazza entrance of the Cathedral in *Child's Play* somehow replicate the illegible markings on the stone door lintel? Or do the terrorist's pistol shots misguidedly strive to eradicate the constitutive ambivalence at the heart of interdependence? Does the violence committed against Gemmy in *Remembering Babylon*, first by the Scots settlers who take him in but cannot accept his part-indigenous identity and later by the perpetrators of the massacres, sacralize the victim as the epitome of a new form of Antipodean belonging? Or does his murder permanently tarnish the narrative of the nascent nation-state beyond any cathartic closure the fiction might propose? Malouf's texts of course do not raise such questions merely to offer neat answers to them.[8] The import of such problematic texts is to remind us that any alternative mode of spatial marking, however salutary it may appear, is also woven into ongoing processes of coercion and control, power and appropriation. Indigenous writing is one of the privileged sites of deiXis as a counter-discourse of spatial reciprocity. Yet it also is exemplary in its constant awareness of the constraints always weighing upon the respectful evocation of 'place'.

In this chapter we address the emergence or re-inscription of deiXis as a mode of writing space. It resonates often with a widespread dissatisfaction regarding the postcolonial nationalist paradigm and a conviction of the bankruptcy of the project of development, two crucial issues discussed in previous chapters. Post-developmental consciousness stressed the necessity of a rejuvenated sensitivity to the specifically African or Asian or American or Australian environments and their natural fabric in the forging of cultural and social political programmes. In the Australian indigenous context, so-called development meant re-settlement, assimilation, education, urbanization, child removal, cultural erasure and the rupture of intergenerational transmission of tradition and language – in other words, a sustained onslaught on the traditional connections of place, culture and community.[9] Spatial coercion and spatial resistance have always been at the core of such struggles. A character in Eva Johnson's play *Murras* reacts angrily to government plans to resettle indigenous people in suburbia: "We don't wanna go ... Better live here outside, we got no doors to lock out family. ... just *wudjellas* [white men] telling us what's good for us. .... [I] not goin' city ... I born here, I die here, this my born place."[10] Development in the framework imposed by the Australian white settler nation has consistently sought the erasure and re-inscription of "my born place" owned by indigenous Australians.

The literary concomitant of this post-post-independence or post-developmental consciousness would be one that moves away from an oppositional deadlock with the colonial moment, that is, from one which merely re-inscribes the spatial parameters of the colony. Instead, it would seek alternative spatial frameworks, ones preceding the colonial paradigm and never entirely elided by it, in an attempt to re-articulate the grounds of cultural identity.

What is deiXis?

Ondaatje's *The English Patient* (1991) includes among its cast of displaced characters thrown together by the contingencies of war a colonial subject in Europe. Kip the Indian sapper and bomb-disposal expert inherits, perhaps from his colonial experience, perhaps from his dangerous job, a certain edginess. He is used to paying attention to the surfaces forming the interfaces between objects and their environment:

> He moves always in relation to things, beside walls, raised terrace hedges. He scans the periphery. When he looks at Hana he sees a fragment of her lean cheek in relation to the landscape behind it. The way he watches the arc of a linnet in terms of the space it gathers away from the surface of the earth. (*English Patient* 218)

Kip sees himself and other entities always within relationships, not as discrete objects. He sacrifices the integrity of being and people for their integration to their context. Individuals become components of a place. This relinquishment of separateness is a first step in the direction of a relinquishment of an exclusive notion of agency. To concede that one is part of place is to concede a less commanding attitude towards that place.

Ondaatje's novel gestures towards an alternative way of belonging to place in one the mysterious meditations of of Almásy, the eponymous patient:

> We die containing a richness of lovers and tribes, tastes we have swallowed, bodies we have plunged into and swum as if rivers of wisdom, characters we have climbed into as if trees, fears we have hidden in

as if caves. I wish for all this to be marked on my body when I am dead. I believe in such cartography – to be marked by nature, not just to label ourselves on a map like the names of rich men and women on buildings. We are communal histories, communal books. ... All I desired was to walk upon such an earth that had no maps. (*English Patient* 261)

The meditation poses the map, a marking of space by humans, one associated irrevocably in the novel with conquest and occupation, against an alternative cartography. That alternative cartography would acknowledge the way the human body is exposed to a process of inscription. This other mapping would be "marked on [the] body ... marked by nature". Ondaatje suggests that human experience is multiple and reciprocal – not merely in its content, but also in the way in marks us and forms us. The body is not merely an 'agens' in the world, it is equally a "patiens" (as the book's title suggests), an object as well as a subject. Human agency marks the environment, but the marker is also marked by the world around.

Ondaatje's English patient is condemned to a supine position which advertises a hiatus in language as a mode of mastery. According to Leroi-Gouhran, it is the upright position which allowed *homo sapiens* to create tools but also to articulate language, both of these revolutions accelerating his increasing mastery of the environment.[11] In the Biblical Genesis-narrative which has legitimized much environmental depredation, Adam's act of naming signalled his separation from and superiority over the natural world. The supine position, in contrast, translates the reflux of the natural world back upon the body and the resurgence within language of a forgotten mode of spatial marking.

In Malouf's lyrical novel *An Imaginary Life* (1978), this supine position becomes the privileged mode of apprehending the natural world. The novel recounts Ovid's exile from Rome and the way he gradually sheds the illusory trappings of a decadent civilization. Freed of the spurious sense of cultural superiority he initially brings to bear upon Tomis, Ovid is free to experience the natural world through a position expressive of bodily intimacy:

The earth, now that I am about to leave it, seems so close at last. ... The earth's warmth under me, as I stretch out at night, is astonishing. It is like the warmth of another body that has absorbed the sun all day. It is softer, darker than I could ever have believed, and when I take a handful of it and smell its extraordinary odors I know suddenly what it is I am composed of, as if the energy that is in this fistful of black soil has suddenly opened, between my body and it, as between it and the grass stalks, some corridor along which our common being flowed. ... I lie down to sleep, and wonder if, in the looseness of sleep, I mightn't strike down roots along all the length of my body, and as I enter the first dream, almost feel it begin to happen, feel my individual pores open to the individual grains of the earth, as the interchange begins.[12]

Via the transmutation of Ovid's sensibility through exile, Malouf sketches the development of a notion of selfhood which is porous to the world, connected to it by "some corridor along which our common being flowed". Prostration reveals the deep links between body and earth: "I know suddenly what it is I am composed of." The moment of lying-down reveals the matter which has supported human existence all along. If speech is predicated upon an erect posture, then it none the less owes much to the ground from which it arose, but whose primitive influence appears to have been elided in the act of imposing language. Ovid's sleep upon the earth lays bare an "interchange" and an interdependence formerly elided by his satirical mastery of language. The hidden substrate of interdependence reveals what the indigenous Australian storyteller Bill Neidjie posits: "this earth, this ground, | this piece of ground e grow you" (*Story About Feeling* 30).

Recast in the visual form of writing, this mode of spatial marking would perhaps resemble the inscriptions Sycorax, the protagonist of Warner's *Indigo*, leaves on the trunks of trees in the Caribbean island jungle. They were "Neither straight downstrokes, like the stems of letters in Kit Everard's log, nor tipped and fledged like the arrows that plotted the course of the *Hopewell* on Kit's portolan, the marks reflected the concept of time and direction Sycorax shared with her people" (*Indigo* 121). Rather than the upright, erect, or linear marks of European script, symptoms of egocentric deictic activity and instruments of invasion and conquest, Sycorax's marking would evince another mode of spatial existence. This concept of existence is predicated upon continuous interaction: "the indigenous islanders could conceive ... of the time and space they occupied ... as a churn or bowl, in which substances and essences were tumbled and mixed" (*Indigo* 122). Egocentric or self-reflexive deixis hardly have a place here. Instead, interdependence and reciprocity are proclaimed by the topos of mixing.

At moments where these respective modes of deictic action collide in Warner's text, she is careful to mark their difference typographically.

A passage which contrasts the natives' and the conqueror's rapport with the island territory employs brackets to demonstrate the different modes of spatial interaction.

> [Sycorax and Ariel] put down their feet firmly, heels first, hitting a fast easy stride and rarely stumbling, though they did not seem to look down at the ground they covered; both of them understood the terrain, the conch-strewn beach, the root-tangled forest floor without the need for a close watch.
>
> (When Kit Everard and one or two of the fourteen men returning with him caught a glimpse of them moving, they marvelled at the easy manner of their progress up the uneven and tangled mountain slopes.) (*Indigo* 113)

Kit Everard and his fellow conquerors are bracketed-off to highlight their exclusion from a mode of intimate contact with the ground at which they can only marvel uncomprehendingly. Sycorax and Ariel "understand" the terrain, according to a mode of intellection which etymologically speaking is derived from "standing under", being sheltered by something (such as in the Old High German "unterstân"). This comprehension is nurtured by the ground and acknowledges that, rather than standing masterfully upon it. The brackets around Kit Everard and his henchmen signal their foreignness not merely as colonizing intruders but as prototypical technocrats bereft of a feeling of interdependence with nature. The parentheses seal them off from the environment they are in the process of appropriating as a rationalized object of possession and subsequent exploitation. Ariel, who later on becomes Kit Everard's lover, "had accepted that she stood on some kind of common ground to which he felt himself a stranger" (*Indigo* 115–16). The brackets around Kit Everard's perception signal a change of perspective. They index an external narrative focalization clearly positioned outside that of the immediate context of the fictional universe. The principal, unbracketed focalization encodes the perspective of Sycorax and Ariel. This latter focalization is not merely a matter of narratorial privilege. It is, far more, the manifestation of a nexus of narrative closeness and deictic intimacy which suggests that the primary task of narrative fiction, wherever possible, is to approximate the connectedness with the contours of the spatial environment that its characters are shown to possess.

Such a narrative nexus is clearly manifest as the close of Malouf's *An Imaginary Life*, to which we briefly return. The final note of the novel is a deictic gesture of fulfillment. Malouf's Ovidian narrator concludes: "I am there" (*An Imaginary Life* 152). The contrast with the grim deple- tion of Naipaul's "You are there. Your journey's over" (*Enigma of Arrival* 188) could not be greater. This sense of spatial immediacy experienced by Malouf's Ovidian narrator is embodied, literally, in his postural atti- tude, his closeness to the earth: "I lie down to sleep, and wonder if ... I mightn't strike down roots along all the length of my body ... [I] feel my individual pores open to the individual grains of the earth, as the interchange begins" (*An Imaginary Life* 147). The "interchange" upon which this deictic gesture reposes is such that we are confronted with that alternative mode of spatial marking, deiXis. The chiastic crux at the heart of this neologism translates the "interchange", the 'eXchange', between environment and body, creating a there-ness which lies lightly on the ground. DeiXis, epitomized in the posedness of "I am there", installs language as the threshold instance between human subject and natural subject, the interstitial site where their respective agencies inter- act and generate each other.

Antiquity

The concept of deiXis assumes a significant paradigm shift from the values of modernity towards those of what might term antiquity. Antiquity is understood here not as a form of archaism, but rather, as the foregrounding of the priority, both temporal and axiological, which deiXis accords to the natural world over above its human inhabitants.

Such a paradigm of precedence is encapsulated remarkably in E. M. Forster's *A Passage to India* (1924). Part two of the novel, "Caves", begins with a section devoted entirely to a description of the landscape of the Marabar hills and its caves.[13] This long landscape description sits oddly with the rest of the novel and its narrative of events and char- acters. There is only one other descriptive "topographical passage", the opening chapter of Part one, "Mosque" (*Passage to India* 9–11). That description surveys the town of Chandrapore and the European town at some distance from it, but in fact serves as a displaced preface to the later description of the caves: "Only in the south, where a group of fists and fingers are thrust up through the soil, is the endless expanse interrupted. These fists and fingers are the Marabar hills, containing the extraordinary caves" (*Passage to India* 11). The earlier topographic description, with its unflattering account of the Indian city and the European settlement, tends inevitably towards the later chapter. That later description perpetuates that depopulating (though none the less anthropomorphizing) tendency, portraying a landscape apparently hostile to human occupation.

The absence of human characters, however, is an index of the "incredible antiquity of these hills" (*Passage to India* 123). The most salient reason why this short descriptive passage sits so strangely with the rest of the novel is that its historical dimensions dwarf the otherwise compact temporal framework of the story. The passage stresses the immense age of the Marabar hills: "the high places of Dravidia have been land since land began ... They are older than anything in the world. No water has ever covered them, and the sun who has watched them for countless aeons may still discern in their outline forms that were his before our globe was torn from his bosom" (*Passage to India* 123). This antiquity generates a sentiment of strangeness whose epistemological significance the text is at pains to underscore:

> There is something unspeakable in these outposts. They are like nothing else in the world, and a glimpse of them makes the breath catch. They rise abruptly, insanely, without the proportion that is kept by the wildest hills elsewhere, they bear no relation to anything dreamt or seen. To call them "uncanny" suggests ghosts, and they are older than all spirit. (*Passage to India* 123–4)

Just as the hills are uncanny, so to the passage describing them sits uneasily within the fabric of the novel. By virtue of this intratextual discrepancy, Forster stresses the unassimilable nature of these geographical features.

It is patently difficult to integrate these passages to the rest of the novel and its action. Perhaps this difficulty, however, is not due to some flaw in Forster's narrative technique, but on the contrary a direct manifestation of the strangeness of the landscape. The landscape cannot be integrated into the human scale and logic of the novel's plot because it remains beyond such minor concerns. Accordingly, the landscape itself is somehow incommensurate with the narrative economy of the realist/ naturalist novel. To that extent it corroborates Fincham's identification of Hindu India in the text as a "chronotope which flickers throughout the novel ... troubling the reader's consciousness ... challenging our preoccupations, ignoring the boundaries of our epistemological categories".[14] This excess that eludes conceptual framing is directly suggested by the text itself:

> Having seen one such cave, having seen two, having seen three, four, fourteen, twenty-four, the visitor returns to Chandrapore

uncertain whether he has had an interesting experience or a dull one or any experience at all. He finds it difficult to discuss the caves, or to keep them apart in his mind, for the pattern never varies ... Nothing, nothing attaches to them, and their reputation – for they have one – does not depend upon human speech. (*Passage to India* 124)

From this perspective, what happens in the caves, Mrs Moore's panic or hysteria, and Miss Quested's subsequent inability to coherently reconstruct that moment, is not be simply ascribable to the characters themselves, nor to the aporia of colonial cross-cultural relationships and the racialist representations governing them. Rather, the landscape itself constitutes an aporetic site within the novel's own representational economy: "It is as if the surrounding plain or the passing birds have taken upon themselves to exclaim 'extraordinary', and the word has taken root in the air, and has been inhaled by mankind" (*Passage to India* 124).

The landscape of the Marabar hills and their caves would constitute the properly Modernist aspect of the novel – that factor which disrupts the smooth running of realist/naturalist narrative technique. One might object that this is to neutralize the aporetic functioning of imperial ideology or the novel's own assault on such ideologies (as in Fielding's iconoclastic "aside to the effect that the so-called white races are really pinko-grey" – *Passage to India* 62). Simultaneously, however, the text itself attributes the force of epistemological critique to the landscape. To suggest that the landscape has a power to confuse the normal workings of racist representations, the attendant roles of white women and black men, and the accusatory stereotyping of the indigenous molestor, is not foreign to postcolonial theory. The landscape itself, like its colonized inhabitants, has been conquered by European invaders, and can be said to possess an agency no less that that of the colonized themselves. Its agency, simply, is different to that of human actors. It has been approached tangentially, for instance, in accounts of the toll taken upon the colonizers by disease.[15]

It is in this context that the stress laid upon the antiquity of the Marabar hills becomes particularly important. The landscape precedes human activity by thousands, indeed millions of years, and that chronological precedence is to be understood as an ethical or axiological precedence. The natural world is prior to its human inhabitants. This does not mean that it is an object already given and representable as a given in discourse. On the contrary, this precedence of the natural world manifests itself in an epistemeological excess that will only ever be partly contained by the subsequent symbolic structures imposed upon it. Forster's description works to highlight the way in which the landscape exceeds discourse precisely because it precedes it. Furthermore, the landscape has a prior existence in such a way as to allow it to make claims upon human inhabitants. Lévinas' anti-ontological ethics, which posits that the Other precedes the existence of the self and thus makes ethical claims upon the self before the self even comes to being, could be transferred here to landscape.[16]

The precedence of landscape is directly addressed by the opening passages of Alexis Wright's *Carpentaria*, an epic novel celebrating the endurance and resilience of the indigenous peoples of the northernmost coast of Australia.[17] The novel opens with a type of Genesis-narrative:

> The ancestral serpent, a creature larger than storm clouds, came down from the stars, laden with its own creative enormity ... long before man was a creature who could contemplate the next moment in time. It came down those billions of years ago, to crawl on its heavy belly, all around the wet clay soils in the Gulf of Carpentaria. ... They say its being is porous; it permeates everything. It is all around in the atmosphere and is attached to the lives of the river people like skin. (*Carpentaria* 1–2)

The quasi-mythological tenor of the opening pages swiftly modulates into the quirky semi-satirical, semi-comic, semi-magical-realist narrative tone of the remaining five hundred pages of Wright's epic. This modulation is by no means a rupture in the style. On the contrary, it is the antiquity and epistemological precedence of the land itself which fuels the satirical undermining of white certainties and the unsettling of empiricist seriousness. The landscape itself founds the book's critical project, a project embedded as much in the manner of narrating as the events that are narrated. The narrative strands thus resemble the track followed by Fishman as he "led the way ... pushing along an ancient path invisible to the naked eye, heading through the foothills. Unquestioningly, instinctively, he was following a map etched on his mind from the times of the many fathers' fathers before him" (*Carpentaria* 366). The serpent of the dreaming stories is the landscape today. The stories themselves remind their custodians and audiences of the antiquity of the landscape and the axiological claims it makes upon them. The landscape itself, laying out tracks for humans to follow as the serpent laid out the water-courses for the tidal rivers to flow along, sets the tone for the lives to come.

With such notions in mind, an Australian indigenous teacher, Carol Oomera Edwards, has organized educational programmes for children in Catholic primary schools to introduce them to indigenous "Guyanggu ('way of being')". This project for transcultural education is "based on the principle that we have a connection with places, with any kind of place. Our habitual and sustained presence, passing through, camping in the lee of a hill, always going to the same place for fishing. All this presence, modulated by absence, establishes a connection." Carol Oomera Edwards goes on to explain the dialogical forms this connectedness might generate:

> Eventually we might address these presences, in a place, with whom we have become familiar, as we approach:
> 'Hello, only us mob coming, OK if we camp here again?'
> Relations can thus be established with any sort of place. Even classrooms. Children might be encouraged to perform a little ceremony each time they enter a place, to modify their behaviour at the threshold. They might be induced to address the room:
> 'Hello, my name is Tommy. OK if I spend a year with you here?'

Stephen Muecke, who cites this story, remarks, "In this example of the approach to place, children keep in mind that the place has a prior existence and history of its own long before they turn up. Their arrival and its impact are considered as addition to the place; in establishing a relationship to the place they acknowledge the prior existence of a context they now seek to become part of."[18] The priority of the natural world over the human, its axiological 'antiquity', results in a de-centring of human subjectivity which is central to the notion of a spatial-social collective 'inter-subjectivity'. In similar vein, Deborah Bird Rose comments on her indigenous mentor from the Yarralin people:

> Jessie Wirpa lived an ethic of intersubjective attention in a sentient world where life happens because living beings take notice. I learnt by walking with her that this ethic is not human-centred. Care of one's country, one's people, one's Dreaming sites, and one's non-human countrymen are not governed by different ethics; they are actions through which people bring forth, and are themselves brought forth by, interacting subjectivities.[19]

A language which is capable of inscribing the spatial relationships which produce and support the human communities who in turn become custodians of space relies upon that mode of spatial signification we are calling deiXis.

In his project of re-thinking landscape in visual representation, W. J. T. Mitchell seeks "to change 'landscape' from a noun to a verb ... [to] think of landscape not as an object to be seen or a text to be read, but as a process by which social and subjective identities are formed."[20] Oddly enough, Mitchell is not attempting anything fundamentally different to Bühler's work on deixis seventy years earlier. Bühler's theory of deixis was innovative in its concern to shift the understanding of spatial language from a focus upon naming and description ("Nennen") towards showing and pointing ("Zeigen").[21] In other words, Bühler effected a shift in the conceptualization of spatial language from the iconic function towards the indexical. This shift from an emphasis upon substance as the essence of spatial language towards process none the less retains the concept of the "origo".

In similar manner, Naipaul's conception of land also stresses the processual over the substantial character of landscape: "Land is not land alone, something that simply is itself. Land partakes of what we breathe into it, is touched by our moods and memories" (*Enigma of Arrival* 366). Yet even this processual conception of space clearly retains the dominance of an human "origo". This conception of land, laudable as it may be in its concern to re-think spatiality as process, none the less leaves intact the centrality of the human subject as the instance anchoring and orienting deictic action.

This fundamentally anthropocentric substrate in deictic theory is betrayed by Mitchell's insistence that "Landscape is a medium of exchange between the human and the natural, the self and the other. As such, it is like money: good for nothing in itself, but expressive of a potentially limitless reserve of value."[22] The notion of landscape as a form of exchange renders it dynamic and processual, but none the less subordinates it to human action. Muecke comments acerbically that "This is a cosmology that places the human too centrally and instrumentally and it fixes the natural as a resource."[23] In competing conceptions of landscape representation, essentialism and constructivism are Enlightenment and post-Enlightenment stances respectively, where the human is primary and place merely secondary. Essentialism and constructivism are models of spatial representation which go hand in hand with the standard and self-reflexive concepts of deixis discussed in Chapters 5 and 6, and 7 and 8 respectively. For all its proclaimed anti-humanism, post-structuralist constructivism, in its re-inscription of space as process rather than substance, nevertheless retains the primacy the human "origo" which ostensibly constructs space. Post-modern theories of space thus evince a fundamentally anti-humanist impulse whose ultimate consequences they have not yet begun to explore. Deborah Bird Rose stresses that "For life, and for the world, the postmodern endeavour to overthrow the pillars of western intellectual/ philosophical traditions requires the subversion of human-centrism. A philosophy that remains human-centred will remain stuck in the mon-ologic space where the voices of the world go unheard."[24] Perhaps what is called for here is a pre-Enlightenment spirit of place where the human is relativized – literally, reminded of the primacy of a *relationship* which grounds the human. Such a cosmology would be one, in the words of Charles Tomlinson, "where space represented possibility and where self would have to embrace that possibility somewhat self-forgetfully, putting aside the more possessive and violent claims of personality."[25]

A pre-Enlightenment spirit of place, one which stresses the antiquity of nature, need not be anachronistic. On the contrary, such a sensibility would appear to be intensely contemporary in its relevance. In the last section of this chapter, we shall look at extracts from two very recent Australian indigenous texts to gain a sense of the modernity of this antiquity. A reading of Kim Scott and Hazel Brown's collaborative oral/ written history, *Kayang & Me* (2005) and Bill Neidjie's *Story About Feeling* (1989) aims to convey the contemporaneity and accessibility of deiXis at work.

DeiXis as immanence and index

Kim Scott is a part-indigenous Australian writer whose work reports on his efforts to retrieve a cultural heritage rendered inaccessible to him, as to many other indigenous people, by government policies of "assimilation".[26] In his project of cultural archaeology, Scott is always careful to sketch the context for the stories which indigenous custodi-ans pass on to him: "We were at a roadhouse, beside a petrol bowser. Across the road a dry, grass-stubbled paddock sloped to a relatively close horizon. I was asking Uncle Lomas about a story in the Hassell memoir, *My Dusky Friends*, in which the moon and the kangaroo talk about what will happen when they die. Uncle Lomas gave me his version."[27] The context is apparently banal. None the less, the process of contextualiza-tion is crucial.

The story details the way in which the kangaroo's bones, though they bleach and crack, become the structure of the landscape, "the hill which grows up around them" (*Kayang & Me* 220). And the moon, though it dies, is continually reborn. "He told me much of the story in Noongar language, which I struggled to understand, and he seemed to suggest that we carry the shape of the new moon at the base of our fingernails. I remember looking at his dark hands, the half-moon bright in his thumbnail" (*Kayang & Me* 220). The human subject is also implicated in the story which is told. The body somehow reflects or resonates with the content of the story. The manner in which theatrical deixis embeds itself in a concrete context by virtue of being carried by a body, that of the actor (thereby overcoming the old distinction between theatrical speech and theatrical gesture, between drama and theatre), in part helps to explain role of corporeal elements in this indigenous story: "the verbal and the spatial, the diegetic and the mimetic, are never separated in the view of linguistics, because speech always involves body, and thus bodily placedness. ... the verbal is always already spatial."[28] More radically, however, the body carries traces which betray its constitutive debts to the environment. The body of the storyteller does not merely relate the hill, the moon, but is of the same fabric as them: "in complete contrast to Western European beliefs, Aboriginal beliefs make no sharp distinction between humanity and nature; both are closely linked. In the Dreaming, the land and its people have a common origin."[29] The body, the story, and the place which the body has the task of relating as story, are part of a single continuum.

Deixis – pointing, indexicality – is facilitated and generated by that continuum: "He pointed across the yellowing paddock. 'That story comes from over there.' Later, we walked to a rock-strewn dome in the middle of a cleared, dusty paddock and I saw the sequence of waning circles in stone" (*Kayang & Me* 220–1). The land gives forth of stories. Telling the story in the place is a mode of making present a narrative which has come from that place. The place generates stories which are its fabric, and which demand to be transmitted by the custodians of place/story. In narratalogical terms, *story*-place is re-generated in the instantiation of *discourse*-place.

Many examples of indigenous storytelling bear out this principle. Bill Neidjie epitomizes the manner in which stories are indentified as emerging from place:

> This story is one of the Woman, from Macassa I think.
> Her name ... Warramurrauungi.
> So that story ... e came from the sea.
> Came up Mali Bay, north from here. (*Story About Feeling* 40)

The story recounts an ancestor who is a place. The identity of ancestors, lands and story is one which is fundamentally foreign to a notion of language which separates signifier and signified. "To describe a country is not to stand back, as if one were not there, but to travel it again. For Aborigines, to travel a country is to *tell* it, to represent it to oneself. ... Here the idea of spatial history is a tautology. Travelling and storytelling are inseparable from one another. The country is not the setting of stories, but the stories and songs themselves."[30] The notion of deiXis which emerges here is one of radical immanence. Language is the place in which this model of spatial marking is encoded, indeed language as it is created by place: "That story comes from over there"; "that story ... e came from the sea". Spatial embedding does not merely anchor a discourse in a context, but tells one about the place to whom its existence is indebted.

In a way, deiXis in this sense no longer belongs to the category of 'shifters'. The deictic "north from here" cannot be implemented anywhere, because the place designated enables the speaking situation. "North from here" is a singular marker which founds the ground upon which the speaker stands, and on the basis of which the speaker can then narrate.

Thus storytelling enacts a personified place, "makes it real" ["réaliser"] as in de Certeau. However, it does not construct place, "project and create [a given situation] in the first place", as a performative theory of deixis might suggest.[31] Quite to the contrary, the story re-enacts place on behalf of the land-ancestor-story. As Galarrwuy Yunipingu explains, speaking of indigenous dance, "When I perform, the land is within me, and I am the only one who can move, land doesn't, so I present the land when I dance. I pretend to be the land, because the land is part of me. So I perform whatever I do on behalf of the land."[32] Yunipingu's formulation makes it clear that this idea can be extended to include narrative as well as dance. The agency awarded to the storyteller, like the dancer, as custodian, always defers to the prior agency of the land-ancestors-story itself.

The teller is a custodian of the story and of the place. "Here" or "there" is an element of a narrative which is given forth by the land – it is the land. Humans are responsible for it, they have to look after it, for the land can't speak by itself. A crucial issue then becomes "how to ensure that the right people speak for country" (*Kayang & Me* 243). But the custodian never forgets that this custodianship is endowed by the place, and that she or he is responsible to that place. The mode of indebted,

reciprocal deiXis which ensues is already from the outset one of point-
ing: "She [the ancestor] pointed ... | 'Look ... goose!' ". The ancestor
points to the goose, as She has "pointed" to everything else and thus
brought it into being: "And e make this, that Woman. | E make this
world. | ... Because She make everything that" (*Story About Feeling* 49).
In this inaugural creative pointing lies a job-description for all future
custodianship.

Paradoxically, though the identity of land-ancestor-story would
appear to imply a metaphorical relationship between these components
of storytelling (land *is* ancestor *is* story) indexicality is equally prominent here. The pointing, as an indexical activity, always leaves a space
between creator and thing created, or subsequently, narrator and thing
narrated. Nothing thus created or narrated can be regarded as a possession. The distance between pointer and thing is one which installs a
relationship of responsibility which is not ownership. Thus the story's
own mode of pointing to the place of its telling perpetuates the process of creation, but not in a mode of possession. Rather, the storyteller
is beholden to a space which enables her or him to tell, and makes her
or him responsible towards that which she or he tells – both story and
place.

Never forget!

The interdependence of land as the sustainer of human community and
human community as the custodian of land is the relation of reciprocity that inhabits deiXis. The stories which concretize this reciprocity are
always anchored in specific places. In Bill Neidjie's narrative, the ancestor woman provides a habitat for the people: "Stone ... this rock ... its
yours. | In the dry e can go hunting. | In the wet season e got to come
back to cave. | Save you building houses." The ancestor woman also
provides nourishment for her people: "Goose ... never leave. | E can eat,
people can eat" (50). Her words create the environment which subsequently sustains the community. The re-telling of those words instructs
the people in the ways that ecosphere can be maintained as a sustaining
and sustainable resource. A narrative segment about wild geese and the
throwing stick used to kill them is exemplary in this respect:

> Time ... you wait there.
> When they fly, knock em down one by one.
> Might be fifteen or ten goose enough,
> big family, might be twenty.

Never miss. Each stick. I seen it myself.
We used to pick im up that stick
and take im back in the water
because still weight there ... heavy, you know.
They used to say ...
  "If you leave im out there, day,
  you can't hit goose.
  That stick be light!
  So chuck im in the water.
  Save you wasting that stick."
I said ...
  "We can cut im new one."
  "No! You can't cut new one.
  You cutting all that tree
  and cutting yourself" (*Story About Feeling* 51)

The dialogical form of the debate between the young (narratorial) persona and the older, wiser interlocutor (italicized) mirrors and replicates the dialogical scenario of the storytelling itself. Nedijie's narratives were recorded and transcribed by Keith Taylor, and though the final product does not include any trace of the listener in the ways Paddy Roe's and Stephen Muecke's *Gularabulu* does,[33] the typography and orthography constantly point to an oral situation of narration. Thus the place of narration, marked out by the presence of at least two participants (indicated by standard and italicized type respectively), is transferred from the level of *story* to that of the performance-recording (*discourse*), and subsequently to that of the reading (next level of *discourse*). Thus the originary place of creation is transformed at the moment of narration into a social site configuring storyteller and listener, as explored in part one of this book.

Yet the 'real' place is not lost through this transformative process. On the contrary, this narration maintains the 'real' place, indeed enhances it. Traditionally, the stories attached to a place are narrated at that particular place so as to explain its sacred character. Story and place, however, are one. Eddie Kneebone explains, "The Dreamtime is there with [the storytellers], it is not a long way away. The Dreamtime is the environment that the Aboriginal lived in, and it still exists today, all around us."[34] The place is told as much as the story. The storytelling does not merely inculcate a sense of respect towards the place, going hand in hand with the inculcation of practices of ecological sustainability. In a much deeper manner, the story perpetuates the place itself, maintains its 'real' symbolic existence. Thus the formal, generic element of dialogue manifest in the differing typological marking is intimately connected with the dispute over cutting a new stick. Traditional storytelling, in its repetitive nature, is like throwing the stick back into the water so as to allow it to regenerate itself. The simile (like) is inadequate, for the story of the stick directly tells the listeners how to manage the landscape so as to make it sustain life – including their own.

> If you pick im up now, lily, you can eat.
> Yam you can dig up.
> You got to ear because ...
> > "Never forget!"
>
> I'm teaching all these kids.
>
> And e make this, that Woman.
> E make this world.
> ...
> Because She make everything that,
> She pointed ...
> "Look ... goose!" (*Story About Feeling* 49)

To tell stories is to re-enact a past which is present spatially in the here and now – with an emphasis upon the here. The past is prior to the extent that it constitutes the very conditions of possibility of the telling which then celebrates it. The imperative "Never forget!" does not rescue memories from the obscurity of a closed-up archive. On the contrary, it is an imperative which addresses something which is patently before the teller's and listeners' eyes. "Never forget!" refers therefore to the mode of relationship to the land present in the here and now. The injunction not to forget implies remaining conscious of one's indebtedness to place and acting in accordance with that consciousness.

It is salutary to conclude with Australian indigenous narratives of place (that is, narratives less *about* place than narratives which *are* place – "Maybe the song is part of him (or articulated with him) rather that circulating *about* him?"[35]) because this conception of spatial narrative resolves the central theoretical conundrum thrown up by the concept of deiXis. How can a theory of the reciprocal interaction of human agents and spatial agency avoid falling back into a pre-constructivist model of space? How can it eschew the Euclidean belief in the 'givenness' of space as a container for things and events? How can it avoid the danger warned of by Lefebvre, namely, that of attributing space an empirical substance?[36]

These difficulties are resolved in indigneous theories of space. Narratives of space remind the listeners of their debt to place. This place is always identified with ancestral actors, awarding it an originary and ongoing agency in the life of the community. Yet place is never substance, it is always narration, performance. Place must be constantly re-activated in acts of narrative performance undertaken by the storyteller – which then recount the prior agency of place in enabling the very act of custodial storytelling.

Conclusion: "Here Fix the Tablet"

In 1822 a group of citizens gathered on the beach at Botany Bay near Sydney to erect a monument to Captain James Cook. Their concern to keep the memory of that first landing bespeaks an understandable anxiety about origins. As an isolated British penal colony in which the number of free settlers was far inferior to that of the convicts and their military guardians, and whose lame economy was yet to see the prosperity brought by the burgeoning wool industry and the mid-century gold rushes, New South Wales had every reason for seeking to embellish its rather tawdry inauguration. This was all the more so that relations between the settlers and the indigenous population had rapidly deteriorated, with latent hostility escalating into armed clashes within a matter of months. Settler–indigenous conflict reached significant proportions as the wool industry drove territorial expansion into the hinterlands around Sydney and eventually beyond the Blue Mountains, devouring enormous swathes of indigenous habitat. How to enoble the only recently established grasp on the new southern continent, and, more pressingly, how to legitimize a process of territorial conquest which to many seemed to have abandoned the rule of law altogether?[1]

The concerned citizens erected a plaque commemorating Cook's landing in 1788, and, as if that was not enough, the early Australian poet Barron Field composed a sonnet celebrating that commemorative gesture: 'On Visiting the Spot where Captain Cook and Sir Joseph Banks First Landed in Botany Bay'.[2] The necessity of commemorating in verse the commemoration in metal betrays anxiety upon anxiety. Apparently, the very need to commemorate an origin already in danger of being lost cannot be adequately satisfied by the metal plaque. A second meta-commemoration is necessary to recuperate the patent lacunae of the first, merely doubling thereby the degrees of cultural anxiety gathered around the putative origin of the colony. Uncertainty is rampant from the very first line on: "Here fix the tablet. This must be the place | Where our Columbus of the South did land." This *must* be the place: is this a gesture of reconstruction on the basis of probability rather than certainty, or, even more disturbingly, a decree which freely acknowledges that the past has been lost and must be recreated in a gesture of ungrounded renewal?

This incertitude has hardly been banished by the end of the sonnet, despite the poet's best efforts to end on a rallying note: "These were the *commelinae* Banks first found; | But where's the tree with the ship's wood-carv'd fame? | Fix then th' Ephesian brass. 'Tis classic ground." The novel flora discovered on the southern continent, albeit perennially blossoming, appear to vitiate any form of more enduring mnemonic inscription. Recording the moment of origin in organic material, the wood of a nearby tree in which a makeshift image of the ship has been carved, offers no resistance to the inevitable processes of decay. This originary marker of colonial origins has been lost. Something more permanent is required: "Fix then th' Ephesian brass. 'Tis classic ground." The allusion to ancient Greece will offer the necessary aura of enduring cultural value – fixity – so desperately needed in this ambience of natural decay. Even so, it is not clear whether this firm declaration at the close of the poem really puts the matter to rest. Does it describe the reason why the plaque should be affixed (because it is *already* classic ground) or does it merely furnish the pre-conditions for that status (*now*, and *only* now, is it classic ground). The imperatives which open and close the poem ("Here fix the tablet", "Fix then . . .") make it a perlocutionary speech act constitutively worried about the potency of its own commands.

Field's verse is often read according to the genetic topos suggesting that early colonial literature is highly derivative and slavishly imitative of metropolitan models.[3] By definition it cannot be original. It must necessarily defer to an origin elsewhere with which it has only the most tenuous affiliation. Such writing is conceived, like the early settlement at Botany Bay, as being dependent upon the mother country and incapable of asserting an origin here. This is indeed what the poem enacts, albeit unwittingly: namely, the need to defer to a classic ideal emanating from another time and another place, in view of the impossibile project of grounding an unambiguous origin-ality in the colonial here-and-now. Paradoxically, in the very moment of seeking a founding origin, the poem dramatizes the metonymic displacement of that origin. The poem bears out Foucault's observation that "What is found at the historical beginning of things is not the inviolable identity of their origin;

it is the dissension of other things. It is disparity" ["Ce qu'on trouve, au commencement historique des choses, ce n'est pas l'identité encore préservée de leur origine – c'est la discorde des autres choses, c'est le disparate"].[4] In cognizance of this aporia, Simon During has proposed an alternative assessment of Field's poety, suggesting that its "'badness' is intentional", even "parodic", and that it should be read "as a joke on the supposed impossibility of transporting sophisticated cultural tastes to the colony".[5] According to this reading, a poem celebrating "classic ground" must be situated in the tension between the anxious impulse to ground translated European culture in the new environment, or to assimilate that environment to a European cultural norm, and the manifest futility of doing so.

Field's poem is an exercise in deictic activity. It epitomizes in its operations many of the varieties of deictic practice reviewed and analysed in this book. It opens with an unmistakeable performance of deixis as a linguistic function: "Here fix the tablet". Deixis 'fixes' the discourse in the 'here' of its enunciation. The 'shifter' here is mobile just as colonial discourse is mobile, just as its bearers the colonizers are mobile. Yet that mobility must seek the permanency of origins and property. Otherwise it would risk appearing as nomadic as the indigenous people whose very nomadism became the colonizers' pretext for dispossessing them of their land. Whence the stark compulsion to "Fix the tablet", repeated again at the end of the poem to prevent any further slippage, but by virtue of that repetition constantly betraying its own insecurity about the hold of deictic anchoring. In the absence of any final fixity of deictic implanting, the poem evinces the "negative deixis" that comes to light in Naipaul's *Enigma of Arrival* (see Chapter 9 above).

The poem's anxiety is surely motivated, however, not just by the fragility of its own deictic activity, but also by the evidence that other forms of deictic activity may be superior. A brief vignette documenting the presence of the indigenous people may be an index of this alternative deixis. The poem's opening lines dramatize the confrontation of Cook-as-Columbus with Aborigines as Indians:

> This must be the place
> Where our Columbus of the South did land;
> He saw the Indian village on that sand,
> And on this rock first met the simple race
> Of Australasia, who presum'd to face
> With lance and spear his musquet.

This is an extremely dense piece of writing, doggerel though it may be. The horizontal axis of conquering vision ("He saw") is immediately countered by a vertical axis of prepositional anchoring. These prepositions localize individual or collectives in space. The first case of prepositional grounding instantiates indigenous belonging ("the Indian village *on* that sand"), while the second instantiates cross-cultural encounter ("And *on* this rock first met the simple race"). The latter site rapidly becomes a site of conflict ("the simple race | Of Australasia, who presum'd to face | With lance and spear his musquet"). The interstitial "on" of fraught encounter displaces the ontological "on" of intrinsic belonging.

The poem offers in this manner a concise narrative of the "fatal impact"[6] of European colonization upon the delicate balance of lifeworlds and the environment long established by indigenous peoples prior to invasion. The poem does not merely comment upon such processes. On the contrary, it is involved in them, and necessarily takes a polemical stance upon them. The prior "on" of indigenous habitation offers a standard against which the poem can measure its own task. The poem embarks upon a belated competition with the erstwhile fixity evinced by indigenous community. Both indigenous belonging and the originary moment of European landing are subject to loss in ways which are intimately connected to each other. What the indigenous people had, namely groundedness in the land, the poem now claims for its own colonizing predecessors. It appropriates indigenous symbolic groundedness, stealing a deictic ground for its poetic discourse just as colonization has stolen indigenous territory.

In analogy with Mitchell's comments on landscape, the range of deictic modes glimpsed in this sonnet might be described as approximating "the 'dreamwork' of imperialism, unfolding its own movement in time and space from a central point of origin and folding back on itself to disclose both utopian fantasies of the perfected imperial prospect and fractured images of unresolved ambivalence and unsuppressed resistance."[7] In other words, the poem enacts the respective modes of deictic activity explored in this book. The sonnet successively dramatizes imperial (egocentric) deixis, self-reflexive deixis, and shadowy traces of deiXis, the latter constituting an object of desire, of envy perhaps, which the text vainly tries to capture for its own deictic task.

Clearly, this is a performative poem. To whom, however, is its performance directed? Presumably, in the first instance, to those who are commemorating the foundation of a settler colony by the affixing of a metal plaque near a presumed place of landing. In later years, the settler nation continues to need to be re-enacted for its citizens. Yet any poem is a "shifter", enacting its deictic work in unpredictable places whose only determination is the site of the current reader. The poem cannot predict where the reader's "here" will be. And the subsequent settler citizens may shift their perspective on these matters, particulary in the wake of renascent indigenous political agitation, and the belated recognition of unextinguished rights of possession of the land.

A significant vignette of these shifting notions of settler deixis can be found in Kate Grenville's immensely successful Booker Prize candidate, *The Secret River* (2005).[8] Grenville's novel tells the story of William Thornhill, an early convict-turned-farmer who settles on the Hawkesbury River near Sydney. In an episode which uncannily echoes Barron Field's anxiety about "the tree with the ship's wood-carv'd fame", Thornhill is assailed by anxiety about representations of his own arrival on "his" territory. On a rocky outcrop overlooking his plot of land, he discovers carved in the rock what he initially takes to be a picture of a fish. Slowly it dawns upon him, however, that this is a picture of his own boat, "a pattern that made no sense until he came around to *look at it from the other side*. Then he saw it as a picture of the *Hope*. There was the curve of the bow, the mast, the sail bulging in a good breeze. ... All that was lacking was William Thornhill holding that tiller, listening to the creak of the ropes and staring out into the forest on his way up the river" (*Secret River* 154; emphasis added). The carving affords a view "from the other side". It is a record, executed by the indigenous inhabitants of the country, of the moment of invasion:

> It came to him that this might look like an empty place, but a man who had walked the length of that fish, seen the tiller and sail of the *Hope* laid down in stone, had to recognize otherwise. This place was no more empty than a parlour in London, from which the master of the house had just stepped into the bedroom. He might not be seen, but he was there. (*Secret River* 155)

Grenville's narrative reverses the vector of observation and inscription of colonial expansion. Significantly, the topos of scopic panoramic mastery belongs here to the inhabitants, not to the colonizers. Here it is the indigenous people who record, in the earth, the arrival of the European intruders. Their record, ironically, does not need to be 'affixed' to the site, it is already carved in the bedrock of the land itself. And it cannot be erased: "With his foot he scraped over the lines, but they were part of the fabric of the rock" (*Secret River* 154).

The rock-carving is at the nexus of two regimes of deictic activity. It depicts colonial mobility (evinced by the boat), gesturing towards the ungrounded and therefore self-reflexive character of imperial deixis. Yet its pictorial *story* is contradicted by its pictorial *discourse*. In its mode of inscription, the rock-carving bespeaks a fundamental integrity with the "fabric" of the land itself. The picture of Thornhill's boat is executed in a mode of deiXis which offers resistance to the very phenomenon it portrays.

It is hardly a coincidence that Thornhill subsequently builds his over-sized colonial mansion upon the site, covering over the carving (*Secret River* 316). Nor is it a coincidence that by the end of the narrative, the text itself has also reverted to calling the ship a "fish", thus displaying its complicity in this erasure. Yet this elision of indigenous deiXis can-not erase the prior mode of spatial marking. DeiXis endures – in all the senses of the word – below the constructions of the settler nation, emerging at significant moments to question European arrogance but also to propose new – but in reality old – ways of imagining and config-uring our common belonging in the landscape.

The indigenous Australian George Tinamin, pointing at a site of religious and cultural significance for his people, says "This is a place where the dreaming comes up, right up from inside the ground."[9] The "coming up" he describes is an archaeological index, explaining how the ground he stands upon underlies and generates the statement itself. The way "the dreaming comes up ... from inside the ground" elucidates the innermost meaning of the ground itself, its investment with life-sustaining meaning. But the "coming up" also indexes an unsettling eruption of prior spatial marking within the semiotic regimes of settler discourse. It makes manifest a process of "coming up" which has been going on ineluctably for millennia, before, during, and after coloniza-tion – a process indexed by the deiXis inherent in his singular declara-tion, "This is a place where ..."

Notes

Introduction: DeiXis

1. Jorge Luis Borges, 'Pierre Menard, Author of the *Quixote'*, trans. James E. Irby, in *Labyrinths*, ed. Donald A. Yates & James E. Irby (Harmondsworth: Penguin, 1971), 66. Spanish original: 'Pierre Menard, Autor del *Quijote'*, *Prosa Completa* (Barcelona: Bruguera, 1980), I, 428–29.
2. Jorge Luis Borges, 'On Rigor in Science', *Dreamtigers*, trans M. Boyer & H. Morland (Austin, TX: University of Texas Press, 1964), 90. Spanish original: 'Del rigor en ciencia', *El hacedor* (Buenos Aires: Emecé Editores, 1969), 103.
3. Louis Marin, *Utopics: The Semiological Play of Textual Spaces*, trans. Robert A. Vollrath (Atlantic Highlands, NJ : Humanities Press, 1990). 234. French original: *Utopiques: Jeux d'espace* (Paris: Minuit, 1973), 292.
4. Italo Calvino, *Invisible Cities*, trans. William Weaver (London: Picador, 1979), 51. Italian original: *Le Città invisibili* (1972; Milan: Oscar Mondadori, 1993), 61.
5. Joseph Grange, quoted in Elmar Schenkel, *Sense of Place: Regionalität und Raumbewußtsein in der neueren britischen Lyrik* (Tübingen: Niemeyer, 1993), 1.
6. Jeff Malpas, *Place and Experience: A Philosophical Topography* (Cambridge: Cambridge University Press, 1999), 35.
7. Luce Irigaray, *L'Oubli de l'air: Chez Martin Heidegger* (Paris: Minuit, 1983), 32.
8. Charles Tomlinson, 'Preface', *Collected Poems* (Oxford: Oxford University Press, 1985), vii.
9. Isabelle Stengers, *Cosmopolitiques. 7. Pour en finir avec la tolérance* (Paris: La Découverte/Les empêcheurs de penser en rond, 1997), 44.
10. Eva Strittmatter & Erwin Strittmatter, *Landschaft aus Wasser, Wacholder und Stein*, ed. Almut Giesecke (Berlin: Aufbau, 2005), 5.
11. Bruno Latour, *We have Never Been Modern*, trans. Catherine Porter (Cambridge, MA: Harvard University Press, 1993), 37. Original French: *Nous n'avons jamais été moderne: Essai d'anthropologie symétrique* (1991; Paris: La Découverte, 1997), 57.
12. Ronald M. Berndt, *Love Songs of Arnhem Land* (Chicago: University of Chicago Press, 1976), 20.
13. Eddie Kneebone quoted in Mudrooroo, *Us Mob: History, Culture, Struggle: An Introduction to Indigenous Australia* (Sydney: Angus & Robertson, 1997), 35.
14. Bill Edwards, 'Living the Dreaming', in Colin Bourke, Eleanor Bourke & Bill Edwards (eds), *Aboriginal Australia: An Introductory Reader in Aboriginal Studies* (St Lucia: University of Queensland Press, 1994), 81.
15. Bill Neidjie, *Story About Feeling*, ed. Keith Taylor (Broome WA: Magabala Books, 1989), 3. All subsequent references in the text.
16. Malpas, *Place and Experience*, 35–6.
17. Paul Carter, *The Lie of the Land* (London: Faber & Faber, 1996), 2.

18. Simon During, *Cultural Studies: A Critical Introduction* (London: Routledge, 2005), 82.
19. W. J. T. Mitchell, 'Introduction', in Mitchell (ed.), *Landscape and Power* (Chicago: University of Chicago Press, 1994), 2.
20. Doreen Massey, *For Space* (London: Sage, 2005), 4.
21. Edward W. Said, *Orientalism* (1978; Harmondsworth: Penguin, 1987), 4–5.
22. Henri Lefebvre, *The Production of Space*, trans. D. Nicolson-Smith (Oxford: Blackwell 1991), 33–9. French original: *La production de l'espace* (Paris: Editions Anthropos, 1974), 42–9.
23. It is worth noting that Lefebvre's *La production de l'espace* (1974) succeeded Lefebvre's *La vie quotidienne dans le monde moderne* (1968: Paris: Gallimard/ Idées, 1970) and *La révolution urbaine* (Paris: Gallimard/Idées, 1968) only by a few years; both of these texts share with de Certeau's *L'Invention du quotidien. 1. Arts de faire* (1980) a concern to rehabilitate the humble everyday practices of ordinary people.
24. Michel de Certeau, *The Practice of Everyday Life*, trans. Steven Rendell (Berkekely: University of California Press, 1984), 97–8. French original: *L'Invention du quotidien. 1. Arts de faire* (1980; Paris: Gallimard/Folio essais, 1990), 148.
25. de Certeau, *The Practice of Everyday Life*, 99; *L'Invention du quotidien*, 149.
26. Meaghan Morris, *The Pirate's Fiancée: Feminism, Reading, Postmodernism* (London: Verso, 1988), 148–9.
27. See Luce Irigaray, *Elemental Passions*, trans. Joanne Collie & Judith Still (London: Athlone, 1992). French original: *Passions élémentaires* (Paris: Minuit, 1982); Paul A. Harris, 'To See with the Mind and Think through the Eye: Deleuze, Folding Architecture, and Simon Rodia's Watts Towers', in Ian Buchanan & Gregg Lambert (eds), *Deleuze and Space* (Toronto: University of Toronto Press, 2005), 36- 60.
28. See Deborah Bird Rose, *Dingo Makes Us Human: Life and Land in an Aboriginal Australian Culture* (Cambridge: Cambridge University Press, 1992).
29. Con Coroneus, *Space, Conrad, and Modernity* (Oxford: Oxford University Press, 2002), 6.
30. Anna McMullan, 'Irish/Postcolonial Beckett', in Lois Oppenheim (ed.), *Palgrave Advances in Beckett Studies* (Basingstoke: Palgrave Macmillan, 2004), 95; see also Colin MacCabe, *James Joyce and the Revolution of the Word* (London/Basingstoke: Macmillan, 1981), 158–71.
31. See Derek Attridge & Marjorie Howes (eds), *Semicolonial Joyce* (Cambridge: Cambridge University Press, 2000).
32. Mark Quigley, 'Unnaming the Subject: Samuel Beckett and Colonial Alterity', in Marius Bruning (ed.), *Historicising Beckett: Issues of Performance* (Amsterdam: Rodopi, 2005), 99.
33. On this topic, see Attie de Lange, Gail Fincham, Jeremy Hawthorn & Jakob Lothe (eds), *Literary Landscapes: From Modernism to Postcolonialism* (Basingstoke: Palgrave Macmillan, 2008).
34. See Michel Foucault, 'Different Spaces', in *Michel Foucault: The Essential Works 2: Aesthetics* (London: Allen Lane/Penguin, 1998), 175–7; French original: 'Des espaces autres', *Dits et écrits 1954–1988*, ed. Daniel Defert & François Ewald (Paris: Gallimard, 1994), IV, 752–54; Joseph Conrad, 'Geography and Some Explorers', *Last Essays* in *Tales of Hearsay and Last Essays* (London: Dent, 1955), 4, 6, 9; Edward W. Soja, *Thirdspace: Journeys to Los Angeles and*

Other Real-and-Imagined Places (Cambridge, MA: Blackwell, 1996); Lefebvre, *The Production of Space*, 33, 38–9; *La Production de l'espace*, 42–3, 48–9.

35. W. J. T. Mitchell, 'Imperial Space', in Mitchell (ed.), *Landscape and Power* (Chicago: University of Chicago Press, 1994), 5–34.

1   Deixis and I

1. James Joyce, *Finnegan's Wake* (1939; London: Faber & Faber, 1975), 152. Subsequent references in the text.

2. Derek Attridge & Marjorie Howes, 'Introduction', in Attridge & Howes (eds), *Semicolonial Joyce*, 1–4; see also Derek Attridge, *Joyce Effects: On Language, Theory and History* (Cambridge: Cambridge University Press, 2000), 1.

3. Samuel Beckett, *En attendant Godot* (1952; Paris: Minuit, 1976); *Waiting for Godot: A Tragicomedy in Two Acts* (1956; London: Faber & Faber, 1971). All subsequent references in the text.

4. See James L. Calderwood, 'Ways of Waiting in *Waiting for Godot*', in Steven Connor (ed.), *Waiting for Godot and Endgame* (Basingstoke: Macmillan, 1992), 29–43.

5. See Joseph Frank, 'Spatial Form in Modern Literature', *The Widening Gyre* (Bloomington: University of Indiana Press, 1968), 3–62.

6. Michel Foucault, 'Questions on Geography', trans. Colin Gordon, in Jeremy W. Crampton & Stuart Elden (eds), *Space Knowledge and Power: Foucault and Geography* (Aldershot: Ashgate, 2007), 177. Also available as 'Questions on Geography', trans. Colin Gordon, in Colin Gordon (ed.) *Power/Knowledge: Selected Interviews and Other Writings 1972–1977* (New York: Pantheon, 1980), 70; *Dits et écrits* III, 34.

7. Randall Stevenson, *Modernist Fiction: An Introduction* (Brighton: Harvester Wheatsheaf, 1992), 80.

8. T. S. Eliot, *The Waste Land*, I, 19–24, *The Complete Poems and Plays of T. S. Eliot* (London: Faber & Faber, 1969), 61.

9. Helen Gardner, 'The Landscapes of Eliot's Poetry', *Critical Quarterly* 10: 4 (Winter 1968), 318.

10. Joseph Conrad, *Heart of Darkness and Other Tales* (1899/1900; Oxford: Oxford University Press/World's Classics, 1990), 172. All subsequent references in the text.

11. Henri Lefebvre, *The Production of Space*, trans. D. Nicolson-Smith (Oxford: Blackwell, 1991), 25; original French: *La production de l'espace* (Paris: Editions Anthropos, 1974), 34.

12. Keir Elam, *The Semiotics of Theatre and Drama* (London: Methuen, 1980), 74.

13. See also Oswald Ducrot & Tzvetan Todorov, *Dictionnaire encyclopédique des sciences du langage* (1972; Paris: Seuil/Points, 1979), 323.

14. John Lyons, *Semantics* (Cambridge: Cambridge University Press, 1977), II, 636.

15. Stephen Levinson, *Pragmatics* (Cambridge: Cambridge University Press, 1983), 54.

16. Barbara Kryk, 'How do indexicals fit into situations? On deixis in English and Polish', in Dieter Kastovsky & A. Szwedock (eds), *Linguistics across Historical and Geographical Boundaries: In Honour of Jacek Fisiak on the Occasion of His Fiftieth Birthday* (Berlin: Mouton de Gruyter, 1986), II, 1289.

17. Peter Jones, 'Philosophical and Theoretical Issues in the Study of Deixis: A Critique of the Standard Account', in Keith Green (ed.), *New Essays in Deixis: Discourse, Narrative, Literature* (Amsterdam: Rodopi, 1995), 32.
18. Gillian Brown & George Yule, *Discourse Analysis* (Cambridge: Cambridge University Press, 1983), 52; empasis added.
19. Jones, 'Philosophical and Theoretical Issues' 35.
20. Karl Bühler, *Theory of Language: The Representational Function of Language*, trans. Donald Fraser Goodwin (Amsterdam/Philadelphia: Benjamins, 1990), 122. German original: *Sprachtheorie* (Jena: Gustav Fischer, 1934), 102, 136.
21. Jones, 'Philosophical and Theoretical Issues' 31.
22. Bertrand Russell, *An Inquiry into Meaning and Truth: The William James Lectures 1940 delivered at Harvard University* (1940; Harmondsworth: Pelican 1965), 102.
23. V. V. Burlakova, 'Deixis', in V. V. Burlakova (ed.), *Controversial Questions* (1988) (in Russian), cited by Peter Jones, 'Philosophical and Theoretical Issues in the Study of Deixis', 28.
24. Keith Green, 'Deixis and the Poetic Persona', *Language and Literature* 1: 2 (1992), 122.
25. Levinson, *Pragmatics* 63.
26. Friedrich Lenz, 'Deictic conceptualisation of time, space and person: Introduction', in Friedrich Lenz (ed.), *Deictic Conceptualisation of Time, Space and Person* (Amsterdam: John Benjamins, 2003), viii.
27. Lyons, *Semantics* II, 638.
28. Jacques Lacan, *Écrits* (Paris: Seuil, 1966), 97; *Écrits*, trans. Bruce Fink (New York: W.W. Norton, 2006), 78. All subsequent references in the text.
29. Jones, 'Philosophical and Theoretical Issues', 32.
30. John Locke, *An Essay Concerning Human Understanding* (1689), ed. Peter Nidditch (Oxford: Clarendon Press, 1975), 13.
31. Levinson, *Pragmatics* 62.
32. Michel Foucault, *The Order of Things: An Archaeology of the Human Sciences*, trans. A. M. Sheridan Smith (London: Routledge, 2004), 351. French original: *Les Mots et les choses: Une archéologie des sciences humaines* (Paris: Gallimard, 1966), 323, 329. All subsequent references in the text.
33. Alexander Pope, *An Essay on Man* (1733), in Herbert Davis (ed.), *Pope: Poetical Works* (Oxford University Press, 1978), 250.
34. Roland Barthes, *The Semiotic Challenge*, trans. Richard Howard (Berkeley: University of California Press, 1994), 81–2, 64–5. French original: *L'Aventure sémiologique* (Paris: Seuil/Points, 1985), 153, 137–8.
35. Liam Davison, *The White Woman* (St Lucia QLD: University of Queensland Press, 1994), 25.
36. Roman Jakobson, 'Shifters, Verbal Categories, and the Russian Verb', *Selected Writings* (The Hague: Mouton, 1971), II, 132.
37. Emile Benveniste, *Problems in General Linguistics*, trans. Mary Elizabeth Meeks (Coral Gables, Florida: University of Miami Press, 1971), 220. French original: *Problèmes de linguistique générale* (Paris: Gallimard, 1966 & 1974), I, 254.
38. Benveniste, *Problems in General Linguistics* 220, *Problèmes de linguistique générale* I, 254.
39. Benveniste, *Problems in General Linguistics* 219, *Problèmes de linguistique generale* I, 253.
40. Levinson, *Pragmatics* 57.
41. Irigaray, *Elemental Passions*, 55, *Passions élémentaires*, 66.

2 From Deictics to DeiXis

1. Jones, 'Philosophical and Theoretical Issues' 38.
2. William F. Hanks, 'The indexical ground of deictic reference', in Alessandro Duranti & Charles Goodwin (eds), *Rethinking Context: Language as an Interactive Phenomenon* (Cambridge: Cambridge University Press, 1992), 70; emphasis added.
3. Günther Grewendorf, Fritz Hamm & Wolfgang Sternefeld, *Sprachliches Wissen: Eine Einführung in moderne Theorien der grammatischen Beschreibung* (Frankfurt am Main: Suhrkamp, 1987), 377.
4. Benveniste, *Problèmes de linguistique generale* II, 82; not available in the single-volume English translation.
5. Jones, 'Philosophical and Theoretical Issues' 37.
6. Anna Fuchs, *Remarks on Deixis* (Heidelberg: Groos, 1993), 48.
7. Fuchs, *Remarks on Deixis* 24.
8. Ibid., 42–6, 49.
9. See for instance, Foucault, *The Order of Things; Les Mots et les choses*.
10. Lyons, *Semantics* II, 637; my emphasis.
11. Jones, 'Philosophical and Theoretical Issues' 35.
12. Maurice Merleau-Ponty, *Phenomenology of Perception*, trans. Colin Smith (London: Routledge, 1995), 243–4. French original: *Phénoménologie de la perception* (1945; Paris: Gallimard/Tel, 1976), 281–2.
13. Karl Marx, *The Eighteenth Brumaire of Louis Bonaparte*, ed. C. P. Dutt (New York: Internationale Publishers, 1940), 13. German original: *Der Achtzehnte Brumaire des Louis Bonaparte* (Leipzig: Reclam, 1982), 15.
14. Edmund Husserl, *Logische Untersuchungen* (Halle an der Saale: Niemeyer, 1901), II, 85, 82.
15. See Elam, *The Semiotics of Theatre and Drama*, 98–109. See also my *Spatial Representations on the Jacobean Stage: From Shakespeare to Webster* (Basingstoke: Palgrave Macmillan, 2002), 1, 42, 57, 72–3, 79, 98, 104–5, 208.
16. Peter Brook, *The Empty Space* (Harmondsworth: Penguin, 1972).
17. See Brian T. Fitch, *Beckett and Babel: An Investigation into the Status of the Bilingual Work* (Toronto: University of Toronto Press, 1988).
18. Michel Foucault, 'Archaeology of a Passion', in Raymond Roussel, *Death and the Labyrinth: The World of Raymond Roussel*, trans. Charles Ruas (New York: Continuum, 2004), 174; *Dits et écrits* IV, 608.
19. See Didier Eribon, *Michel Foucault (1926–1984)* (Paris: Flammarion/Champs, 1991), 79; James Miller, *The Passion of Michel Foucault* (London: HarperCollins, 1993), 64–5; David Macey, *The Lives of Michel Foucault* (London: Hutchinson, 1993), 41.
20. Michel Foucault, 'What is an Author?', trans. Josué Harari, in Josué Harari (ed.), *Textual Strategies: Perspective in Post-Structuralist Criticism* (London: Methuen, 1980), 141–2; *Dits et écrits* I, 792.
21. Foucault, *Dits et écrits* II, 410: "l'espace de la salle du Collège de France".
22. Michel Foucault, 'The Discourse on Language' in *The Archaeology of Knowledge and the Discourse on Language*, trans, A. M. Sheridan Smith (New York: Pantheon, 1972), 215. French original: *L'Ordre du discours: Leçon inaugurale au Collège de France prononcée le 2 décembre 1970* (Paris: Gallimard, 1972), 10.

23. Foucault, 'The Discourse on Language', 215. French Original: *L'Ordre du discours*, 8. Foucault quotes (not entirely accurately) from Samuel Beckett, *L'Innommable: Roman* (Paris: Minuit, 1953), 261–2; *The Unnameable* (1958; New York: The Grove Press, 1970), 179.
24. Mikhail Bakhtin/V. N. Vološinov, *Marxism and the Philosophy of Language*, trans. Ladislav Matejka and I. R. Titurik (1929; Cambridge, MA: Harvard University Press, 1986), 85–6.
25. Wolfgang Klein & Konstanze Jungbluth, 'Einleitung', Thematic issue on Deixis, *Zeitschrift für Literaturwissenschaft und Linguistik* 125 (March 2002), 8.
26. Malpas, *Place and Experience*, 35.
27. See Michael Issacharoff, *Discourse as Performance* (Stanford: Stanford University Press, 1989), 68ff; Michael Issacharoff, 'Space and Reference in Drama', *Poetics Today* 2: 3 (Spring 1981), 211–24; Hanna Scolnicov, *Women's Theatrical Space* (Cambridge: Cambridge University Press, 1994), 6–7.
28. Jakobson, 'Shifters, Verbal Categories, and the Russian Verb', II, 131–2.
29. Charles Sanders Peirce, *Collected Writings*, ed. Charles Hartshore, Paul Weiss & Arthur W. Burks (Cambridge, MA: Harvard University Press, 1931–58), II, 135.
30. Jakobson, 'Shifters, Verbal Categories, and the Russian Verb', II, 131.
31. Louis Althusser, 'A letter on art in reply to Andre Daspre', trans. Ben Brewster, *Lenin and Philosophy and Other Essays* (New York: Monthly Review Press, 1971), 225. French original: 'Lettre sur la connaisance de l'art (réponse à André Daspre)', *Ecrits philosophiques et politiques* (Paris: Stock/IMEC, 1995), II, 564.
32. Julia Kristeva, *Desire in Language: A Semiotic Approach to Literature and Art*, ed. Leon Roudiez, trans. Thomas Gora, Alice Jardine & Leon Roudiez (New York: Columbia University Press, 1980), 68. French original: Σημειωτικη: *Recherches pour une sémanalyse* (1969; Paris: Seuil/Points, 1978), 88.
33. Richard Aczel, 'Rhetorical Figures as Narrative Strategies in English Renaissance Prose Fiction', in Bernhard Reitz & Sigrid Rieuwerts (eds), *Anglistentag 1999 Mainz: Proceedings* (Trier: WVT, 2000), 451, 460.
34. Foucault, *Dits et écrits* III, 581.
35. Doreen Massey, *For Space* (London: Sage, 2005), 45.
36. Ibid., 47–8.

3 Narrative Space

1. T. S. Eliot, 'The Hollow Men' (1925), *Complete Poems and Plays of T. S. Eliot*, 81; Louis Ferdinand Céline, *Voyage au bout de la nuit* (1932; Paris: Livre de poche, 1962); Michel Leiris, *L'Afrique fantôme* (1934; Paris: Gallimard/tel, 1988); V. S. Naipaul, *An Area of Darkness* (1964; Harmondsworth: Penguin, 1970), *A Bend in the River* (1979; London: Picador, 2002); Timothy Findley, *Headhunter* (Toronto: Random House, 1993); Liam Davison, *The White Woman* (St. Lucia QLD: University of Queensland Press, 1994); Zakes Mda, *Heart of Redness* (New York: Picador, 2000).
2. Walter Benjamin, 'The Task of the Translator: An Introduction to the Translation of Baudelaire's *Tableaux Parisiens*', trans. Harry Zorn, in *Illuminations*, ed. Hannah Arendt (London: Pimlico, 1999), 72. German original: 'Die Aufgabe des Übersetzers', in *Illuminationen: Ausgewählte Schriften I*, ed. Siegfried Unseld (Frankfurt am Main: Suhrkamp), 51.

3. Edward W. Said, *The World, the Text, and the Critic* (London: Faber & Faber, 1983), 93, 92.

4. André Gide, *The Immoralist*, trans. Dorothy Bussy (New York: Alfred Knopf, 1930). French original: *L'Immoraliste* (1902), in *Romans* (Paris: NRF/Pleiade, 1958). All subsequent references in the text.

5. See Dorrit Cohn, *Fictional Minds: Narrative Modes for Presenting Consciousness in Fiction* (Princeton NJ: Princeton University Press, 1978), 158–60; Tzvetan Todorov, 'Knowledge of the Void: Heart of Darkness', trans. Walter C. Putnam III, *Conradania* 21 (1989), 161–72. French original: 'Coeur des ténèbres', *Les genres du discours* (Paris: Seuil, 1978), 172–83.

6. See my *Conrad and Gide: Translation, Transference and Intertextuality* (Amsterdam/Atlanta, GA: Rodopi, 1996), chapters 1 and 5; André Gide, *Le Retour du Tchad* in *Journal 1939–1949, Souvenirs* (Paris: Gallimard/NRF, Pléiade, 1981), 679, 941.

7. André Gide, *Journal 1939–1949; Souvenirs* (Paris: Gallimard/NRF, Pléiade, 1954), 14.

8. Kristeva, *Desire in Language*, 66, Σημειωτική, 85. See also Kristeva, Σημειωτική 74, 83–112, 194–6, 272–7; *Desire in Language* 53, 64–91. French original: *Le Texte du roman: Approche sémiologique d'une structure discursive transformationelle* (Den Haag/Paris: Mouton, 1970), 139–76. See also *Revolution in Poetic Language*, trans. Margaret Waller (New York: Columbia University Press, 1984), 59. French original: *La Révolution du langage poétique: L'avant-garde à la fin du XIXe siècle: Lautréamont et Mallarmé* (Paris: Seuil, 1974), 59.

9. Kristeva, *Desire in Language* 65, Σημειωτική 83.

10. Kristeva, *Desire in Language* 65, Σημειωτική 84.

11. Kristeva, *Desire in Language* 65–6, Σημειωτική 84.

12. Kristeva, *Desire in Language* 65–6, Σημειωτική 84.

13. Kristeva, *Desire in Language* 66, Σημειωτική 84.

14. Kristeva, *Desire in Language* 66, Σημειωτική 84.

15. Kristeva, *Desire in Language* 81, Σημειωτική 103.

16. See Seymour Chatman, *Story and Discourse: Narrative Structure in Fiction and Film* (Ithaca: Cornell University Press, 1978).

17. Viktor Shklovsky, *Theory of Prose*, trans. Benjamin Sher (Elmswood Park, IL: Dalkey Archive Press, 1990), 170. Russian original: Viktor Shklovskij, *O Teorii Prozy* (Moskva: Isdatelstovo Federacija, 1929) [Виктор Шкловский, О Теории Прозы (Москва: Издательство Федерация, 1929)], 204.

18. Victor Erlich, *Russian Formalism: History – Doctrine*, 4th edn. (The Hague: Mouton, 1980), 240.

19. Theodore Baird, 'The Time Scheme of Tristram Shandy and a Source', *PMLA* 51 (1936), 803–20.

20. Laurence Sterne, *The Life and Opinions of Tristram Shandy* (Harmondsworth: Penguin, 1985), 65; see Terry Eagleton, *Walter Benjamin: Or, Towards a Revolutionary Criticism* (London: Verso, 1981), 16–18.

21. Richard Sherwood, 'Viktor Shklovsky and the Development of Early Formalist Theory on Prose Literature', in Stephen Bann and John E. Bowlt (eds), *Russian Formalism: A Collection of Articles and Texts in Translation* (Edinburgh: Scottish Academic Press, 1973), 28, 32.

22. Peter Steiner, *Russian Formalism: A Metapoetics* (Ithaca: Cornell University Press, 1984), 44–7.

23. Conrad's letter to Cunningham Graham of 20 December 1897, in C. T. Watts (ed.), *Joseph Conrad's Letters to R. B. Cunningham Graham* (Cambridge: Cambridge University Press, 1969), 56–7.
24. Terry Eagleton, *Marxism and Literary Theory* (London: Methuen, 1976), Ch. 4; *Criticism and Ideology: A Study in Marxist Literary Theory* (London: Verso, 1978), Ch. 3.
25. Shklovsky, *Theory of Prose* 20, О Теории Прозы [*O Theorii Prosy*], 32.
26. See Chatman, *Story and Discourse*, 96–105.
27. Theodor W. Adorno, *Aesthetic Theory*, trans. Robert Hullot-Kentor (London: Athlone Press, 1997), 228. German original: *Ästhetische Theorie* (Frankfurt am Main: Suhrkamp, 1973), 338–9.
28. Wolfgang Iser, *Prospecting: From Reader Response to Literary Anthropology* (Baltimore: Johns Hopkins University Press, 1989), 28. German original: 'Die Appellstruktur der Texte: Unbestimmtheit als Wirkungsbedingung literarischer Prosa', in Rainer Warning (ed.), *Rezeptionsästhetik: Theorie und Praxis* (München: Fink/UTB, 1993), 248.
29. Kristeva, Σημειωτική 164. This text is not translated in *Desire in Language*.
30. Kristeva, *Desire in Language* 74, Σημειωτική 95.
31. Benveniste, *Problems in General Linguistics* 218, *Problèmes de linguistique générale I*, 252.
32. Kristeva, Σημειωτική 164. This text is not translated in *Desire in Language*.
33. See Julia Kristeva, *Polylogue* (Paris: Seuil, 1977), 487.
34. Shklovsky, *Theory of Prose* 169, О Теории Прозы [*O Theorii Prosy*] 203; see Sterne, *Tristram Shandy*, 435.

4 Anadiplosis

1. V. S. Naipaul, *An Area of Darkness* (1964; Harmondsworth: Penguin, 1970); 'Conrad's Darkness and Mine', *Literary Occasions: Essays*, ed. Pankaj Mishra (New York: Knopf, 2003), 162–80.
2. David Dabydeen, *The Intended* (1991; London: Vintage, 1993); Christa Wolf, *Störfall: Nachrichten eines Tages* (Frankfurt am Main: Luchterhand, 1987); English translation: *Accident: A Day's News*, trans. Heike Schwarzbauer & Rick Takvorian (New York: Farrar, Straus & Giroux, 1989). All subsequent references to these works in the text.
3. See Harold Bloom, *The Anxiety of Influence* (New York: Oxford University Press, 1973); Laurent Jenny, 'La stratégie de la forme', *Poétique* 27 (1976), 261.
4. Gérard Genette, *The Architext: An Introduction*, trans. Jane E. Lewin (Berkeley: University of California Press, 1992), 81–2; French original: *Introduction à l'architext* (Paris: Seuil, 1979), 87–8; Juri Lotman, *Universe of the Mind: A Semiotic Theory of Culture*, trans. Ann Shukman (London: J. B. Tauris, 1990), 143–50.
5. See Pierre Bourdieu & Jean-Claude Passeron, *The Inheritors: French Students and their Relation to Culture*, trans. Richard Nice (Chicago: University of Chicago Press, 1979); Pierre Bourdieu, *Reproduction in Education, Society and Culture*, trans. Richard Nice (London: Sage, 1990); Pierre Bourdieu, *Distinction: A Social Critique of the Judgement of Taste*, trans. Richard Nice

(London: Routledge, 1984). French originals : Pierre Boudieu & Jean-Claude Passeron, *Les héritiers: Les étudiants et la culture* (Paris: Minuit, 1964), Pierre Bourdieu, *La Réproduction: Eléments pour une théorie du système d'enseignement* (Paris: Minuit, 1970); Pierre Bourdieu, *La distinction: Critique sociale du jugement* (Paris: Minuit, 1979).

6. Kwame Dawes, Interview with David Dabydeen, in Kevin Grant (ed.), *The Art of David Dabydeen* (London: Peepal Tree Press, 1997), 210–11; Tobias Döring, 'The Passage of the I/Eye: David Dabydeen, V. S. Naipaul and the Tombstones of Parabiography', in Alfred Hornung and Ernstpeter Ruhe (eds), *Postcolonialism & Autobiography: Michelle Cliff, David Dabydeen, Opal Palmer Adisa* (Amsterdam/Atlanta, GA: Rodopi, 1998), 150–66; Tobias Döring, *Caribbean-English Passages: Intertextuality in a Postcolonial Tradition* (London: Routledge, 2002), 109–36, 115.

7. See Jörg Helbig, *Intertextualität und Markierung: Untersuchungen zur Systematik und Funktion der Signalisierung von Intertextualität* (Heidelberg: Winter, 1996).

8. See Paul Ricoeur, *The Conflict of Interpretations: Essays in Hermeneutics*, trans. Willis Domingo et al. (Evanston, IL: Northwestern University Press, 1974). French original: *Le conflit des interprétations: Essais d'herméneutique I* (Paris: Seuil, 1969).

9. Laurent Jenny, 'La stratégie de la forme', *Poétique* 27 (1976), 257.

10. Michael Worton, 'Intertextuality: to Inter Textuality or to Resurrect it?', in David Kelley & Isabelle Llasera (eds), *Cross-References: Modern French Theory and the Practice of Criticism* (London: Society for French Studies, 1986), 18; Michael Riffaterre, 'Sémiotique intertextuelle: l'interprétant', *Rhétoriques, Sémiotiques: Revue d'esthétique* 1/2 (1979), (Paris: UGE 10/18, 1979), 128–50.

11. See Sigmund Freud, *The Interpretation of Dreams* (1900), in *The Complete Psychological Works of Sigmund Freud*, trans. and ed. James Strachey (1963; London: Hogarth Press, 1973), IV, 293–4, 303. German original: *Die Traumdeutung* (1900), in *Gesammelte Werke* (Frankfurt am Main: Fischer, 1999), I/II, 301–2, 309.

12. Julia Kristeva, 'Quelques problèmes de sémiotique littéraire à propos d'un texte de Mallarmé: Un coup de dés', in A. J. Greimas (ed.), *Essais de sémiotique poétique* (Paris: Larousse, 1972), 208–34.

13. David Dabydeen & Nana Wilson-Tagoe, *A Reader's Guide to West Indian and Black British Literature* (London: Hansib Publishing/Rutherford Press, 1988), 9.

14. See Monika Fludernik's comprehensive overview in *The Fictions of Language and the Languages of Fiction: The Linguistic Representation of Speech and Consciousness* (London: Routledge, 1993), 60–4.

15. Lubomír Doležel, *Heterocosmica: Fiction and Possible Worlds* (Baltimore MD: Johns Hopkins University Press, 1998), 33.

16. See for instance Dorit Cohn, *Transparent Minds: Narrative Modes for Presenting Consciousness in Fiction* (Princeton NJ: Princeton University Press, 1978).

17. Alan Palmer, *Fictional Minds* (Lincoln: University of Nebraska Press, 2004), 11, 194.

18. Lotman, *Universe of the Mind*, 140.

19. See Julia Kristeva, *Au risque de la pensée* (Paris: L'Aube, 2001), 96; Michael Riffaterre, *La Production du texte* (Paris: Seuil, 1979).

20. Charles Sanders Peirce, *Collected Papers*, I/II, 51.
21. Ibid., 50.
22. Gregory L. Ulmer, *Applied Grammatology: Post(e)-Pedagogy from Jacques Derrida to Joseph Beuys* (Baltimore: Johns Hopkins University Press, 1984), 162.
23. Antoine Compagnon, *La seconde main: ou le travail de la citation* (Paris: Seuil, 1979), 60–1; see also Russell West-Pavlov, *Transcultural Graffiti: Diasporic Writing and the Teaching of Literary Studies* (Amsterdam: Rodopi, 2005), 103, 118.
24. See André Gide, *Voyage au Congo* in *Journal 1939–1949, Souvenirs* (Paris: Gallimard/Pléiade, 1954), for instance 736, 769, 794.
25. Gérard Genette, *Narrative Discourse*, trans. Jane E. Levin (Oxford: Blackwell 1980), 215. French originals: *Discours du récit* in *Figures III* (Paris: Seuil, 1972), 228; *Discours du récit/Nouveau discours du récit* (1972, 1983; Paris: Seuil/folio essais, 2007), 223. See also, however, Gérard Genette, 'Espace et langage', *Figures I* (Paris: Seuil, 1966), 101–8, and 'La littérature et l'espace', *Figures II: Essais* (Paris: Seuil, 1969), 43–8.
26. See Peter Brooks, *Reading for the Plot: Design and Interpretation in Narrative* (Oxford: Clarendon Press, 1984), 238–63.
27. Stéphane Mallarmé, 'Λ Throw of Dice', trans. Daisy Aldan, in *The Anchor Anthology of French Poetry*, ed. Angel Flores (1958; New York: Anchor, 2000), 190–1. French original: 'Un Coup de dés', *Oeuvres*, ed. Yves-Alain Favre (Paris: Garnier, 1985), 444–5.
28. Christa Wolf, *Im Dialog: Aktuelle Texte* (Frankfurt am Main: Luchterhand, 1990), 140–1.
29. Robert Young, *White Mythologies: History, Writing and the West* (London: Routledge, 1990), 17, ostensibly quoting Emmanuel Lévinas, *Ethique et infini: Dialogues avec Philippe Nemo* (Paris: Livre de poche/biblio essais, 1988), 115; *Ethics and Infinity: Conversations with Philippe Nemo*, trans. Richard A. Cohen (Pittsburgh: Duquesne University Press, 1991), 117.
30. Joseph Conrad, Preface to *The Nigger of the 'Narcissus'* (1897; London: Dent, 1960), 5.
31. Dieter Saalman, 'Christa Wolf and and Joseph Conrad's *Heart of Darkness*: The Curse of the Blind Spot', *Neophilologus* 76: 1 (1992), 19–20; 'Elective Affinities: Christa Wolf's *Störfall* and Joseph Conrad's *Heart of Darkness*', *Comparative Literature Studies* 29: 3 (1992), 244.
32. Kristeva, Σημειωτική 164; this chapter is not translated in *Desire in Language*.
33. Kristeva, *Desire in Language* 66, Σημειωτική 85.
34. Roland Barthes, 'From Work to Text', *The Rustle of Language*, trans. Richard Howard (Berkeley: University of California Press, 1989), 60. French original: 'De l'oeuvre au texte', *Le Bruissement de la langue* (Paris: Seuil, 1984), 77.

5 Spatial Amnesia

1. Michael Ondaatje, *The English Patient* (1992; London: Picador, 1993), 246. Subsequent references in the text.
2. Bill Ashcroft, *Post-Colonial Transformation* (London: Routledge, 2001), 151.

3. See Lefebvre, *The Production of Space*, 33, 38–9; *La Production de l'espace*, 42–3, 48–9.
4. Smith, Neil, *Uneven Development: Nature, Capital and the Production of Space* (Oxford: Blackwell, 1984); Edward W. Soja, *Postmodern Geographies* (London: Verso, 1989).
5. Foucault, *Power/Knowledge* 70, *Dits et écrits* III, 34.
6. Julian Murphet, 'Postmodern Space' in Stephen Connor (ed.), *The Cambridge Companion to Postmodernism* (Cambridge: Cambridge University Press, 2004), 116.
7. Foucault, *Aesthetics* 175–6, *Dits et écrits* IV, 752.
8. Soja, *Postmodern Geographies*, 1.
9. Massey, *For Space* 30; see also Nigel Thrift, 'Overcome by Space: Reworking Foucault', in Jeremy W. Crampton & Stuart Elden (eds), *Space, Knowledge and Power: Foucault and Geography* (Aldershot: Ashgate, 2007), 53–8 for a similar argument.
10. Massey, *For Space*, 49.
11. Julia Kristeva, *Au risqué de la pensée* (Paris: L'Aube, 2001), 36.
12. Anne Godlewska & Neil Smith, 'Introduction: Critical Histories of Geography', in Godlewska & Smith (eds), *Geography and Empire* (Oxford: Blackwell, 1994), 1–2.
13. Lefebvre, *The Production of Space*, 27–30, *La Production de l'espace* 36–9.
14. Sabine Buchholz & Manfred Jahn, 'Space in Narrative', in David Herman, Manfred Jahn & Marie Laure Ryan (eds), *Routledge Encyclopedia of Narrative Theory* (London: Routledge, 2005), 551.
15. Genette, *Narrative Discourse*, 215. Original French: *Discours du récit* in *Figures III* (Paris: Seuil, 1972), 228 ; *Discours du récit/Nouveau discours du récit*, 223.
16. Shlomith Rimmon-Kenan, *Narrative Fiction: Contemporary Poetics* (London: Methuen, 1983), 14–15.
17. Issacharoff, *Discourse as Performance*, 55.
18. See Young, *White Mythologies*, 17.
19. Couze Venn, *The Postcolonial Challenge: Towards Alternative Worlds* (London: Sage, 2006), 55.
20. Kirwan Desai, *The Inheritance of Loss* (London: Hamish Hamilton/Penguin, 2006), 31, 34.
21. Lucretius, *The Nature of the Universe*, trans. R. E. Latham (Harmondsworth: Penguin, 1951), 39.
22. John Rickard, *Australia: A Cultural History*, 2nd edn. (London: Longman, 1996), 4.
23. See Mitchell, 'Imperial Space', in Mitchell (ed.), *Landscape and Power*, 5–34.
24. A. J. Greimas, 'Pour une sémiotique topologique', in *Sémiotique de l'espace: Architecture, urbanisme, sortir de l'impasse*, eds Manar Hammad, Eric Proovost & Michel Vernin (Paris: Denoël/Gonthier, 1979), 11.
25. Greimas, 'Pour une sémiotique topologique', 14.
26. See for instance B. Hillier & H. Janson, *The Social Logic of Space* (Cambridge: Cambridge University Press, 1984).
27. Stephen Muecke, *Ancient & Modern: Time, Culture and Indigenous Philosophy* (Sydney: UNSW Press, 2004), 9.
28. Niklas Luhmann, *Soziale Systeme: Grundriß einer allgemeinen Theorie* (Frankfurt/Main: Suhrkamp, 1984), 114 (in English in the German original).

For an extended reading, see my *Bodies and their Spaces: System, Crisis and Transformation in Early Modern Drama* (Amsterdam: Rodopi, 2006), 52–83.

29. Greimas, 'Pour une sémiotique topologique', 15.
30. See Chatman, *Story and Discourse*, 96–105.
31. Jakob Lothe, 'Space, Time, Narrative: From Thomas Hardy to Franz Kafka and J. M. Coetzee', in Gail Fincham, Jeremy Hawthorn, Attie de Lange & Jakob Lothe (eds), *Literary Landscapes: From Modernism to Postcolonialism* (Basingstoke: Palgrave Macmillan, 2008), 3.
32. The best known example is Gaston Bachelard, *The Poetics of Space*, trans. Maria Jolas (Boston, MA: Beacon Press, 1994). Original French: *La Poétique de l'espace* [1957] (Paris: PUF/Quadrige, 1994), Most other work in this vein has been done in German: see for instance Gerhard Hoffmann, *Raum, Situation, erzählte Wirklichkeit: Poetologische und historische Studien zum englischen und amerikanischen Roman* (Stuttgart: Metzler, 1978); Norbert Reichel, *Der erzählte Raum: Zur Verflechtung von sozialem und poetischem Raum in erzählender Literatur* (Darmstadt: Wissenschaftliche Buchgesellschaft, 1987); Alexander Ritter (ed.), *Landschaft und Raum in der Erzählkunst* (Darmstadt; Wissenschaftliche Buchgesellschaft, 1975).
33. Franco Moretti, *Atlas of the European Novel 1800–1900* (London: Verso, 1998), 3.
34. Barbara Piatti, *Die Geographie der Literatur: Schauplätze, Handlungsräume, Raumphantasien* (Göttingen: Wallstein, 2008), 126–31.
35. Carol Clarkson, 'Remains of the Name', in Gail Fincham, Jeremy Hawthorn, Attie de Lange & Jakob Lothe (eds), *Literary Landscapes: From Modernism to Postcolonialism* (Basingstoke: Palgrave Macmillan, 2008), 126.
36. Gerald Prince, 'Narratology, Narratological Criticism, and Gender', in Calin-Andrei Mihailescu & Walid Harmaneh (eds), *Fiction Updated: Theories of Fictionality, Narratology, and Poetics* (Toronto: University of Toronto Press, 1996), 163.
37. See Jürgen Osterhammel, *Colonialism: A Theoretical Overview*, trans. Shelley L. Frisch (Princeton NJ: Marcus Wiener, 1997), 10–12. Original German: *Kolonialismus: Geschichte – Formen – Folgen* (München: Beck, 1995), 16–18.
38. Mikhail Bakhtin, 'Forms of Time and the Chronotope in the Novel', in Michael Holquist (ed.), *The Dialogic Imagination: Four Essays by M. M. Bakhtin* (Austin, TX: The University of Texas Press, 1981), 84.
39. Mitchell, 'Imperial Space', 5–34.
40. See for instance James Ferguson, 'Decomposing Modernity: History and Hierarchy after Development', in Ania Loomba et al. (eds), *Postcolonial Studies and Beyond* (Durham: Duke University Press, 2005), 166–81.
41. Raymond Williams, *Marxism and Literature* (Oxford: Oxford University Press, 1977), 120–7.

6 Imperial Deixis

1. Achille Mbembe, *On the Postcolony*, trans. A. M. Berett, Janet Roitman, Murray Last & Steven Rendall (Berkeley: University of California Press, 2001), 4.

2. John Acton, *Lectures on Modern History* (1906), cited in Ashcroft, *Post-Colonial Transformation*, 96.
3. Partha Chatterjee, *Nationalist Thought and the Colonial World: A Derivative Discourse* (London: Zed Books, 1986), 17.
4. G. W. F. Hegel, *The Philosophy of History*, trans. J. Sibree (New York: Dover, 1956), 91 (translation modified). Original German: *Philosophie der Geschichte*, ed. Theodor Litt (Stuttgart: Reclam, 1961), 163.
5. Karl Marx, 'The Future Results of British Rule in India', *New York Daily Tribune*, 8 August 1853, quoted in Shlomo Avineri (ed.), *Karl Marx on Colonization & Modernization* (New York: Doubleday Anchor, 1969), 132–3.
6. Edouard Glissant, *Caribbean Discourse: Selected Essays*, trans. J. Michael Dash (Charlottesville: University Press of Virginia, 1989), 60, 62. Original French: *Le Discours antillais* (Paris: Seuil, 1981), 131, 133.
7. V. S. Naipaul, *A Bend in the River* (1979; London: Picador, 2002), 4. All subsequent page references in the text.
8. See John Agnew & Stuart Corbridge, *Mastering Space: Hegemony, Territory and International Political Economy* (London: Routledge, 1995), 207; Zygmunt Bauman, *Wasted Lives: Modernity and its Outcasts* (London: Polity, 2004).
9. V. S. Naipaul, 'A New King for the Congo: Mobutu and the Nihilism of Africa', *The Return of Eva Perón with The Killings in Trinidad* (Harmondsworth: Penguin, 1981), 196.
10. Edward Said, 'Always on Top', *London Review of Books* 25: 6 (20 March 2003).
11. Derek Walcott, 'The Spoiler's Return', in *The Fortunate Traveller* (New York: Farrar, Strauss & Giroux, 1981), 54.
12. Massey, *For Space*, 4.
13. From Robert Dunbar, *The Cruise, or A Prospect of the West Indian Archipelago* (1835) in Paula Burnett (ed.), *The Penguin Book of Caribbean Verse* (Harmondsworth: Penguin, 1986), 121.
14. David Spurr, *The Rhetoric of Empire: Colonial Discourse in Journalism, Travel Writing and Imperial Administration* (Durham NC: Duke University Press, 1993), 16.
15. Morris, *The Pirate's Fiancée*, 144–5.
16. See Victor Burgin, *In/Different Spaces: Place and Memory in Visual Culture* (Berkeley: University of California Press, 1996), 142–3.
17. See for instance, Bernhard Klein, *Maps and the Writing of Space in Early Modern England and Ireland* (Basingstoke: Palgrave Macmillan, 2001); Peter Hulme: 'Beyond the Straits: Postcolonial Allegories of the Globe' in Ania Loomba et al. (eds), *Postcolonial Studies and Beyond* (Durham: Duke University Press, 2005), 41–61.
18. Samuel Y. Edgerton, *The Renaissance Rediscovery of Perspective* (New York: Basic Books, 1975), 9–10.
19. Mark J. Bruhn, 'Place Deixis and the Schematics of Imagined Space: Milton to Keats', *Poetics Today* 26: 3 (Fall 2005), 387–432.
20. Bruhn, 'Place Deixis and the Schematics of Imagined Space', 387–8, 399 n24.
21. Jonathan Culler, *Structuralist Poetics: Structuralism, Linguistics and the Study of Literature* (London: Routledge & Kegan Paul, 1975), 165, 166; *Literary Theory: A Very Short Introduction* (Oxford: Oxford University Press, 1997), 31.

22. Bruhn, 'Place Deixis and the Schematics of Imagined Space', 389.
23. Liliach Lachman, 'Keats's *Hyperion*: Time, Space and the Long Poem', *Poetics Today* 22 (2001), 105.
24. See for instance Eric Williams, *Capitalism and Slavery* (Chapel Hill, NC: The University of North Carolina Press, 1944).
25. Raymond Williams, *The Country and the City* (London: Hogarth Press, 1985), 2.
26. Dorothy Wordsworth, 'Floating Island' (1842), in Paul Keegan (ed.), *The New Penguin Book of English Verse* (Harmondsworth: Penguin, 2001), 670.
27. Bruhn, 'Place Deixis and the Schematics of Imagined Space', 392.
28. See Ian Baucom, *Specters of the Atlantic: Finance Capital, Slavery, and the Philosophy of History* (Durham NC: Duke University Press, 2005).
29. John Keats, 'On First Looking into Chapman's Homer' (1816), in Robert Gittings (ed.), *Selected Poems and Letters of Keats* (London: Heinemann, 1982), 25.
30. Mary Louise Pratt, *Imperial Eyes: Travel Writing and Transculturation* (London: Routledge, 1992), 61.
31. Rudyard Kipling, *Kim*, ed. Edward Said (1901; Penguin: Harmondsworth, 2000), 49.
32. Edward W. Said, *Culture and Imperialism* (1993; London: Vintage, 1994), 162.
33. Aimé Césaire, *Cahier d'un retour au pays natal/Return to My Native Land*, trans. Emile Snyder (1956; Paris: Présence africaine, 1971), 28, 29; translation modified.
34. Jean Rhys, *Wide Sargasso Sea* (1962; Harmondsworth: Penguin, 1968), 106.
35. Henry Reynolds, *The Other Side of the Frontier: Aboriginal Resistance to the European Invasion of Australia* (1981; Ringwood VIC: Penguin, 1995).
36. Glissant, *Caribbean Discourse* 66, *Discours antillais* 134.
37. Foucault, *Dits et écrits* III, 581.
38. Arundhati Roy, *The God of Small Things* (London: Flamingo/HarperCollins, 1997), [ix]. Subsequent references in the text.
39. Salman Rushdie, *Midnight's Children* (1981; London: Vintage, 1995), 9. Subsequent references in the text.
40. See Stephen Connor, *The English Novel in History 1950–1995* (London: Routledge, 1996), 2–8.
41. Michel Foucault, *Archaeology of Knowledge*, trans. Alan M. Sheridan Smith (1970; London: Routledge, 2002), 8. Original French: *L'archéologie du savoir* (Paris: Gallimard, 1969), 15.

7 Self-reflexive Deixis and the Aporias of the Nation

1. J. E. Clare McFarlane, 'On National Vanity', circa 1948, in Burnett (ed.), *The Penguin Book of Caribbean Verse*, 153.
2. Homi K. Bhabha, *The Location of Culture* (London: Routledge, 1994), 145.
3. See for instance, Jonathan Gathorne-Hardy, *The Public School Phenomenon, 597–1977* (1977; Harmondsworth: Penguin, 1979), 150–7, 209–13.
4. Judith Butler, *Gender Trouble: Feminism and the Subversion of Identity* (New York: Routledge, 1990), 33.

5. Basil Davidson, *The Black Man's Burden: Africa and the Curse of the Nation-State* (New York: Times Books, 1992), 215.

6. Frantz Fanon, *The Wretched of the Earth*, trans. Contance Farrington (1961; Harmondsworth: Penguin, 1967), 119; *Les Damnés de la terre* (Paris: Maspero, 1961), 113.

7. On this topic see Benedict Anderson, *Imagined Communities: Reflections on the Origin and Spread of Nationalism*, rev. ed. (London: Verso, 1991), 47–65; Tom Nairn, *The Break-Up of Britain: Crisis and Neo-Nationalism*, 2nd edn. (London: Verso, 1981), 38–44.

8. Fanon, *The Wretched of the Earth*, 150; *Les Damnés de la terre*, 139.

9. Thierry G. Verhelst, *No Life Without Roots: Culture and Development*, trans. Bob Cumming (London: Zed, 1990), 38.

10. Robert J. C. Young, *Postcolonialism: An Historical Introduction* (Oxford: Blackwell, 2001), 125, 240.

11. See Agnew & Corbridge, *Mastering Space*, 36–40.

12. Stuart Hall, 'When Was "The Post-Colonial"? Thinking at the Limit', in Iain Chambers & Lidia Curti (eds), *The Post-Colonial Question: Common Skies, Divided Horizons* (London: Routledge, 1996), 250.

13. Neil Lazarus, *Nationalism and Cultural Practice in the Postcolonial World* (Cambridge: Cambridge University Press, 1999), 108–9.

14. Homi K. Babha, 'DissemiNation: Time, Narrative, and the Margins of the Modern Nation', in Bhabha (ed.), *Nation and Narration* (London: Routledge, 1990), 315.

15. A salutary exception is Gayatri Chakravorty Spivak, who always links these issues: see for instance *A Critique of Postcolonial Reason: Towards a History of the Vanishing Present* (Cambridge, MA: Harvard University Press, 1999), 256–66.

16. Ania Loomba, *Colonialism/Postcolonialism* (London: Routledge, 1998), 11–12.

17. Chinua Achebe, *Things Fall Apart* (1958; London: Heinemann, 1986), 147–8.

18. Roland Oliver & J. D. Fage, *A Short History of Africa*, rev. ed. (1962; 1978; Harmondsworth: Penguin, 1995), 246.

19. Mbembe, *On the Postcolony*, 2.

20. Joseph Frank, 'Spatial Form in Modern Literature', *The Widening Gyre: Crisis and Mastery in Modern Literature* (New Brunswick, NJ: Rutgers University Press, 1963), 3–62; Jeffrey R. Smitten & Ann Daghistany, 'Editors' preface', in Smitten & Daghistany (eds), *Spatial Form in Narrative* (Ithaca/London: Cornell University Press, 1981), 13.

21. Joseph Frank, 'Spatial Form: Some Further Reflections', *Critical Inquiry* 5:2 (Winter 1978), 281.

22. Sharon Spencer, *Space, Time and Structure in the Modern Novel* (New York: New York University Press, 1971), xx.

23. W. B. Yeats, *Selected Poetry*, ed. A. Norman Jeffares (London: Pan Macmillan, 1978), 99.

24. Nadine Gordimer, *A Guest of Honour* (1970; Harmondsworth: Penguin, 1973), 525.

25. Franco Moretti, *Atlas of the European Novel 1800–1900* (London: Verso, 1998), 17, see also 20; Fredric Jameson, *Fables of Aggression: Wyndham Lewis,*

The Modernist as Fascist (Berkeley: University of California Press, 1979), 94. By contrast, for a content-based reading which explicitly eschews connections between the "political" nation and literary form see Patrick Parrinder's none the less marvellously readable *Nation & Novel: The English Novel from its Origins to the Present Day* (Oxford: Oxford University Press, 2006), in particular 15–20.

26. See Oswald Spengler, *The Decline of the West: An Abridged Edtion*, trans. Charles Francis Atkinson (New York: Oxford University Press, 1991), 97. Original German: *Der Untergang des Abendlandes: Umrisse einer Morphologie der Weltgeschichte* (1923; München: dtv, 1997), 234.

27. George Eliot, *Silas Marner: The Weaver of Raveloe* (Oxford: Oxford University Press/The World's Classics, 1996), 21.

28. Ngũgĩ wa Thiong'o, *A Grain of Wheat*, rev. ed. (1967, 1986; Harmondsworth: Penguin, 2002). All subsequent references in the text.

29. Kwame Anthony Appiah, 'Is the post- in postmodernism the post- in postcolonial?', *Critical Inquiry* 17: 2 (Winter 1991), 336–57.

30. See for instance Elikia M'Bokolo, *L'Afrique au XXe siècle: Le continent convoité* (Paris: Seuil/Points, 1985), 334–41.

31. Appiah, 'Is the post- in postmodernism the post- in postcolonial?', 352.

32. See Max Weber, *Max Weber: Essays in Sociology*, trans. and ed. H. H. Gerth & C. Wright Mills (New York: Oxford University Press, 1946), 155. Original German: *Soziologie – Weltgeschichtliche Analysen – Politik*, ed. Eduard Baumgarten (Stuttgart: Kroner, 1968), 317, 338; Anthony Giddens, *The Consequences of Modernity* (Stanford, Cal.: Stanford University Press, 1991), 18.

33. See Franco Moretti, *The Way of the World: The Bildungsroman in European Culture* trans. Albert Sbragia (London: Verso, 2000); Original Italian: *Il romanzo de formazione* (Milan: Garzanti, 1986).

34. James Ngugi, *Weep Not, Child* (London: Heineman, 1964), 92–3.

35. Quoted in Spurr, *The Rhetoric of Empire*, 93.

36. Bill Ashcroft, *On Post-Colonial Futures: Transformations of Colonial Culture* (New York: Continuum, 2001), 40.

37. See Tirop Simatei, 'Colonial Violence, Postcolonial Violations: Violence, Landscape and Memory in Kenyan Fiction', *Research in African Literatures* 36: 2 (Summer 2005), 88–9.

38. Mahmood Mamdami, 'Lessons of Zimbawe', *London Review of Books* 23: 4 (4 December 2008), 17.

39. Aimé Césaire, *Cahier d'un retour au pays natal/Return to My Native Land*, 42, 43.

8 Critiques of National Narratives

1. Liam Davison, *The White Woman* (St Lucia: University of Queensland Press, 1994), 138–9.

2. See Pat Grimshaw, 'Federation as a Turning Point in Australian History', *Australian Historical Studies*, 33: 118 (2002), 25–41.

3. Paul Carter, *The Road to Botany Bay: An Essay in Spatial History* (London: Faber & Faber, 1987). All subsequent references in the text.

4. See Paul Carter, *Living in a New Country: History, Travelling and Language* (London: Faber, 1992), 1–8.

5. Carter, *The Lie of the Land*, 2.

6. Bill Ashcroft, Gareth Griffiths, & Helen Tiffin, *The Empire Writes Back: Theory and Practice in Post-Colonial Literatures* (London: Routledge, 1989), 2.

7. Fanon, *The Wretched of the Earth*, 29–30, *Les damnés de la terre*, 31–2.

8. Frantz Fanon, *Sociologie d'une révolution (L'an V de la révolution algérienne)* (1959; Paris: Maspero, 1968), 34–5.

9. Ahmadou Kourouma, *Les Soleils des indépendances* (1970; Paris: Seuil/Points, 1990), 18.

10. See Mark Sanders, *Complicities: The Intellectual and Apartheid* (Durham NC: Duke University Press, 2001), 16–17.

11. Zoë Wicomb, *David's Story* (2000; New York: Feminist Press at The City University of New York, 2001). All subsequent references in the text. I am grateful to Rebecca Fasselt for making this text known to me, and to the members of the Postcolonial Studies Forum at the Free University of Berlin for exchanging their readings of it.

12. See Zoë Wicomb, 'Shame and Identity: the Case of the Coloured in South Africa' in Mary Jolley & Derek Attridge (eds), *Writing South Africa: Literature, Apartheid, and Democracy, 1970–1995* (Cambridge: Cambridge University Press, 1998), 91–107.

13. For a cogent and sobering discussion of the ANC and its legacy, see R. W. Johnson, 'End of the Road', *London Review of Books* 30: 22 (20 November 2008), 13–16.

14. See the interview with Zoë Wicomb, 'Zoë Wicomb in conversation with Hein Willemse', *Research in African Literatures* 33: 1 (Spring 2002), 144–52.

15. M. G. Vassanji, *The In-Between World of Vikram Lall* (2003; London: Cannongate, 2008). All subsequent references in the text. I am indebted to Justus Makokha for drawing my attention to this text.

16. Ashcroft, *On Post-Colonial Futures*, 129.

17. See Edward Said, *The World, the Text, and the Critic* (London: Faber & Faber, 1984), 16–20.

18. Paul Gilroy, *The Black Atlantic: Modernity and Double Consciousness* (London: Verso, 1993), 4.

19. James Clifford cited by Iain Chambers, *Migrancy, Culture, Identity* (London: Routledge/Comedia, 1994), 1.

20. See Jackson Kennel, '"Impossible to ignore their Greatness": Survival Craft in the Mau Mau Forest Movement', in E. S. Atieno Odhiambo & John Lonsdale (eds), *Mau Mau and Nationhood* (London: James Currey, 2005), 176–90.

21. On this topic, see my 'Exile as Origin: Definitions of Australian Identity in David Malouf's *12 Edmondstone Street*', *Anglia* 119: 1 (2001), 77–92.

9   DeiXis and Loss

1. Carter, *The Lie of the Land*, 2.

2. Femi Fatoba, 'In America', in Burnet (ed.), *The Penguin Book of Modern African Poetry*, 270.

3. Stephen Muecke, *No Road (bitumen all the way)* (Fremantle: Fremantle Arts Centre Press, 1997), 18.

4. See Stuart Hall, 'When Was "The Post-Colonial"? Thinking at the Limit', in Iain Chambers & Lidia Curti (eds), *The Post-Colonial Question: Common Skies, Divided Horizons* (London: Routledge, 1996), 242–60.

5. Amilcar Cabral, *Return to the Source: Selected Speeches by Amilcar Cabral*, ed. Africa Information Service (New York: Monthly Review Press, 1973), 60.

6. V. S. Naipaul, *The Enigma of Arrival* (1987; London: Picador, 2002), 247. Subsequent references in the text.

7. See Agnew & Corbridge, *Mastering Space*, 36–40.

8. Bart Moore-Gilbert, *Postcolonial Theory: Contexts, Practices, Politics* (London: Verso, 1997), 121.

9. Weber, *Max Weber: Essays in Sociology*, 155; Original German: *Soziologie – Weltgeschichtliche Analysen – Politik*, 317, 338.

10. See Herbert Marcuse, *One-Dimensional Man: Studies in the Ideology of Advanced Industrial Society* (London: Routledge & Kegan Paul, 1964).

11. Contrast Jürgen Habermas, 'Modernity: An Unfinished Project', in Charles Jencks (ed.), *The Post-Modern Reader* (London: Academy Editions, 1992), 158–69; Original German in *Die Moderne – ein unvollendetes Projekt: Philosophisch-politische Aufsätze 1977–1990* (Leipzig; Reclam, 1990), 32–54.

12. Marina Warner, *Indigo* (1992; London: Vintage, 1993), 131–2 (emphasis added). Subsequent references in the text.

13. See Maurice Blanchot, *The Writing of the Disaster*, trans. Anne Smock (Lincoln NE: University of Nebraska Press, 1986). Original French: *L'Ecriture du désastre* (Paris: Gallimard, 1980).

14. Patrick Chamoiseau, *Solibo Magnifique* (1988; Paris: Gallimard/folio, 1995), 207. Subsequent references in the text.

15. Gail Fincham, 'Orality, Literacy and Community: Conrad's *Nostromo* and Ngugi's *Petals of Blood*', *Conradian* 17: 1 (1992), 45–71. On narrative exchange, see Ian Reid, *Narrative Exchanges* (London: Routledge, 1992).

16. Edouard Glissant, *Mahogany* (Paris: Seuil, 1987), 24. All subsequent references in the text.

17. Jakobson, *Selected Writings*, II, 27.

18. Glissant, *Caribbean Discourse* 67, *Discours antillais* 134.

19. See for instance Eliot, 'Burnt Norton', *Four Quartets*, in *The Collected Poems and Plays of T. S. Eliot*, 172.

10 DeiXis Rediscovered

1. David Malouf, *Child's Play/Eustace/The Prowler* (1982; Ringwood VIC: Penguin, 1985), 90, 92. All subsequent references in the text.

2. Giorgio Agamben, *Homo Sacer: Sovereign Power and Bare Life*, trans. Daniel Heller-Roazen (1995; Stanford: Stanford University Press, 1998), 105.

3. David Malouf, *Remembering Babylon* (1993; New York: Vintage, 1994), 196. Subsequent references in the text.

4. See for instance Peter Otto, 'Forgetting Colonialism', *Meanjin* 52: 3 (1993), 545–58.

5. See René Girard, *Deceit, Desire and the Novel: Self and Other in Literary Structure*, trans. Yvonne Freccero (Baltimore ML: Johns Hopkins University Press, 1966) and *Violence and the Sacred*, trans. Patrick Gregory (Baltmore, ML: Johns Hopkins University Press, 1977). Original French: *Mensonge*

romantique et vérité romanesque (Paris: Grasset, 1961) and *La Violence et le sacré* (Paris: Grasset, 1972).

6. On this topic see David Punter, *Postcolonial Imaginings: Fictions of a New World Order* (Edinburgh: Edinburgh University Press, 2000).

7. Rukmini Bhaya Nair, *Lying on the Postcolonial Couch: The Idea of Indifference* (Minneapolis: University of Minnesota Press, 2002), 191.

8. See Graham Huggan, *Australian Literature: Postcolonialism, Racism, Transnationalism* (Oxford: Oxford University Press, 2007), 104–5.

9. See for instance C. D. Rowley, *The Destruction of Aboriginal Society* (Ringwood, Victoria: Penguin, 1972); Basil Sansom, *The Camp at Wallaby Cross: Aboriginal Fringe Dwellers in Darwin* (Canberra: Australian Institute of Aboriginal Studies, 1980); *Bringing them Home*: Report of the National Inquiry into the Separation of Aboriginal and Torres Strait Islander Children from Their Families (April 1997). http://www.hreoc.gov.au/Social_Justice/bth_report/report/index.html (accessed 9 September 2008); Anna Haebich, *Broken Circles: Fragmenting Indigenous Families, 1800–2000* (Fremantle: Fremantle Arts Centre Press, 2001).

10. Eva Johnson, *Murras*, in Justine Saunders (ed.) *Plays from Black Australia: Jack Davis, Eva Johnson, Jack Walley, Bob Mazza* (Sydney: Currency, 1989), 85, 87–8.

11. See André Leroi-Gourhan, *Le Geste et la parole: la mémoire et les rythmes* (Paris: Albin Michel, 1965).

12. David Malouf, *An Imaginary Life* (1978; Woolahra, NSW: Pan/Picador, 1982), 146–7.

13. E. M. Forster, *A Passage to India* (1924; Harmondsworth: Penguin, 1967), 123–5. All subsequent references in the text.

14. Gail Fincham, 'Space and Place in the Novels of E. M. Forster', in Gail Fincham, Jeremy Hawthorn, Attie de Lange & Jakob Lothe (eds), *Literary Landscapes: From Modernism to Postcolonialism* (Basingstoke: Palgrave Macmillan, 2008), 52, 54.

15. See for instance Alfred W. Cosby, *Ecological Imperialism: The Biological Expansion of Europe 900–1900* (Cambridge: Cambridge University Press/Canto, 1993).

16. See François Poirié, *Emmanuel Lévinas: qui êtes-vous?* (Lyon: La Manufacture, 1987), 28; Emmanuel Lévinas, *Humanism of the Other*, trans. Nidra Poller (Urbana IL: University of Illinois Press, 2006), 45–58. Original French: *Humanisme de l'autre homme* (1972; Paris: Livre de poche/biblio essais, 1987), 71–91.

17. Alexis Wright, *Carpentaria* (2006; London: Constable, 2008). Subsequent page references in the text.

18. Muecke, *Ancient and Modern*, 69.

19. Deborah Bird Rose, 'Taking Notice', *Worldview: Environment, Culture, Religion* 3: 2 (August 1999), 100.

20. Mitchell, 'Introduction', 1.

21. Dietrich Krusche, *Zeigen im Text: Anschauliche Orientierung in literarischen Modellen von Welt* (Würzburg: Königshausen & Neumann, 2001), 70–1.

22. Mitchell, 'Imperial Space', 5.

23. Muecke, *Ancient and Modern*, 93.

24. Rose, 'Taking Notice', 102.

25. Charles Tomlinson, 'Preface', *Collected Poems* (Oxford: Oxford University Press, 1985), vii.
26. See for instance Kim Scott, *True Country* (Fremantle WA: Fremantle Arts Centre Press, 1993).
27. Kim Scott & Hazel Brown, *Kayang & Me* (Fremantle: Fremantle Arts Centre Press, 2005), 220. All subsequent references in the text.
28. Vimala Herman, 'Deixis and Space in Drama', *Social Semiotics* 7: 3 (1997), 271.
29. Philip Clarke, *Where the Ancestors Walked: Australia as an Aboriginal Landscape* (Crows Nest NSW: Allen & Unwin, 2005), 18.
30. Carter, *The Road to Botany Bay*, 346.
31. Manfred Pfister, '"As an unperfect actor on the stage": Notes Towards a Definition of Performance and Performativity in Shakespeare's *Sonnets*', in Eva Müller-Zettelmann & Margarete Rubik (eds), *Theory into Poetry: New Approaches to the Lyric* (Amsterdam: Rodopi, 2005), 211.
32. Quoted in Ashcroft, *Post-colonial Transformation*, 140.
33. Paddy Roe, *Gularabulu: Stories from the West Kimberely*, ed. Stephen Muecke (Fremantle: Fremantle Arts Centre Press, 1983).
34. Eddie Kneebone quoted in Mudrooroo, *Us Mob*, 35.
35. Stephen Muecke, 'A Chance to Hear a Nyigina Song', in Judith Ryan & Chris Wallace-Crabbe (eds) *Imagining Australia: Literature and Culture in the New World* (Cambridge, MA: Harvard University Press, 2004), 129.
36. Lefebvre, *The Production of Space*, 27–30, *La Production de l'espace* 36–9.

Conclusion: "Here Fix the Tablet"

1. See Henry Reynolds, *Aboriginal Sovereignty: Three Nations, One Australia?* (Crows Nest, NSW: Allen & Unwin, 1996).
2. Barron Field, 'On Visiting the Spot where Captain Cook and Sir Joseph Banks First Landed in Botany Bay', *Sydney Gazette*, 22 March 1822. Many thanks to Anja Schwarz for drawing my attention to this poem. See Anja Schwarz, 'Beached: A Postcolonial Reading of the Australian Shore', unpublished PhD thesis, Free University of Berlin, 2008, 201–4.
3. See Ashcroft, Griffith & Tiffin, *The Empire Writes Back*, 4–6.
4. Foucault, *Language, Counter-Memory, Practice: Selected Essays and Interviews*, ed. Donald F. Bouchard, trans. Donald F. Bouchard & Sherry Simon (Ithaca: Cornell University Press, 1977), 142, *Dits et écrits 1954–1988*, II, 138.
5. Simon During, 'Out of England: Literary Subjectivity in the Australian Colonies, 1788–1867', in Judith Ryan & Chris Wallace-Crabbe (eds), *Imagining Australia: Literature and Culture in the New World* (Cambridge, MA: Harvard University Press, 2004), 9–10.
6. Alan Moorehead, *The Fatal Impact: The Invasion of the South Pacific 1767–1840* (London: Hamish Hamilton, 1966).
7. Mitchell, 'Imperial Space', 10.
8. Kate Grenville, *The Secret River* (Melbourne: Text, 2005). References in the text.
9. Quoted in Philip Toyne & Daniel Vachon, *Growing up the Country: The Pitjantjatjara Struggle for their Land* (Melbourne: McPhee Gribble, 1984), 5.

Bibliography

Primary Literature

Achebe, Chinua, *Things Fall Apart* (1958; London: Heinemann, 1986).

Beckett, Samuel, *The Unnameable* (1958; New York: The Grove Press, 1970). French original: *L'Innommable: Roman* (Paris: Minuit, 1953).

Beckett, Samuel, *Waiting for Godot: A Tragicomedy in Two Acts* (1956; London: Faber & Faber, 1971). French original: *En attendant Godot* (1952; Paris: Minuit, 1976).

Borges, Jorge Luis, *Dreamtigers*, trans. M. Boyer & H. Morland (Austin, TX: University of Texas Press, 1964); Spanish original: *El hacedor* (Buenos Aires: Emecé Editores, 1969).

Borges, Jorge Luis, *Labyrinths*, ed. Donald A. Yates & James E. Irby (Harmondsworth: Penguin, 1971); Spanish original: *Prosa Completa* (Barcelona: Bruguera, 1980), I.

Calvino, Italo, *Invisible Cities*, trans. William Weaver (London: Picador, 1979); Italian original: *Le Città invisibili* (1972; Milan: Oscar Mondadori, 1993).

Céline, Louis Ferdinand, *Voyage au bout de la nuit* (1932; Paris: Livre de poche, 1962).

Césaire, Aimé, *Cahier d'un retour au pays natal/Return to My Native Land*, trans. Emile Snyder (1956; Paris: Présence africaine, 1971).

Chamoiseau, Patrick, *Solibo Magnifique* (1988; Paris: Gallimard/folio, 1995).

Conrad, Joseph, *Heart of Darkness and Other Tales* (1899/1900; Oxford: Oxford University Press/World's Classics, 1990).

Conrad, Joseph, *Last Essays* in *Tales of Hearsay and Last Essays* (London: Dent, 1955).

Conrad, Joseph, *The Nigger of the 'Narcissus'* (1897; London: Dent, 1960).

Dabydeen, David, *The Intended* (1991; London: Vintage, 1993).

Davison, Liam, *The White Woman* (St Lucia QLD: University of Queensland Press, 1994).

Desai, Kirwan, *The Inheritance of Loss* (London: Hamish Hamilton/Penguin, 2006).

Eliot, George, *Silas Marner: The Weaver of Raveloe* (Oxford: Oxford University Press/The World's Classics, 1996).

Eliot, T. S., *The Complete Poems and Plays of T. S. Eliot* (London: Faber & Faber, 1969).

Field, Barron, 'On Visiting the Spot where Captain Cook and Sir Joseph Banks First Landed in Botany Bay', *Sydney Gazette*, 22 March 1822.

Findley, Timothy, *Headhunter* (Toronto: Random House, 1993).

Forster, E. M., *A Passage to India* (1924; Harmondsworth: Penguin, 1967).

Gide, André, *Journal 1939–1949; Souvenirs* (Paris: Gallimard/NRF, Pléiade, 1954).

Gide, André, *The Immoralist*, trans. Dorothy Bussy (New York: Alfred Knopf, 1930). French original: *L'Immoraliste* (1902), in *Romans* (Paris: NRF/Pleiade, 1958).

Glissant, Edouard, *Mahogany* (Paris: Seuil, 1987).

Gordimer, Nadine, *A Guest of Honour* (1970; Harmondsworth: Penguin, 1973).

Grenville, Kate, *The Secret River* (Melbourne: Text, 2005).

Joyce, James, *Finnegan's Wake* (1939; London: Faber & Faber, 1975).

Keats, John, *Selected Poems and Letters of Keats*, ed. Robert Gittings (London: Heinemann, 1982).

Kipling, Rudyard, *Kim*, ed. Edward Said (1901; Penguin: Harmondsworth, 2000).

Kourouma, Ahmadou, *Les Soleils des indépendances* (1970; Paris: Seuil/Points, 1990).

Leiris, Michel, *L'Afrique fantôme* (1934; Paris: Gallimard/tel, 1988).

Mallarmé, Stéphane, 'A Throw of Dice', trans. Daisy Aldan, in *The Anchor Anthology of French Poetry*, ed. Angel Flores (1958; New York: Anchor, 2000). French original: 'Un Coup de dés', *Oeuvres*, ed. Yves-Alain Favre (Paris: Garnier, 1985).

Malouf, David, *An Imaginary Life* (1978; Woolahra, NSW: Pan/Picador, 1982).

Malouf, David, *Child's Play/Eustace/The Prowler* (1982; Ringwood VIC: Penguin, 1985).

Malouf, David, *Remembering Babylon* (1993; New York: Vintage, 1994).

Mda, Zakes, *Heart of Redness* (New York: Picador, 2000).

Naipaul, V. S., *An Area of Darkness* (1964; Harmondsworth: Penguin, 1970).

Naipaul, V. S., *A Bend in the River* (1979; London: Picador, 2002).

Naipaul, V. S., *The Return of Eva Perón with The Killings in Trinidad* (Harmondsworth: Penguin, 1981).

Naipaul, V. S., *The Enigma of Arrival* (1987; London: Picador, 2002).

Naipaul, V. S., *Literary Occasions: Essays*, ed. Pankaj Mishra (New York: Knopf, 2003).

Neidjie, Bill, *Story About Feeling*, ed. Keith Taylor (Broome WA: Magabala Books, 1989).

Ngũgĩ wa Thiong'o, *A Grain of Wheat*, rev. edn. (1967, 1986; Harmondsworth: Penguin, 2002).

Ngũgĩ, James, *Weep Not, Child* (London: Heineman, 1964).

Ondaatje, Michael, *The English Patient* (1992; London: Picador, 1993).

Pope, Alexander, *Poetical Works*, ed. Herbert Davis (Oxford University Press, 1978).

Rhys, Jean, *Wide Sargasso Sea* (1962; Harmondsworth: Penguin, 1968).

Roe, Paddy, *Gularabulu: Stories from the West Kimberely*, ed. Stephen Muecke (Fremantle: Fremantle Arts Centre Press, 1983).

Roy, Arundhati, *The God of Small Things* (London: Flamingo/HarperCollins, 1997).

Rushdie, Salman, *Midnight's Children* (1981; London: Vintage, 1995).

Saunders, Justine (ed.) *Plays from Black Australia: Jack Davis, Eva Johnson, Jack Walley, Bob Mazza* (Sydney: Currency, 1989).

Scott, Kim, *True Country* (Fremantle: Fremantle Arts Centre Press, 1993).

Scott, Kim & Hazel Brown, *Kayang & Me* (Fremantle: Fremantle Arts Centre Press, 2005).

Sterne, Laurence, *The Life and Opinions of Tristram Shandy* (Harmondsworth: Penguin, 1985).

Strittmatter, Eva & Erwin Strittmatter, *Landschaft aus Wasser, Wacholder und Stein*, ed. Almut Giesecke (Berlin: Aufbau, 2005).

Tomlinson, Charles, *Collected Poems* (Oxford: Oxford University Press, 1985).

Vassanji, M. G., *The In-Between World of Vikram Lall* (2003; London: Cannongate, 2008).
Walcott, Derek, *The Fortunate Traveller* (New York: Farrar, Strauss & Giroux, 1981).
Warner, Marina, *Indigo* (1992; London: Vintage, 1993).
Wicomb, Zoë, *David's Story* (2000; New York: Feminist Press at The City University of New York, 2001).
Wolf, Christa, *Accident: A Day's News*, trans. Heike Schwarzbauer & Rick Takvorian (New York: Farrar, Straus & Giroux, 1989). German original: *Störfall: Nachrichten eines Tages* (Frankfurt am Main: Luchterhand, 1987).
Wolf, Christa, *Im Dialog: Aktuelle Texte* (Frankfurt am Main: Luchterhand, 1990).
Wright, Alexis, *Carpentaria* (2006; London: Constable, 2008).
Yeats, W. B., *Selected Poetry*, ed. A. Norman Jeffares (London: Pan Macmillan, 1978).

Secondary literature

Aczel, Richard, 'Rhetorical Figures as Narrative Strategies in English Renaissance Prose Fiction', in Bernhard Reitz & Sigrid Rieuwerts (eds), *Anglistentag 1999 Mainz: Proceedings* (Trier: WVT, 2000), 451–61.
Adorno, Theodor W., *Aesthetic Theory*, trans. Robert Hullot-Kentor (London: Athlone Press, 1997). German original: *Ästhetische Theorie* (Frankfurt am Main: Suhrkamp, 1973).
Agamben, Giorgio, *Homo Sacer: Sovereign Power and Bare Life*, trans. Daniel Heller-Roazen (1995; Stanford: Stanford University Press, 1998).
Agnew, John, & Stuart Corbridge, *Mastering Space: Hegemony, Territory and International Political Economy* (London: Routledge, 1995).
Althusser, Louis, 'A letter on art in reply to Andre Daspre', trans. Ben Brewster, *Lenin and Philosophy and Other Essays* (New York: Monthly Review Press, 1971), 221–8. French original: 'Lettre sur la connaisance de l'art (réponse à André Daspre)', *Ecrits philosophiques et politiques* (Paris: Stock/IMEC, 1995), II, 559–66.
Anderson, Benedict, *Imagined Communities: Reflections on the Origin and Spread of Nationalism*, rev. edn. (London: Verso, 1991).
Appiah, Kwame Anthony, 'Is the post- in postmodernism the post- in postcolonial?', *Critical Inquiry* 17: 2 (Winter 1991), 336–57.
Ashcroft, Bill, *On Post-Colonial Futures: Transformations of Colonial Culture* (New York: Continuum, 2001).
Ashcroft, Bill, *Post-Colonial Transformation* (London: Routledge, 2001).
Ashcroft, Bill, Gareth Griffiths, & Helen Tiffin, *The Empire Writes Back: Theory and Practice in Post-Colonial Literatures* (London: Routledge, 1989), 2.
Attridge, Derek, *Joyce Effects: On Language, Theory and History* (Cambridge: Cambridge University Press, 2000).
Attridge, Derek & Marjorie Howes (eds), *Semicolonial Joyce* (Cambridge: Cambridge University Press, 2000).
Bachelard, Gaston, *The Poetics of Space*, trans. Maria Jolas (Boston, MA: Beacon Press, 1994). Original French: *La Poétique de l'espace* (1957; Paris: PUF/Quadrige, 1994).

Baird, Theodore, 'The Time Scheme of Tristram Shandy and a Source', *PMLA* 51 (1936), 803–20.

Bakhtin, Mikhail, *The Dialogic Imagination: Four Essays by M. M. Bakhtin*, ed. Michael Holquist (Austin, TX: The University of Texas Press, 1981).

Bakhtin, Mikhail/V. N. Vološinov, *Marxism and the Philosophy of Language*, trans. Ladislav Matejka and I. R. Titurik (1929; Cambridge, MA: Harvard University Press, 1986).

Barthes, Roland, 'From Work to Text', *The Rustle of Language*, trans. Richard Howard (Berkeley: University of California Press, 1989), 49–82. French original: 'De l'oeuvre au texte', *Le Bruissement de la langue* (Paris: Seuil, 1984), 69–78.

Barthes, Roland, *The Semiotic Challenge*, trans. Richard Howard (Berkeley: University of California Press, 1994). French original: *L'Aventure sémiologique* (Paris: Seuil/Points, 1985).

Baucom, Ian, *Specters of the Atlantic: Finance Capital, Slavery, and the Philosophy of History* (Durham NC: Duke University Press, 2005).

Bauman, Zygmunt, *Wasted Lives: Modernity and its Outcasts* (London: Polity, 2004).

Benjamin, Walter, 'The Task of the Translator: An Introduction to the Translation of Baudelaire's *Tableaux Parisiens*', trans. Harry Zorn, in *Illuminations*, ed. Hannah Arendt (London: Pimlico, 1999), 70–82. German original: 'Die Aufgabe des Übersetzers', in *Illuminationen: Ausgewählte Schriften I*, ed. Siegfried Unseld (Frankfurt am Main: Suhrkamp, 1969), 56–69.

Benveniste, Emile, *Problems in General Linguistics*, trans. Mary Elizabeth Meeks (Coral Gables, Florida: University of Miami Press, 1971). French original: *Problèmes de linguistique générale* (Paris: Gallimard, 1966 & 1974), 2 volumes.

Berndt, Ronald M., *Love Songs of Arnhem Land* (Chicago: University of Chicago Press, 1976).

Bhabha, Homi K. (ed.), *Nation and Narration* (London: Routledge, 1990).

Bhabha, Homi K., *The Location of Culture* (London: Routledge, 1994).

Bloom, Harold, *The Anxiety of Influence* (New York: Oxford University Press, 1973).

Bourdieu, Pierre, *Distinction: A Social Critique of the Judgement of Taste*, trans. Richard Nice (London: Routledge, 1984). French original: *La distinction: Critique sociale du jugement* (Paris: Minuit, 1979).

Bourdieu, Pierre, *Reproduction in Education, Society and Culture*, trans. Richard Nice (London: Sage, 1990). French original: *La Réproduction: Eléments pour une théorie du système d'enseignement* (Paris: Minuit, 1970).

Bourdieu, Pierre & Jean-Claude Passeron, *The Inheritors: French Students and their Relation to Culture*, trans. Richard Nice (Chicago: University of Chicago Press, 1979). French original: *Les héritiers: Les étudiants et la culture* (Paris: Minuit, 1964).

Bourke, Colin, Eleanor Bourke & Bill Edwards (eds), *Aboriginal Australia: An Introductory Reader in Aboriginal Studies* (St Lucia: University of Queensland Press, 1994).

Bringing them Home: Report of the National Inquiry into the Separation of Aboriginal and Torres Strait Islander Children from Their Families (April 1997). http://www.hreoc.gov.au/Social_Justice/bth_report/report/index.html (accessed 9 September 2008).

Brook, Peter, *The Empty Space* (Harmondsworth: Penguin, 1972).

Brooks, Peter, *Reading for the Plot: Design and Interpretation in Narrative* (Oxford: Clarendon Press, 1984).

Brown, Gillian, & George Yule, *Discourse Analysis* (Cambridge: Cambridge University Press, 1983).

Bruhn, Mark J., 'Place Deixis and the Schematics of Imagined Space: Milton to Keats', *Poetics Today* 26: 3 (Fall 2005), 387–432.

Bucholz, Sabine, & Manfred Jahn, 'Space in Narrative', in David Herman, Manfred Jahn & Marie Laure Ryan (eds), *Routledge Encyclopedia of Narrative Theory* (London: Routledge, 2005), 551–5.

Bühler, Karl, *Theory of Language: The Representational Function of Language*, trans. Donald Fraser Goodwin (Amsterdam/Philadelphia: John Benjamins, 1990). German original: *Sprachtheorie* (Jena: Gustav Fischer, 1934).

Burgin, Victor, *In/Different Spaces: Place and Memory in Visual Culture* (Berkeley: University of California Press, 1996).

Burnett, Paula (ed.), *The Penguin Book of Caribbean Verse* (Harmondsworth: Penguin, 1986).

Butler, Judith, *Gender Trouble: Feminism and the Subversion of Identity* (New York: Routledge, 1990).

Cabral, Amilcar, *Return to the Source: Selected Speeches by Amilcar Cabral*, ed. Africa Information Service (New York: Monthly Review Press, 1973).

Calderwood, James L., 'Ways of Waiting in *Waiting for Godot*', in Steven Connor (ed.), *Waiting for Godot and Endgame* (Basingstoke: Macmillan – now Palgrave Macmillan, 1992), 29–43.

Carter, Paul, *The Road to Botany Bay: An Essay in Spatial History* (London: Faber & Faber, 1987).

Carter, Paul, *Living in a New Country: History, Travelling and Language* (London: Faber, 1992), 1–8.

Carter, Paul, *The Lie of the Land* (London: Faber & Faber, 1996).

Certeau, Michel de, *The Practice of Everyday Life*, trans. Steven Rendell (Berkekely: University of California Press, 1984). French original: *L'Invention du quotidien. 1. Arts de faire* (1980; Paris: Gallimard/Folio essais, 1990).

Chambers, Iain, *Migrancy, Culture, Identity* (London: Routledge/Comedia, 1994).

Chatman, Seymour, *Story and Discourse: Narrative Structure in Fiction and Film* (Ithaca: Cornell University Press, 1978).

Chatterjee, Partha, *Nationalist Thought and the Colonial World: A Derivative Discourse* (London: Zed Books, 1986).

Clarke, Philip, *Where the Ancestors Walked: Australia as an Aboriginal Landscape* (Crows Nest NSW: Allen & Unwin, 2005).

Clarkson, Carol, 'Remains of the Name', in Gail Fincham, Jeremy Hawthorn, Attie de Lange & Jakob Lothe (eds), *Literary Landscapes: From Modernism to Postcolonialism* (Basingstoke: Palgrave Macmillan, 2008), 125–42.

Cohn, Dorrit, *Fictional Minds: Narrative Modes for Presenting Consciousness in Fiction* (Princeton NJ: Princeton University Press, 1978).

Compagnon, Antoine, *La seconde main: ou le travail de la citation* (Paris: Seuil, 1979).

Connor, Stephen, *The English Novel in History 1950–1995* (London: Routledge, 1996).

Conrad, Joseph, *Joseph Conrad's Letters to R. B. Cunningham Graham*, ed. C. T. Watts (Cambridge: Cambridge University Press, 1969).

Coroneus, Con, *Space, Conrad, and Modernity* (Oxford: Oxford University Press, 2002).

Cosby, Alfred W., *Ecological Imperialism: The Biological Expansion of Europe 900–1900* (Cambridge: Cambridge University Press/Canto, 1993).

Crampton, Jeremy W. & Stuart Elden (eds), *Space Knowledge and Power: Foucault and Geography* (Aldershot: Ashgate, 2007).

Culler, Jonathan, *Structuralist Poetics: Structuralism, Linguistics and the Study of Literature* (London: Routledge & Kegan Paul, 1975).

Culler, Jonathan, *Literary Theory: A Very Short Introduction* (Oxford: Oxford University Press, 1997).

Dabydeen, David, & Nana Wilson-Tagoe, *A Reader's Guide to West Indian and Black British Literature* (London: Hansib Publishing/Rutherford Press, 1988).

Davidson, Basil, *The Black Man's Burden: Africa and the Curse of the Nation-State* (New York: Times Books, 1992).

Dawes, Kwame, Interview with David Dabydeen, in Kevin Grant (ed.), *The Art of David Dabydeen* (London: Peepal Tree Press, 1997), 210–1.

Döring, Tobias, 'The Passage of the I/Eye: David Dabydeen, V. S. Naipaul and the Tombstones of Parabiography', in Alfred Hornung and Ernstpeter Ruhe (eds), *Postcolonialism & Autobiography: Michelle Cliff, David Dabydeen, Opal Palmer Adisa* (Amsterdam/Atlanta, GA: Rodopi, 1998), 150–66.

Döring, Tobias, *Caribbean-English Passages: Intertextuality in a Postcolonial Tradition* (London: Routledge, 2002).

Doležel, Lubomir, *Heterocosmica: Fiction and Possible Worlds* (Baltimore MD: Johns Hopkins University Press, 1998).

Ducrot, Oswald, & Tzvetan Todorov, *Dictionnaire encyclopédique des sciences du langage* (1972; Paris: Seuil/Points, 1979).

During, Simon, 'Out of England: Literary Subjectivity in the Australian Colonies, 1788–1867', in Judith Ryan & Chris Wallace-Crabbe (eds), *Imagining Australia: Literature and Culture in the New World* (Cambridge, MA: Harvard University Press, 2004), 3–21.

During, Simon, *Cultural Studies: A Critical Introduction* (London: Routledge, 2005).

Eagleton, Terry, *Marxism and Literary Theory* (London: Methuen, 1976).

Eagleton, Terry, *Criticism and Ideology: A Study in Marxist Literary Theory* (London: Verso, 1978).

Eagleton, Terry, *Walter Benjamin: Or, Towards a Revolutionary Criticism* (London: Verso, 1981).

Edgerton, Samuel Y., *The Renaissance Rediscovery of Perspective* (New York: Basic Books, 1975).

Elam, Keir, *The Semiotics of Theatre and Drama* (London: Methuen, 1980).

Eribon, Didier, *Michel Foucault (1926–1984)* (Paris: Flammarion/Champs, 1991).

Erlich, Victor, *Russian Formalism: History – Doctrine*, 4th edn. (The Hague: Mouton, 1980).

Fanon, Frantz, *Sociologie d'une révolution (L'an V de la révolution algérienne)* (1959; Paris: Maspero, 1968).

Fanon, Frantz, *The Wretched of the Earth*, trans. Contance Farrington (1961; Harmondsworth: Penguin, 1967). Original French: *Les Damnés de la terre* (Paris: Maspero, 1961).

Ferguson, James, 'Decomposing Modernity: History and Hierarchy after Development', in Ania Loomba et al. (eds), *Postcolonial Studies and Beyond* (Durham: Duke University Press, 2005), 166–81.

Fincham, Gail, 'Orality, Literacy and Community: Conrad's *Nostromo* and Ngugi's *Petals of Blood*', *Conradian* 17: 1 (1992), 45–71.

Fincham, Gail, 'Space and Place in the Novels of E. M. Forster', in Gail Fincham, Jeremy Hawthorn, Attie de Lange & Jakob Lothe (eds), *Literary Landscapes: From Modernism to Postcolonialism* (Basingstoke: Palgrave Macmillan, 2008), 38–57.

Fincham, Gail, Jeremy Hawthorn, Attie de Lange, & Jakob Lothe (eds), *Literary Landscapes: From Modernism to Postcolonialism* (Basingstoke: Palgrave Macmillan, 2008).

Fitch, Brian T., *Beckett and Babel: An Investigation into the Status of the Bilingual Work* (Toronto: University of Toronto Press, 1988).

Fludernik, Monika, *The Fictions of Language and the Languages of Fiction: The Linguistic Representation of Speech and Consciousness* (London: Routledge, 1993).

Foucault, Michel, *The Order of Things: An Archaeology of the Human Sciences*, trans. A. M. Sheridan Smith (London: Routledge, 2004). French original: *Les Mots et les choses: Une archéologie des sciences humaines* (Paris: Gallimard, 1966).

Foucault, Michel, *Archaeology of Knowledge*, trans. Alan M. Sheridan Smith (1970; London: Routledge, 2002). Original French: *L'archéologie du savoir* (Paris: Gallimard, 1969).

Foucault, Michel, 'The Discourse on Language' in *The Archaeology of Knowledge and the Discourse on Language*, trans, A. M. Sheridan Smith (New York: Pantheon, 1972), 215–37. French original: *L'Ordre du discours: Leçon inaugurale au Collège de France prononcée le 2 décembre 1970* (Paris: Gallimard, 1972).

Foucault, Michel, *Language, Counter-Memory, Practice: Selected Essays and Interviews*, ed. Donald F. Bouchard, trans. Donald F. Bouchard & Sherry Simon (Ithaca: Cornell University Press, 1977).

Foucault, Michel, 'What is an Author?', trans. Josué Harari, in Josué Harari (ed.), *Textual Strategies: Perspective in Post-Structuralist Criticism* (London: Methuen, 1980), 141–60.

Foucault, Michel, *Power/Knowledge: Selected Interviews and Other Writings 1972–1977*, ed. Colin Gordon (New York: Pantheon, 1980).

Foucault, Michel, *Dits et écrits 1954–1988*, ed. Daniel Defert & François Ewald (Paris: Gallimard, 1994), 4 volumes.

Foucault, Michel, *Michel Foucault: The Essential Works 2: Aesthetics*, ed. James Faubion (London: Allen Lane/Penguin, 1998).

Foucault, Michel, 'Archaeology of a Passion', in Raymond Roussel, *Death and the Labyrinth: The World of Raymond Roussel*, trans. Charles Ruas (New York: Continuum, 2004), 169–186.

Frank, Joseph, 'Spatial Form in Modern Literature', *The Widening Gyre* (Bloomington: University of Indiana Press, 1968), 3–62.

Frank, Joseph, 'Spatial Form: Some Further Reflections', *Critical Inquiry* 5:2 (Winter 1978), 275–90.

Freud, Sigmund, *The Interpretation of Dreams* (1900), in *The Complete Psychological Works of Sigmund Freud,* trans. and ed. James Strachey (1963; London: Hogarth Press, 1973). German original: *Die Traumdeutung* (1900), in *Gesammelte Werke* (Frankfurt am Main: Fischer, 1999), I/II.

Fuchs, Anna, *Remarks on Deixis* (Heidelberg: Groos, 1993).

Gardner, Helen, 'The Landscapes of Eliot's Poetry', *Critical Quarterly* 10: 4 (Winter 1968), 313–30.

Gathorne-Hardy, Jonathan, *The Public School Phenomenon, 597–1977* (1977; Harmondsworth: Penguin, 1979).

Genette, Gérard, 'Espace et langage', *Figures I* (Paris: Seuil, 1966), 101–8.

Genette, Gérard, 'La littérature et l'espace', *Figures II: Essais* (Paris: Seuil, 1969), 43–8.

Genette, Gérard, *Narrative Discourse*, trans. Jane E. Levin (Oxford : Blackwell 1980). French originals: *Discours du récit* in *Figures III* (Paris: Seuil, 1972); *Discours du récit/Nouveau discours du récit* (1972, 1983; Paris: Seuil/folio essais, 2007).

Genette, Gérard, *The Architext: An Introduction*, trans. Jane E. Lewin (Berkeley: University of California Press, 1992). French original: *Introduction à l'architext* (Paris: Seuil, 1979).

Giddens, Anthony, *The Consequences of Modernity* (Stanford, CA.: Stanford University Press, 1991).

Gilroy, Paul, *The Black Atlantic: Modernity and Double Consciousness* (London: Verso, 1993).

Girard, René, *Deceit, Desire and the Novel: Self and Other in Literary Structure*, trans. Yvonne Freccero (Baltimore ML: Johns Hopkins University Press, 1966). Original French: *Mensonge romantique et vérité romanesque* (Paris: Grasset, 1961).

Girard, René, *Violence and the Sacred*, trans. Patrick Gregory (Baltimore, ML: Johns Hopkins University Press, 1977). Original French: *La Violence et le sacré* (Paris: Grasset, 1972).

Glissant, Edouard, *Caribbean Discourse: Selected Essays*, trans. J. Michael Dash (Charlottesville: University Press of Virginia, 1989). Original French: *Le Discours antillais* (Paris: Seuil, 1981).

Godlewska, Anne, & Neil Smith, 'Introduction: Critical Histories of Geography', in Godlewska & Smith (eds), *Geography and Empire* (Oxford: Blackwell, 1994), 1–8.

Green, Keith, 'Deixis and the Poetic Persona', *Language and Literature* 1: 2 (1992), 121–34.

Greimas, A. J., 'Pour une sémiotique topologique', in *Sémiotique de l'espace: Architecture, urbanisme, sortir de l'impasse*, eds Manar Hammad, Eric Proovost & Michel Vernin (Paris: Denoël/Gonthier, 1979), 11–43.

Grewendorf, Günther, Fritz Hamm & Wolfgang Sternefeld, *Sprachliches Wissen: Eine Einführung in moderne Theorien der grammatischen Beschreibung* (Frankfurt am Main: Suhrkamp, 1987).

Grimshaw, Pat, 'Federation as a Turning Point in Australian History', *Australian Historical Studies* 33: 118 (2002), 25–41.

Habermas, Jürgen, 'Modernity: An Unfinished Project', in Charles Jencks (ed.), *The Post-Modern Reader* (London: Academy Editions, 1992), 158–69; Original German in *Die Moderne – ein unvollendetes Projekt: Philosophisch-politische Aufsätze 1977–1990* (Leipzig; Reclam, 1990), 32–54.

Haebich, Anna, *Broken Circles: Fragmenting Indigenous Families, 1800–2000* (Fremantle: Fremantle Arts Centre Press, 2001).

Hall, Stuart, 'When Was "The Post-Colonial"? Thinking at the Limit', in Iain Chambers & Lidia Curti (eds), *The Post-Colonial Question: Common Skies, Divided Horizons* (London: Routledge, 1996), 242–60.

Hanks, William F., 'The Indexical Ground of Deictic Reference', in Alessandro Duranti & Charles Goodwin (eds), *Rethinking Context: Language as an Interactive Phenomenon* (Cambridge: Cambridge University Press, 1992), 43–76.

Harris, Paul A., 'To See with the Mind and Think through the Eye: Deleuze, Folding Architecture, and Simon Rodia's Watts Towers', in Ian Buchanan & Gregg Lambert (eds), *Deleuze and Space* (Toronto: University of Toronto Press, 2005), 36–60.

Hegel, G. W. F., *The Philosophy of History*, trans. J. Sibree (New York: Dover, 1956). Original German: *Philosophie der Geschichte*, ed. Theodor Litt (Stuttgart: Reclam, 1961).

Helbig, Jörg, *Intertextualität und Markierung: Untersuchungen zur Systematik und Funktion der Signalisierung von Intertextualität* (Heidelberg: Winter, 1996).

Herman, Vimala, 'Deixis and Space in Drama', *Social Semiotics* 7: 3 (1997), 269–83.

Hillier, B. & H. Janson, *The Social Logic of Space* (Cambridge: Cambridge University Press, 1984).

Hoffmann, Gerhard, *Raum, Situation, erzählte Wirklichkeit: Poetologische und historische Studien zum englischen und amerikanischen Roman* (Stuttgart: Metzler, 1978).

Huggan, Graham, *Australian Literature: Postcolonialism, Racism, Transnationalism* (Oxford: Oxford University Press, 2007).

Hulme, Peter, 'Beyond the Straits: Postcolonial Allegories of the Globe' in Ania Loomba et al. (eds), *Postcolonial Studies and Beyond* (Durham: Duke University Press, 2005), 41–61.

Husserl, Edmund, *Logische Untersuchungen* (Halle an der Saale: Niemeyer, 1901), volume 2.

Irigaray, Luce, *Elemental Passions*, trans. Joanne Collie & Judith Still (London: Athlone, 1992). French original: *Passions élémentaires* (Paris: Minuit, 1982).

Irigaray, Luce, *L'Oubli de l'air: Chez Martin Heidegger* (Paris: Minuit, 1983).

Iser, Wolfgang, *Prospecting: From Reader Response to Literary Anthropology* (Baltimore: Johns Hopkins University Press, 1989).

Iser, Wolfgang, 'Die Appellstruktur der Texte: Unbestimmtheit als Wirkungsbedingung literarischer Prosa', in Rainer Warning (ed.), *Rezeptionsästhetik: Theorie und Praxis* (München: Fink/UTB, 1993), 228–52.

Issacharoff, Michael, 'Space and Reference in Drama', *Poetics Today* 2: 3 (Spring 1981), 211–24.

Issacharoff, Michael, *Discourse as Performance* (Stanford: Stanford University Press, 1989).

Jakobson, Roman, *Selected Writings* (The Hague: Mouton, 1971), 8 volumes.

Jameson, Fredric, *Fables of Aggression: Wyndham Lewis, The Modernist as Fascist* (Berkeley: University of California Press, 1979).

Jenny, Laurent, 'La stratégie de la forme', *Poétique* 27 (1976), 257–81.

Johnson, R. W., 'End of the Road', *London Review of Books* 30: 22 (20 November 2008), 13–16.

Jones, Peter, 'Philosophical and Theoretical Issues in the Study of Deixis: A Critique of the Standard Account', in Keith Green (ed.), *New Essays in Deixis: Discourse, Narrative, Literature* (Amsterdam: Rodopi, 1995), 43–76.

Keegan, Paul (ed.), *The New Penguin Book of English Verse* (Harmondsworth: Penguin, 2001).

Kennel, Jackson, '"Impossible to ignore their Greatness": Survival Craft in the Mau Mau Forest Movement', in E. S. Atieno Odhiambo & John Lonsdale (eds), *Mau Mau and Nationhood* (London: James Currey, 2005), 176–90.

Klein, Bernhard, *Maps and the Writing of Space in Early Modern England and Ireland* (Basingstoke: Palgrave Macmillan, 2001).

Kristeva, Julia, *Desire in Language: A Semiotic Approach to Literature and Art*, ed. Leon Roudiez, trans. Thomas Gora, Alice Jardine & Leon Roudiez (New York: Columbia University Press, 1980). French original: Σημειωτικη: *Recherches pour une sémanalyse* (1969; Paris: Seuil/Points, 1978).

Kristeva, Julia, *Le Texte du roman: Approche sémiologique d'une structure discursive transformationelle* (Den Haag/Paris: Mouton, 1970).

Kristeva, Julia, 'Quelques problèmes de sémiotique littéraire à propos d'un texte de Mallarmé: Un coup de dés', in A. J. Greimas (ed.), *Essais de sémiotique poétique* (Paris: Larousse, 1972), 208–34.

Kristeva, Julia, *Revolution in Poetic Language* trans. Margaret Waller (New York: Columbia University Press, 1984). French original: *La Révolution du langage poétique: L'avant-garde à la fin du XIXe siècle: Lautréamont et Mallarmé* (Paris: Seuil, 1974).

Kristeva, Julia, *Polylogue* (Paris: Seuil, 1977).

Kristeva, Julia, *Au risque de la pensée* (Paris: L'Aube, 2001).

Krusche, Dietrich, *Zeigen im Text: Anschauliche Orientierung in literarischen Modellen von Welt* (Würzburg: Königshausen & Neumann, 2001).

Kryk, Barbara, 'How do Indexicals fit into Situations? On Deixis in English and Polish', in Dieter Kastovsky & A. Szwedock (eds), *Linguistics across Historical and Geographical Boundaries: In Honour of Jacek Fisiak on the Occasion of His Fiftieth Birthday* (Berlin: Mouton de Gruyter, 1986), II, 1289–301.

Lacan, Jacques, *Écrits*, trans. Bruce Fink (New York: W.W. Norton, 2006); French original: *Écrits* (Paris: Seuil, 1966).

Lachman, Liliach, 'Keats's *Hyperion*: Time, Space and the Long Poem', *Poetics Today* 22 (2001), 88–127.

Latour, Bruno, *We Have Never Been Modern*, trans. Catherine Porter (Cambridge, MA: Harvard University Press, 1993). Original French: *Nous n'avons jamais été moderne: Essai d'anthropologie symétrique* (1991; Paris: La Découverte, 1997).

Lazarus, Neil, *Nationalism and Cultural Practice in the Postcolonial World* (Cambridge: Cambridge University Press, 1999).

Lefebvre, Henri, *La révolution urbaine* (Paris: Gallimard/Idées, 1968).

Lefebvre, Henri, *La vie quotidienne dans le monde moderne* (1968: Paris: Gallimard/ Idées, 1970).

Lefebvre, Henri, *The Production of Space*, trans. D. Nicolson-Smith (Oxford: Blackwell 1991). Original French: *La production de l'espace* (Paris: Editions Anthropos, 1974).

Lenz, Friedrich, 'Deictic Conceptualisation of Time, Space and Person: Introduction', in Friedrich Lenz (ed.), *Deictic Conceptualisation of Time, Space and Person* (Amsterdam: John Benjamins, 2003), vii-xiv.

Leroi-Gouhran, André, *Le Geste et la parole: la mémoire et les rythmes* (Paris: Albin Michel, 1965).

Lévinas, Emmanuel, *Ethics and Infinity: Conversations with Philippe Nemo*, trans. Richard A. Cohen (Pittsburgh: Duquesne University Press, 1991). French original: *Ethique et infini: Dialogues avec Philippe Nemo* (Paris: Livre de poche/biblio essais, 1988).

Lévinas, Emmanuel, *Humanism of the Other*, trans. Nidra Poller (Urbana IL: University of Illinois Press, 2006). Original French: *Humanisme de l'autre homme* (1972; Paris: Livre de poche/biblio essais, 1987).

Levinson, Stephen, *Pragmatics* (Cambridge: Cambridge University Press, 1983).

Locke, John, *An Essay Concerning Human Understanding* (1689), ed. Peter Nidditch (Oxford: Clarendon Press, 1975).

Loomba, Ania, *Colonialism/Postcolonialism* (London: Routledge, 1998).

Lothe, Jakob, 'Space, Time, Narrative: From Thomas Hardy to Franz Kafka and J. M. Coetzee', in Gail Fincham, Jeremy Hawthorn, Attie de Lange & Jakob Lothe (eds), *Literary Landscapes: From Modernism to Postcolonialism* (Basingstoke: Palgrave Macmillan, 2008), 1–18.

Lotman, Juri, *Universe of the Mind: A Semiotic Theory of Culture*, trans. Ann Shukman (London: J. B. Tauris, 1990).

Lucretius, *The Nature of the Universe*, trans. R. E. Latham (Harmondsworth: Penguin, 1951).

Luhmann, Niklas, *Soziale Systeme: Grundriß einer allgemeinen Theorie* (Frankfurt am Main: Suhrkamp, 1984).

Lyons, John, *Semantics* (Cambridge: Cambridge University Press, 1977), 2 volumes.

M'Bokolo, Elikia, *L'Afrique au XXe siècle: Le continent convoité* (Paris: Seuil/Points, 1985).

MacCabe, Colin, *James Joyce and the Revolution of the Word* (Basingstoke: Macmillan – now Palgrave Macmillan, 1981).

Macey, David, *The Lives of Michel Foucault* (London: Hutchinson, 1993).

Malpas, Jeff, *Place and Experience: A Philosophical Topography* (Cambridge: Cambridge University Press, 1999).

Mamdami, Mahmood, 'Lessons of Zimbawe', *London Review of Books* 23: 4 (4 December 2008), 17–18.

Marcuse, Herbert, *One-Dimensional Man: Studies in the Ideology of Advanced Industrial Society* (London: Routledge & Kegan Paul, 1964).

Marin, Louis, *Utopics: The Semiological Play of Textual Spaces*, trans. Robert A. Vollrath (Atlantic Highlands, NJ : Humanities Press, 1990). French original: *Utopiques: Jeux d'espace* (Paris: Minuit, 1973).

Marx, Karl, *Karl Marx on Colonization & Modernization*, ed. Shlomo Avineri (New York: Doubleday Anchor, 1969).

Marx, Karl, *The Eighteenth Brumaire of Louis Bonaparte*, ed. C. P. Dutt (New York: Internationale Publishers, 1940). German original: *Der Achtzehnte Brumaire des Louis Bonaparte* (Leipzig: Reclam, 1982).

Massey, Doreen, *For Space* (London: Sage, 2005).

Maurice Blanchot, *The Writing of the Disaster*, trans. Anne Smock (Lincoln NE: University of Nebraska Press, 1986). Original French: *L'Ecriture du désastre* (Paris: Gallimard, 1980).

Mbembe, Achille, *On the Postcolony,* trans. A. M. Berett, Janet Roitman, Murray Last & Steven Rendall (Berkeley: University of California Press, 2001).

McMullan, Anna, 'Irish/Postcolonial Beckett', in Lois Oppenheim (ed.), *Palgrave Advances in Beckett Studies* (Basingstoke: Palgrave Macmillan, 2004), 89–109.

Merleau-Ponty, Maurice, *Phenomenology of Perception*, trans. Colin Smith (London: Routledge, 1995). French original: *Phénoménologie de la perception* (1945; Paris: Gallimard/Tel, 1976).

Miller, James, *The Passion of Michel Foucault* (London: HarperCollins, 1993).

Mitchell, W. J. T. (ed.), *Landscape and Power* (Chicago: University of Chicago Press, 1994).

Moore-Gilbert, Bart, *Postcolonial Theory: Contexts, Practices, Politics* (London: Verso, 1997).

Moorehead, Alan, *The Fatal Impact: The Invasion of the South Pacific 1767–1840* (London: Hamish Hamilton, 1966).

Moretti, Franco, *Atlas of the European Novel 1800–1900* (London: Verso, 1998).

Moretti, Franco, *The Way of the World: The Bildungsroman in European Culture*, trans. Albert Sbragia (London: Verso, 2000). Original Italian: *Il romanzo de formazione* (Milan: Garzanti, 1986).

Morris, Meaghan, *The Pirate's Fiancée: Feminism, Reading, Postmodernism* (London: Verso, 1988).

Mudrooroo, *Us Mob: History, Culture, Struggle: An Introduction to Indigenous Australia* (Sydney: Angus & Robertson, 1997).

Muecke, Stephen, *No Road (bitumen all the way)* (Fremantle: Fremantle Arts Centre Press, 1997).

Muecke, Stephen, 'A Chance to Hear a Nyigina Song', in Judith Ryan & Chris Wallace-Crabbe (eds), *Imagining Australia: Literature and Culture in the New World* (Cambridge, MA: Harvard University Press, 2004), 123–35.

Muecke, Stephen, *Ancient & Modern: Time, Culture and Indigenous Philosophy* (Sydney: UNSW Press, 2004).

Murphet, Julian, 'Postmodern Space' in Stephen Connor (ed.), *The Cambridge Companion to Postmodernism* (Cambridge: Cambridge University Press, 2004), 116–35.

Nair, Rukmini Bhaya, *Lying on the Postcolonial Couch: The Idea of Indifference* (Minneapolis: University of Minnesota Press, 2002).

Nairn, Tom, *The Break-Up of Britain: Crisis and Neo-Nationalism*, 2nd edn. (London: Verso, 1981).

Oliver, Roland & J. D. Fage, *A Short History of Africa*, rev. edn. (1962; 1978; Harmondsworth: Penguin, 1995).

Osterhammel, Jürgen, *Colonialism: A Theoretical Overview*, trans. Shelley L. Frisch (Princeton NJ: Marcus Wiener, 1997). Original German: *Kolonialismus: Geschichte – Formen – Folgen* (München: Beck, 1995).

Otto, Peter, 'Forgetting Colonialism', *Meanjin* 52: 3 (1993), 545–58.

Palmer, Alan, *Fictional Minds* (Lincoln: University of Nebraska Press, 2004).

Parrinder, Patrick, *Nation & Novel: The English Novel from its Origins to the Present Day* (Oxford: Oxford University Press, 2006).

Peirce, Charles Sanders, *Collected Writings*, ed. Charles Hartshore, Paul Weiss & Arthur W. Burks (Cambridge, MA: Harvard University Press, 1931–58), Volume 2.

Pfister, Manfred, '"As an unperfect actor on the stage": Notes Towards a Definition of Performance and Performativity in Shakespeare's *Sonnets*', in Eva Müller-Zettelmann & Margarete Rubik (eds), *Theory into Poetry: New Approaches to the Lyric* (Amsterdam: Rodopi, 2005), 207–28.

Piatti, Barbara, *Die Geographie der Literatur: Schauplätze, Handlungsräume, Raumphantasien* (Göttingen: Wallstein, 2008).

Poirié, François, *Emmanuel Lévinas: qui êtes-vous?* (Lyon: La Manufacture, 1987).

Pratt, Mary Louise, *Imperial Eyes: Travel Writing and Transculturation* (London: Routledge, 1992).

Prince, Gerald, 'Narratology, Narratological Criticism, and Gender', in Calin-Andrei Mihailescu & Walid Harmaneh (eds), *Fiction Updated: Theories of*

Fictionality, Narratology, and Poetics (Toronto: University of Toronto Press, 1996), 159–64.

Punter, David, *Postcolonial Imaginings: Fictions of a New World Order* (Edinburgh: Edinburgh University Press, 2000).

Quigley, Mark, 'Unnaming the Subject: Samuel Beckett and Colonial Alterity', in Marius Bruning (ed.), *Historicising Beckett: Issues of Performance* (Amsterdam: Rodopi, 2005), 87–100.

Reichel, Norbert, *Der erzählte Raum: Zur Verflechtung von sozialem und poetischem Raum in erzählender Literatur* (Darmstadt: Wissenschaftliche Buchgesellschaft, 1987).

Reid, Ian, *Narrative Exchanges* (London: Routledge, 1992).

Reynolds, Henry, *Aboriginal Sovereignty: Three Nations, One Australia?* (Crows Nest, NSW: Allen & Unwin, 1996).

Reynolds, Henry, *The Other Side of the Frontier: Aboriginal Resistance to the European Invasion of Australia* (1981; Ringwood VIC: Penguin, 1995).

Rickard, John, *Australia: A Cultural History*, 2nd edn. (London: Longman, 1996).

Ricoeur, Paul, *The Conflict of Interpretations: Essays in Hermeneutics,* trans. Willis Domingo et al. (Evanston, IL: Northwestern University Press, 1974). French original: *Le conflit des interprétations: Essais d'herméneutique I* (Paris: Seuil, 1969).

Riffaterre, Michael, 'Sémiotique intertextuelle: l'interprétant', *Rhétoriques, Sémiotiques: Revue d'esthétique* 1/2 (1979), (Paris: UGE 10/18, 1979), 128–50.

Riffaterre, Michael, *La Production du texte* (Paris: Seuil, 1979).

Rimmon-Kenan, Shlomith, *Narrative Fiction: Contemporary Poetics* (London: Methuen, 1983).

Ritter, Alexander (ed.), *Landschaft und Raum in der Erzählkunst* (Darmstadt: Wissenschaftliche Buchgesellschaft, 1975).

Rose, Deborah Bird, *Dingo Makes Us Human: Life and Land in an Aboriginal Australian Culture* (Cambridge: Cambridge University Press, 1992).

Rose, Deborah Bird, 'Taking Notice', *Worldview: Environment, Culture, Religion* 3: 2 (August 1999), 97–103.

Rowley, C. D., *The Destruction of Aboriginal Society* (Ringwood, VIC: Penguin, 1972).

Russell, Bertrand, *An Inquiry into Meaning and Truth: The William James Lectures 1940 delivered at Harvard University* (1940; Harmondsworth: Pelican 1965).

Saalman, Dieter, 'Christa Wolf and and Joseph Conrad's *Heart of Darkness*: The Curse of the Blind Spot', *Neophilologus* 76: 1 (1992), 19–28.

Saalman, Dieter, 'Elective Affinities: Christa Wolf's *Störfall* and Joseph Conrad's *Heart of Darkness*', *Comparative Literature Studies* 29: 3 (1992), 238–58.

Said, Edward W., *Orientalism* (1978; Harmondsworth: Penguin, 1987).

Said, Edward W., *The World, the Text, and the Critic* (London: Faber & Faber, 1984).

Said, Edward W., *Culture and Imperialism* (1993; London: Vintage, 1994).

Said, Edward, 'Always on Top', *London Review of Books* 25: 6 (20 March 2003).

Sanders, Mark, *Complicities: The Intellectual and Apartheid* (Durham NC: Duke University Press, 2001).

Sansom, Basil, *The Camp at Wallaby Cross: Aboriginal Fringe Dwellers in Darwin* (Canberra: Australian Institute of Aboriginal Studies, 1980).

Schenkel, Elmar, *Sense of Place: Regionalität und Raumbewußtsein in der neueren britischen Lyrik* (Tübingen: Niemeyer, 1993).

Schwarz, Anja, 'Beached: A Postcolonial Reading of the Australian Shore', unpublished PhD thesis, Free University of Berlin, 2008.

Scolnicov, Hanna, *Women's Theatrical Space* (Cambridge: Cambridge University Press, 1994).

Sherwood, Richard, 'Viktor Shklovsky and the Development of early Formalist Theory on Prose Literature', in Stephen Bann & John E. Bowlt (eds), *Russian Formalism: A Collection of Articles and Texts in Translation* (Edinburgh: Scottish Academic Press, 1973), 26–40.

Shklovsky, Viktor, *Theory of Prose*, trans. Benjamin Sher (Elmswood Park, IL: Dalkey Archive Press, 1990). Russian original: Viktor Shklovskij, *O Teorii Prozy* (Moskva: Isdatelstovo Federacija, 1929) [Виктор Шкловский, *О Теории Прозы* (Москва: Издательство Федерация, 1929)].

Simatei, Tirop, 'Colonial Violence, Postcolonial Violations: Violence, Landscape and Memory in Kenyan Fiction', *Research in African Literatures* 36: 2 (Summer 2005), 85–94.

Smith, Neil, *Uneven Development: Nature, Capital and the Production of Space* (Oxford: Blackwell, 1984).

Smitten, Jeffrey R. & Ann Daghistany (eds), *Spatial Form in Narrative* (Ithaca/London: Cornell University Press, 1981).

Soja, Edward W., *Postmodern Geographies* (London: Verso, 1989).

Soja, Edward W., *Thirdspace: Journeys to Los Angeles and Other Real-and-Imagined Places* (Cambridge, MA: Blackwell, 1996).

Spencer, Sharon, *Space, Time and Structure in the Modern Novel* (New York: New York University Press, 1971).

Spengler, Oswald, *The Decline of the West: An Abridged Edtion*, trans. Charles Francis Atkinson (New York: Oxford University Press, 1991). Original German: *Der Untergang des Abendlandes: Umrisse einer Morphologie der Weltgeschichte* (1923; München: dtv, 1997).

Spivak, Gayatri Chakravorty, *A Critique of Postcolonial Reason: Towards a History of the Vanishing Present* (Cambridge, MA: Harvard University Press, 1999).

Spurr, David, *The Rhetoric of Empire: Colonial Discourse in Journalism, Travel Writing and Imperial Administration* (Durham NC: Duke University Press, 1993).

Steiner, Peter, *Russian Formalism: A Metapoetics* (Ithaca: Cornell University Press, 1984).

Stengers, Isabelle, *Cosmopolitiques. 7. Pour en finir avec la tolérance* (Paris: La Découverte/Les empêcheurs de penser en rond, 1997).

Stevenson, Randall, *Modernist Fiction: An Introduction* (Brighton: Harvester Wheatsheaf, 1992).

Thrift, Nigel, 'Overcome by Space: Reworking Foucault', in Jeremy W. Crampton & Stuart Elden (eds), *Space, Knowledge and Power: Foucault and Geography* (Aldershot: Ashgate, 2007), 53–8.

Todorov, Tzvetan, 'Knowledge of the Void: Heart of Darkness', trans. Walter C. Putnam III, *Conradiana* 21 (1989), 161–72. French original: 'Coeur des ténèbres', *Les genres du discours* (Paris: Seuil, 1978), 172–83.

Toyne, Philip & Daniel Vachon, *Growing up the Country: The Pitjantjatjara Struggle for their Land* (Melbourne: McPhee Gribble, 1984).

Ulmer, Gregory L., *Applied Grammatology: Post(e)-Pedagogy from Jacques Derrida to Joseph Beuys* (Baltimore: Johns Hopkins University Press, 1984).

Venn, Couze, *The Postcolonial Challenge: Towards Alternative Worlds* (London: Sage, 2006).

Verhelst, Thierry G., *No Life Without Roots: Culture and Devlopment*, trans. Bob Cummings (London: Zed Books, 1990).

Weber, Max, *Max Weber: Essays in Sociology*, trans. and ed. H. H. Gerth & C. Wright Mills (New York: Oxford University Press, 1946).

Weber, Max, *Soziologie – Weltgeschichtliche Analysen – Politik*, ed. Eduard Baumgarten (Stuttgart: Kroner, 1968).

West, Russell, *Conrad and Gide: Translation, Transference and Intertextuality* (Amsterdam/Atlanta, GA: Rodopi, 1996).

West, Russell, 'Exile as Origin: Definitions of Australian Identity in David Malouf's *12 Edmondstone Street'*, *Anglia* 119: 1 (2001), 77–92.

West, Russell, *Spatial Representations on the Jacobean Stage: From Shakespeare to Webster* (Basingstoke: Palgrave Macmillan, 2002).

West-Pavlov, Russell, *Transcultural Graffiti: Diasporic Writing and the Teaching of Literary Studies* (Amsterdam: Rodopi, 2005).

West-Pavlov, Russell, *Bodies and their Spaces: System, Crisis and Transformation in Early Modern Drama* (Amsterdam: Rodopi, 2006).

Wicomb, Zoë, 'Shame and Identity: the Case of the Coloured in South Africa' in Mary Jolley & Derek Attridge (eds), *Writing South Africa: Literature, Apartheid, and Democracy, 1970–1995* (Cambridge: Cambridge University Press, 1998), 91–107.

Wicomb, Zoë, 'Zoë Wicomb in conversation with Hein Willemse', *Research in African Literatures* 33: 1 (Spring 2002), 144–52.

Williams, Eric, *Capitalism and Slavery* (Chapel Hill, NC: The University of North Carolina Press, 1944).

Williams, Raymond, *Marxism and Literature* (Oxford: Oxford University Press, 1977).

Williams, Raymond, *The Country and the City* (London: Hogarth Press, 1985).

Wolfgang Klein & Konstanze Jungbluth (eds), Thematic issue on Deixis, *Zeitschrift für Literaturwissenschaft und Linguistik* 125 (March 2002).

Worton, Michael, 'Intertextuality: to Inter Textuality or to Resurrect it?', in David Kelley & Isabelle Llasera (eds), *Cross-References: Modern French Theory and the Practice of Criticism* (London: Society for French Studies, 1986), 14–23.

Young, Robert, *White Mythologies: History, Writing and the West* (London: Routledge, 1990).

Young, Robert J. C., *Postcolonialism: An Historical Introduction* (Oxford: Blackwell, 2001).

Index